CONTENTS

2000
A NEW MILLENNIUM—
A NEW TOMORROW!

Enter Sydney Omarr's world of accurate day-by-day predictions for every aspect of your life. With expert readings and forecasts, you can chart a course to romance, adventure, good health, or career opportunities while gaining valuable insight into yourself and others. Offering a daily outlook for 18 full months, this fascinating guide shows you:

- The important dates in your life
- What to expect from an astrological reading
- The initials of people who will be influential in your life
- How the stars can help you stay healthy and fit
- Your lucky lottery numbers
  And more!

Let this expert's sound advice guide you through a year of heavenly possibilities—for today and for every day of 2000!

SYDNEY OMARR'S DAY-BY-DAY
ASTROLOGICAL GUIDE FOR

ARIES—March 21–April 19
TAURUS—April 20–May 20
GEMINI—May 21–June 20
CANCER—June 21–July 22
LEO—July 23–August 22
VIRGO—August 23–September 22
LIBRA—September 23–October 22
SCORPIO—October 23–November 21
SAGITTARIUS—November 22–December 21
CAPRICORN—December 22–January 19
AQUARIUS—January 20–February 18
PISCES—February 19–March 20

IN 2000

WIN A PERSONALIZED HOROSCOPE FROM SYDNEY OMARR!

Enter the Sydney Omarr Horoscope Sweepstakes!

No Purchase necessary.
Details below.

Name _____

Address _____

City _____ State _____ Zip _____

Mail to:

SYDNEY OMARR HOROSCOPE SWEEPSTAKES
P.O. BOX 9248
Medford, NY 11763

Offer expires August 31, 1999

Official Rules

1. NO PURCHASE NECESSARY TO ENTER OR WIN A PRIZE. To enter the SYDNEY OMARR HOROSCOPE SWEEPSTAKES, complete this official entry form (original or photocopy), or, on a 3" × 5" piece of paper, print your name and complete address. Mail your entry to: SYDNEY OMARR HOROSCOPE SWEEPSTAKES, P.O. Box 9248, Medford, NY 11763. Enter as often as you wish, but mail each entry in a separate envelope. All entries must be received by 8/31/99 to be eligible. Not responsible for illegal entries, lost or misdirected mail.

2. Winners will be selected from all valid entries in a random drawing on or about 9/14/99, by Marden-Kane, Inc., an independent judging organization whose decisions are final and binding. Odds of winning are dependent upon the number of entries received. Winners will be notified by mail and may be required to execute an affidavit of eligibility and release which must be returned within 14 days of notification or an alternate winner will be selected.

3. One (1) Grand Prize winner will receive a personalized prediction for one (1) year from Sydney Omarr. One (1) Second Prize winner will receive a personalized prediction for (1) month from Sydney Omarr. Twenty-five (25) Third Prize winners will receive a free phone call to Sydney Omarr's 1-900 number to hear a personal prediction. No transfer or substitution for prize offered. Estimated value of all prizes: $250.

4. Sweepstakes open to residents of the U.S. and Canada 18 years of age or older, except employees and the immediate families of Penguin Putnam Inc., its affiliated companies, advertising and promotion agencies. Void in the Province of Quebec and wherever else prohibited by law. All Federal, State, Local, and Provincial laws apply. Taxes, if any, are the sole responsibility of the prize winners. Canadian winners will be required to answer an arithmetical skill testing question administered by mail. Winners consent to the use of their name and/or photos or likenesses for advertising purposes without additional compensation (except where prohibited).

5. For the names of the major prize winners, send a self-addressed, stamped envelope after 9/28/99, to: SYDNEY OMARR HOROSCOPE SWEEPSTAKES WINNERS, P.O. Box 4319, Manhasset, NY 11030-4319.

Penguin Putnam Inc. ▲ Mass Market

⓪ SIGNET
A member of Penguin Putnam Inc.
A PEARSON COMPANY

SYDNEY OMARR'S

DAY-BY-DAY ASTROLOGICAL GUIDE
FOR THE NEW MILLENNIUM

GEMINI

May 21–June 20

2000

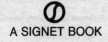

A SIGNET BOOK

SIGNET
Published by New American Library, a division of
Penguin Putnam Inc., 375 Hudson Street,
New York, New York 10014, U.S.A.
Penguin Books Ltd, 27 Wrights Lane,
London W8 5TZ, England
Penguin Books Australia Ltd, Ringwood,
Victoria, Australia
Penguin Books Canada Ltd, 10 Alcorn Avenue,
Toronto, Ontario, Canada M4V 3B2
Penguin Books (N.Z.) Ltd, 182–190 Wairau Road,
Auckland 10, New Zealand

Penguin Books Ltd, Registered Offices:
Harmondsworth, Middlesex, England

First published by Signet, an imprint of New American Library,
a division of Penguin Putnam Inc.

First Printing, July 1999
10 9 8 7 6 5 4 3 2 1

Sydney Omarr is syndicated worldwide by
Los Angeles Times Syndicate.

 REGISTERED TRADEMARK—MARCA REGISTRADA

Printed in the United States of America

INTRODUCTION:

The Year 2000—Business as Usual?

The year 2000 will be ushered in with celebration like never before. However, the very next day could mark one of the biggest snafus in history!

Unless millions of computer users and businesses worldwide have prepared in advance, the change in the initial digits from 19 to 20 of the date 2000 could shut down the technology that regulates every aspect of our lives. Now referred to as the "Y2K bug," this critical flaw that keeps computers locked in the 20th century has nearly every organization that depends on computers racing to beat the clock to avoid a major shutdown. Billions of lines of code must be rewritten before the chimes strike midnight. And suspense will mount during the hours before the century officially closes, as we wait to see what will happen.

The Millennium takes on even more significance when we realize that we're initiating a new era by making critical changes in the technology we've come to depend on. Because of the urgent time factor, everyone from government computer experts to teenage hackers must pull together to guarantee a smooth transition before the midnight deadline. In an extraordinary way, the technology is drawing us together as we make a global effort to resolve this problem.

Astrologers forecasted the union of technology and global cooperation with the entrance of the planet Uranus (technology) into the sign of Aquarius (humanitarian consciousness) in 1996. And it is also the harbinger of the next century, one where remarkable technological advances will be available to more people than ever before; however, the inevitable problems that will occur may also happen on a global scale and require us to work more closely together to discover solutions.

So the stroke of midnight will be a test of whether we are prepared for the challenges of the next century. Will there be shutdowns, accidents, faulty calculations, inaccurate data? Will you just be frustrated temporarily by not being able to use your bank card or by the store losing track of the Christmas gift you returned? Working together for a smooth crossing of the threshold of the Millennium might set the stage for cooperation in other areas, paving the way for better international communications and mutual understanding.

Astrologers have been looking at the horoscope for the Millennium for other clues to what lies ahead. We find that the first day of the Millennium is marked by an alignment of two tiny but powerful forces in astrology, the distant planet Pluto and the tiny planetoid Chiron. In astrology, Pluto is associated with transformation by renewal, Chiron with healing our wounds and helping others to heal. They are aligned in the sign of Sagittarius, which speaks of wide-reaching aspirations and long-term goals, and they are placed in the communications area of the horoscope as the clock chimes 12:01 EST. Let's hope that this Millennium will be a time of global healing and transformation, so that we may greet the new century with hope and enthusiasm.

In this year's guide, we show you some ways that you can harmonize your own life and goals to the rapid changes taking place. For fun, you can compare your planets with our extensive celebrity list, get a new leap-year lease on love, or find out how to use the Internet to connect with the wide world of astrology.

Besides learning the basic information, you can go beyond your sun sign to find out what astrology is all about. Using this book, you can look up your other planets and rising sign and find out what they mean.

2

The sometimes confusing symbols you see on a horo-scope are explained in the chapter on the astrological glyphs. And, of course, there is all you need to know about your sun sign.

Let this guide help you use astrology as a valuable tool to create prosperity, happiness, and growth in the Millennium!

CHAPTER 1

Leaping into the Millennium—Predictions

In the U.S. Capitol building, there is a famous frieze of the shooting death of the Indian chief, Tecumseh, who figures prominently in this year's predictions. Every twenty years, there's a fateful lineup of two huge planets, Jupiter and Saturn, which coincides with an old prophecy of gloom and doom known as "Tecumseh's Curse."

Tecumseh, whose name, ironically, means "shooting star," was a brilliant Shawnee chief and orator. Threatened by the rapid territorial expansion of the white man and the concept of land division and property ownership, he attempted to unite the native American tribes to fight off the foreign invaders, but was shot in Canada in 1813 by American forces. Later, William Henry Harrison, who had defeated Indian attacks led by Tecumseh's brother at the famous battle of Tippecanoe, became the first U.S. president to die in office. But some believed that Tecumseh had put a curse on the United States presidency. Seemingly a coincidence, the list of American presidents who did not complete their term in office at twenty-year intervals after Harrison's death gave rise to the legend of "Tecumseh's Curse."

The next conjunction of Jupiter and Saturn after Harrison's term came during Lincoln's term, followed in twenty years by Garfield, then by McKinley, all assassinated by shooting. Both Presidents Harding and Franklin Delano Roosevelt died in office. The seventh president whose term fell under a Jupiter/Saturn conjunction was John F. Kennedy, also assassinated by shooting. And the last was President Reagan, who was shot during his term but survived.

At this writing, the term of current President Bill Clinton lasts until the time of the next conjunction in May 2000. However, he is experiencing a kind of "character assassination" leading to impeachment hearings that threaten his presidency and could result in his leaving office. The president taking office in 2001 will also be under the influence of this conjunction, which happens twice more in that year.

Long before Tecumseh, this conjunction has been regarded as one that brings sweeping and traumatic social and political events, wars, and destruction. The conjunction on May 28, 2000 follows several ominous celestial events and a pileup of seven planets in the sign of Taurus on May 3. So those of you who are born in fixed signs (Taurus, Leo, Scorpio, and Aquarius) can expect to be most influenced.

On a more positive note, it is important to recognize that lineups of planets are not events that happen in isolation. They are part of a natural, cyclical growth process. The stage for the events in the year 2000 has been set in motion by major astrological events in the past. So think of this event in context of what has been building up for some time.

What Types of Experiences Can You Expect?

The Millennium itself produces optimism, forward thinking, and futurism, all encouraged by Jupiter. But then Saturn, the taskmaster of the zodiac, brings reality checks, obstacles, demands for responsibility, duty, organization, structure, and follow-through into the picture. So this year we will all be concerned with the tradeoffs, the prices to be paid for all our growth and expansion. We will be setting limits on negative growth, such as overpopulation, destruction of the environment, and overspending of any kind.

The Saturn/Jupiter conjunction in the fixed earth sign of Taurus suggests that, as in the days of Tecumseh, there will be issues of territory, including land rights and physical boundaries—claiming it, gaining it, expanding it, fighting over it. In 1940–41, when the last Taurus meeting of these two planets happened, World War II was under way. At this moment, in Eastern Europe and in the Middle East, there are rumblings of global involvement in local territorial wars.

In your personal life, big plans run up against obstacles and bureaucratic red tape. You may be at odds with authority figures. In other words, when you try to spread your wings and fly, you may have trouble getting off the ground. Unless you bring practicality and discipline into play, you will run into restrictions that result in frustration.

As you may notice from the glyph chapter in this book, Jupiter's symbol is a variation on Saturn's glyph upside down. This is your clue that the two planets actually complement each other. Saturn, the planet associated with constriction, discipline, rules, obligations, and limitations, is the reverse of Jupiter, which is associated with expansion, optimism, options, opportunities, and luck. Saturn's long-lasting rewards come to you with hard work; Jupiter's rewards come to you with little effort—they're lucky breaks. Without Saturn's limitation, however, Jupiter is like a vehicle with no brakes. Saturn without Jupiter is like a vehicle stalled. In other words, Jupiter's enthusiasm needs Saturn's emphasis on structure and discipline in order to accomplish its goals, and vice versa.

At the same time, these planets can work at cross purposes. Saturn's fears and limitations can dampen Jupiter's hope and enthusiasm. Jupiter's expansion can come to a halt under Saturn's demand for reality checks and authority figures. Saturn can be a real drag on Jupiter.

The key is to find a balance to harmonize both of these complementary principles, bringing dreams down to earth and getting a wider perspective on fears that are the basis of our limitations. When Saturn and Jupiter work together, we can adjust our expectations to reality, give form to our hopes, and overcome our fears. As Franklin D. Roosevelt said, "We have nothing to fear but fear itself." With this conjunction, there should be a dialogue between structure and opportunity, and between ideals and reality, that can be very fruitful in preparing us to meet the challenges of the next century. Together, these planets promise great accomplishments, but there is a tradeoff, a price to be paid by meeting obligations and taking on responsibilities.

Where Might It Affect Your Life?

The people who will be most affected will be those born during the previous conjunction in Taurus (1940–1941), who will have both Saturn and Jupiter returning to their natal positions. This second "Saturn Return" is a time of maturity, of leadership and responsibility, the beginning of assuming the duties of the wise elder of the community.

Here is where the conjunction might most affect your life according to your sun sign and rising sign. First look up your rising sign in the chart on page 134 in this book then read the following descriptions.

If Your Sun or Rising Sign Is Aries—

The principles of expansion vs. contraction will be evident in your second house of possessions, income, and self-esteem. You can make financial progress by combining new ideas with discipline, organization, and structure. Schemes that promise great rewards with no practical basis will not fly. It will also be important to balance your budget, stick to an investment plan, and guard against extravagance.

If Your Sun or Rising Sign Is Taurus—

Since the conjunction, and a major pileup of planets, takes place in your sign in May, you hold the power cards. This means you'll be in an authority position; you may be imposing structures on others or shaking others up. Though you will have many opportunities and a good deal of luck coming your way, you will also be aware that there will be a tradeoff, a price to pay. You'll be highly visible, so be sure that you look and feel your best.

If Your Sun or Rising Sign Is Gemini—

This conjunction falls in your most spiritual and vulnerable place, making this a time to open up and examine past experiences. Many of you may delve deeply into your subconscious. Watch what you put your faith in, for there is a potential for disillusion here. Something you believe in fervently will be tested, but this could take you into a new dimension. More Geminis may be involved with charity, hospitals, prisons, and religious institutions, creating much-needed changes in these places.

If Your Sun or Rising Sign Is Cancer—

The Saturn/Jupiter conjunction will fall in your house of goals, values, and group activities. This is a time when you will test your ideals in relationship to society. You will be forced out of your shell in some way. You will have opportunities to get involved in clubs, unions, or politics, but you may have some conflict between being popular and playing by the rules. You might discover talents you didn't know you had, such as organizing groups or public speaking. It's a year to shine before the public.

If Your Sun or Rising Sign Is Leo—

You will have many new opportunities in your career or public life, but along with the prestige, these bring extra responsibilities and hard work. You may feel that the job of your dreams is at last attainable, only to find that your workload will also be doubled. You'll be especially concerned about your public image, so show yourself at your very best. Keep your energy high by cultivating good habits.

If Your Sun or Rising Sign Is Virgo—

Though you may love your own comfortable home turf, you could find that you are challenged to accept a position in a new and different atmosphere. It is important to open your mind to other cultural or religious points of view. This would be an excellent time to study something new, to apply your mind in a disciplined way. There could be a conflict between new ideas and the traditional ways of thinking, between keeping yourself on the cutting edge versus clinging to the past. Be cautious, but also give way to adventure.

If Your Sun or Rising Sign Is Libra—

The conjunction will fall in the area of life where you share resources with others, and this is where issues of power and control dominate in your financial and most intimate life. This could complicate investments, savings, and the cost of living. It is a very important time to deal with funds from outside sources, inheritance, or with tax matters. You could be pushing to increase your income as this year begins, but not getting the backing or funding you need, or the funds may come with restrictions. Wheeling and dealing will face many challenges, but the results could bring you long-term security.

If Your Sun or Rising Sign Is Scorpio—

You'll get more accomplished if you do it with someone else. The pileup of planets in Taurus in May falls in your partnership sector, where you'll be making some lasting and permanent changes. Go for long-term benefits, perhaps turning over the reins to another for a while. The emphasis is on changing or improving relationships, making and meeting commitments, and on legal issues.

If Your Sun or Rising Sign Is Sagittarius—

Pay special attention to the care and maintenance department of your life. This is not the time to take your health for granted or burn the candle at both ends, so listen to your body and make sure everything is in working order. Consider alternate methods of healing that are pleasurable and uplifting as well as effective. Take courses to improve yourself. The events of May 2000 mean that you will be rethinking your job situation. Routine may weigh you down, but you can enhance your reputation by getting the job done and upgrading your skills if necessary. Don't promise more than you can deliver.

If Your Sun or Rising Sign Is Capricorn—

Since Capricorn is a Saturn-ruled sign, you may be especially favored by this conjunction, benefiting from the up-side of both planets. Your self-expression and creativity can take leaps forward now. It's an excellent time to expose your talents to a larger audience. Though you may have extra opportunities for romance, there may also be restrictions involved. The object of your affections may have other obligations or you may attract lovers who are not free to follow their hearts. Matters involving children—both the joys and responsibilities of their upbringing—will be more important than ever to you.

If Your Sun or Rising Sign Is Aquarius—

Your home and personal life will be emphasized by this conjunction, which could give you conflicting emotions about your domestic scene. Perhaps you'll want to move or sell, yet there will be an equally strong pull that might hold you back from taking the decisive step. The grass may look greener elsewhere, but not prove to be so. You may have some wonderful ideas about practical home products or interior design, and you could be highly successful here. You could also resolve some long-standing family issues if you keep an open mind.

If Your Sun or Rising Sign Is Pisces—

How you communicate with others will be emphasized by this conjunction. The buildup of planets in Taurus, a fixed earth sign, indicates a tendency toward stubbornness, so make an extra effort to be flexible and to listen to other points of view. Friends and relatives could be more demanding, perhaps imposing extra duties and responsibilities for their care. There may be elderly friends or family that require your attention. There may be some changes in your neighborhood that require you to get involved. Take extra care of your car and matters concerning local transportation. Taking up new studies or hobbies now could be especially beneficial. Consider learning a new language or computer skills, or taking a writing course to broaden your horizons. The discipline of Saturn and the good luck of Jupiter might help you write that novel or play you've had on the back burner.

CHAPTER 2

The Leap Year Guide to Love

Though the year 2000 is a leap year, when ladies traditionally make the first romantic moves, today it's no longer unusual for women to chase the object of their desire aggressively, no matter what the year. One of the main reasons women turn to astrology is to help them attract a lover or to figure out what's going wrong in a relationship.

Probably the question astrologers hear most is: What sign is best for me in love? Or: I'm a Taurus and my lover is a Gemini. What are our prospects? You might be wondering if you can trust that first spark of chemistry—should you lower your expectations if you're a Leo with a fatal attraction to a sexy Scorpio? Old-fashioned astrologers would warn ominously, "This relationship is doomed from the start!" It used to be that some sun-sign combinations were treated like champagne and tomato juice—never the twain should meet. Others were considered blessed by the stars with perfect compatibility. Today's astrologers are more realistic, acknowledging that, though some combinations will be more challenging, there are too many long-lasting relationships between so-called incompatible sun signs to brand any combination as totally unworkable. We've gone far beyond stereotyping to respecting and enjoying the differences between people and using astrology to help us get along with them.

Each sun sign does have certain predictable characteristics in love, however, which can help you better understand the dynamics of the relationship. But we must be careful not to oversimplify. Just because someone is a so-called "incompatible" sign is no reason the relationship can't work out. For a true in-depth comparison, an astrologer considers the interrelationships of all the planets and houses (where they fall in your respective horoscopes).

Since romantic bonds between other planets can offset difficulties between sun signs, it's worthwhile to analyze several of the most important ones. You can do this by making a very simple chart that compares the moon, Mars, and Venus, as well as the sun signs of the partners in a relationship. You can find the signs for Mars and Venus in the tables in this book. Unfortunately complete moon tables are too long for a book of this size, so it might be worth your while to consult an astrological ephemeris (a book of planetary tables) in your local library or to have a computer chart cast to find out each other's moon placement.

Simply look up the signs of Mars and Venus in this book (and the moon, if possible) for each person and list them, with the sun sign, next to each other. Then add the element (earth, air, fire, or water) of each sign. The earth signs are Taurus, Virgo, and Capricorn. The air signs are Gemini, Libra, and Aquarius. The fire signs are Aries, Leo, and Sagittarius. And the water signs are Cancer, Scorpio, and Pisces.

Here's an example:

	SUN	MOON	MARS	VENUS
ROMEO	Aries/Fire	Leo/Fire	Scorpio/Water	Taurus/Earth
JULIET	Pisces/Water	Leo/Fire	Aries/Fire	Aquarius/ Air

As a rule of thumb, signs of the *same* element or *complementary* elements (fire with air and earth with water) get along best. So you can see that this particular Romeo and Juliet could have some challenges ahead, with an emotional bond (the moon) creating a strong tie.

The Lunar Link—
The Person You Need

The planet in your chart that governs your emotions is the moon. (Note: The moon is not technically a planet, but is usually referred to as one by astrologers.) So you would naturally take this into consideration when evaluating a potential romantic partnership. If a person's moon is in a good relationship to your sun, moon, Venus, or Mars, preferably in the same sign or element, you should relate well on some emotional level. Your needs will be compatible; you'll understand each other's feelings without much effort. If the moon is in a compatible element, such as earth with water or fire with air, you may have a few adjustments, but you will be able to make them easily. With a water–fire or earth–air combination, you'll have to make a considerable effort to understand where the other is coming from emotionally.

The Venus Attraction—
The One You Want

Venus is what you respond to, so if you and your partner have a good Venus aspect, you should have much in common. You'll enjoy doing things together. The same type of lovemaking will turn you both on, so you'll have no trouble pleasing each other.

Look up both partners' Venus placements in the charts on page 78. Your lover's Venus in the same sign or a sign of the same element as your own Venus, Mars, moon, or sun is best. Second-best is a sign of a compatible element (earth with water, air with fire). Venus in water with air, or earth with fire means that you may have to make a special effort to understand what appeals to each other. And you'll have to give each other plenty of space to enjoy activities that don't particularly appeal to you. By the way, this chart can work not only for

15

lovers, but for any relationship where compatibility of tastes is important to you.

The Mars Connection— This One Lights Your Fire!

Mars positions reveal your sexual energy—how often you like to make love, for instance. It also shows your temper—do you explode or do a slow burn? Here you'll find out if your partner is direct, aggressive, and hot-blooded or more likely to take the cool, mental approach. Mutually supportive partners have their Mars working together in the same or complementary elements. But *any* contacts between Mars and Venus in two charts can strike sexy sparks. Even the difficult aspects—your partner's Mars three or six signs away from your sun, Mars, or Venus—can offer sexual stimulation. Who doesn't get turned on by a challenge from time to time? Sometimes the easy Mars relationships can drift into dullness.

The Solar Bond

The sun is the focus of our personality and therefore the most powerful component involved in astrology. Once again, earth and water or fire and air combinations will have an easier time together. Mixtures earth and water with fire and air can be much more challenging. However, each pair of sun signs has special lessons to teach and learn from each other. There is a negative side to the most ideal couple and a positive side to the most unlikely match—Each has an up and a down side. So if the outlook for you and your beloved (or business associate) seems like an uphill struggle, take heart! Such legendary lovers as Juan and Eva Peron, Ronald and Nancy Reagan, Harry and Bess Truman, Julius Caesar and Cleopatra, Billy and Ruth Graham, and George and

Martha Washington are among the many who have made successful partnerships between supposedly incompatible sun signs.

How to Seduce Every Sign . . .

The Aries Lover

It's not easy to make the first move on an Aries, since this sign always likes to be first. Try challenging your Aries in some way—this sign loves the chase almost as much as the conquest. So don't be too easy or accommodating—let them feel a sense of accomplishment when they've won your heart.

Be sure your interests and appearance are up to the minute. You can wear the latest style off the fashion show runway with an Aries, especially if it's bright red. Aries is a pioneer, an adventurer, always ahead of the pack. Play up your frontier spirit. Present the image of the two of you as an unbeatable team, one that can conquer the world, and you'll keep this courageous sign at your side.

Since they tend to idealize their lovers, Aries is especially disillusioned when their mates flirt. Be sure they always feel like number one in your life.

The Taurus Lover

Taurus is often seduced by surface physical beauty alone. Their five senses are highly susceptible, so find ways to appeal to all of them! Your home should be a restful haven from the outside world. Get a great sound system, some comfortable furniture to sink into, and keep the refrigerator stocked with treats. Most Taureans would rather entertain on their own turf than gad about town, so it helps if you're a good host or hostess.

Taurus like a calm, contented, committed relationship. This is not a sign to trifle with. Don't flirt or tease if you want to please. Don't rock the boat or try to make this sign jealous. Instead, create a steady, secure environment with lots of shared pleasures.

Taurus is an extremely sensual, affectionate, nurturing lover, but can be quite possessive. Taurus likes to "own" you, so don't hold back with them or play power games. If you need more space in the relationship, be sure to set clear boundaries, letting them know exactly where they stand. When ambiguity in a relationship makes Taurus uneasy, they may go searching for someone more solid and substantial. A Taurus romance works best where the limits are clearly spelled out. Taurus needs physical demonstrations of affection—so don't hold back on hugs.

The Gemini Lover

Variety is the spice of life to this flirtatious sign. Guard against jealousy—it is rarely justified. Provide a stimulating sex life—this is a very experimental sign—to keep them interested. Be a bit unpredictable. Don't let lovemaking become a routine. Most of all, sharing lots of laughs together can make Gemini take your relationship very seriously.

Keeping Gemini interested is like walking a tightrope. Though this sign needs stability and a strong home base to accomplish their goals, they also require a great deal of personal freedom. A great role model is Barbara Bush, a Gemini successfully married to another Gemini.

This is a sign that loves to communicate, so sit down and talk things over. Be interested in your partner's doings, but have a life of your own and ideas to contribute. Since this is a gadabout social sign, don't insist on quiet nights at home when your Gemini is in a party mood.

Gemini needs a steady hand, but at the same time plenty of rope. Focus on common goals and abstract ideals. Gemini likes to share, so be a twin soul and do things together. Keep up on their latest interests. Stay in touch mentally and physically, using both your mind and your hands to communicate.

The Cancer Lover

The song "Try a Little Tenderness" must have been written by a Cancer. This is probably the water sign that requires the most TLC. Cancers tend to be very private people who may take some time to open up. They are extremely self-protective and will rarely tell you what is truly bothering them. They operate indirectly, like the movements of the crab. You may have to divine their problem by following subtle clues, then draw them out gently and try to voice any criticism in the most tactful, supportive way possible.

Family ties are especially strong for Cancer. They will rarely break a strong family bond. Create an intimate family atmosphere, with the emphasis on food and family get-togethers. You can get valuable clues to Cancer appeal from their mothers and their early family situation. If their early life was unhappy, it's even more important that they feel they have found a close family with you.

Encouraging their creativity can counter Cancer's moodiness, which is also a sure sign of emotional insecurity. Find ways to distract them from negative moods. Calm them with a good meal for instance, or a trip to the seashore. Cancers are usually quite nostalgic and attached to the past. So be careful not to throw out their old treasures or photos.

The Leo Lover

Appeal to Leo pride by treating this sign royally. Be well groomed and dressed, someone they're proud to show off.

Leo thinks big, and likes to live like a king, so don't you be petty or miserly. Remember special occasions with a beautifully wrapped gift or flowers. Make an extra effort to treat them royally. Keep a sense of fun and playfulness, and loudly applaud Leo's creative efforts. React, respond, be a good audience! If Leo's ignored, this sign will seek a more appreciative audience—fast!

(Cheating Leos are almost always looking for an ego boost.)

Be generous with compliments. You can't possibly overdo here. Always accentuate the positive. Make them feel important by asking for advice and consulting them often. Leo enjoys a charming sociable companion, but be sure to make them the center of attention in your life.

The Virgo Lover

Virgos love to feel needed, so give them a job to do in your life. They are great fixer-uppers. Take their criticism as a form of love and caring, of noticing what you do. Bring them out socially—they're often very shy. Calm their nerves with good food, a healthy environment, trips to the country.

Virgos may seem cool and conservative on the surface, but underneath you'll find a sensual romantic. Think of Raquel Welch, Sophia Loren, Jacqueline Bisset, Garbo—it's amazing how seductive this practical sign can be! They are idealists, however, looking for someone who meets their high standards. If you've measured up, they'll do anything to serve and please you.

Mental stimulation is a turn-on to this Mercury-ruled sign. An intellectual discussion could lead to romantic action, so stay on your toes and keep well informed. This sign often mixes business with pleasure, so it helps if you share the same professional interests—you'll get to see more of your busy mate. With Virgo, the couple who works and plays together, stays together.

The Libra Lover

Do not underestimate Libra's need for beauty and harmony. To keep them happy, avoid scenes. Opt for calm, impersonal discussion of problems (or a well-reasoned debate) over an elegant dinner. Pay attention to the niceties of life. Send little gifts on Valentines Day and don't forget birthdays and anniversaries. Play up the romance to the hilt—with all the lovely gestures and trimmings—but tone down intensity and emotional drama (Aries, Scorpio take note). Surround your Libra with a physically tasteful atmosphere—elegant, well-designed furnishings and calm colors. Be well groomed and tastefully dressed and be sure to emphasize good conversation and good manners.

Bear in mind that Libra truly enjoys life with a mate and needs the harmony of a steady relationship. Outside affairs can throw them off balance. However, members of this sign are natural charmers who love to surround themselves with admirers, and this can cause a very possessive partner to feel insecure. Most of the time, Librans are only testing their charms with harmless flirtations and will rarely follow through, unless they are not getting enough attention or there is an unattractive atmosphere at home.

Mental compatibility is what keeps Libra in tune. Unfortunately this sign, like Taurus, often falls for physical beauty or someone who provides an elegant lifestyle, rather than someone who shares their ideals and activities, the kind of compatibility that will keep you together in the long run.

The Scorpio Lover

Pluto-ruled Scorpio is fascinated by power and control in all its forms. They don't like to compromise—it's "all or nothing." They don't trust or respect anything that comes too easily, so be a bit of a challenge and keep them guessing. Maintain your own personal identity in spite of Scorpio's desire to probe your innermost secrets.

Sex is especially important to this sign, which will demand fidelity from you (though they may not deliver it themselves). Communication on this level is critical. Explore Scorpio's fantasies together. Scorpio is a detective, so watch your own flirtations—don't play with fire. This is a jealous and vengeful sign, so you'll live to regret it. Scorpios rarely flirt for the fun of it themselves. There is usually a strong motive behind their actions.

Scorpios are often deceptively cool and remote on the

outside, but don't be fooled: This sign always has a hidden agenda and feels very intensely about most things. The disguise is necessary because Scorpio does not trust easily; but when they do, they are devoted and loyal and will stick with you through the toughest times. You can lean on this very intense and focused sign. The secret is in first establishing that basic trust through mutual honesty and respect.

Scorpio has a fascination with the dark, mysterious side of life. If unhappy, they are capable of carrying on a secret affair. So try to emphasize positive, constructive solutions with them. Don't fret if they need time alone to sort out problems. They may also prefer time alone with you to socializing with others, so plan romantic getaways together to a private beach or a secluded wilderness spot.

The Sagittarius Lover

Be a mental and spiritual traveling companion. Sagittarius is a footloose adventurer whose ideas know no boundaries, so don't try to fence them in. Sagittarians resent restrictions of any kind. For a long-lasting relationship, be sure you are in harmony with Sagittarius's ideals and spiritual beliefs. They like to feel that their life is constantly being elevated and taken to a higher level. Since down-to-earth matters often get put aside in the Sagittarian's scheme of things, get finances under control (money matters upset more relationships with Sagittarians than any other problem), but try to avoid being the stern disciplinarian in this relationship (find a good accountant).

Sagittarius is not generally a homebody—unless there are several homes. Be ready and willing to take off on the spur of the moment, or they'll go without you! Sports, outdoor activities, and physical fitness are important—stay in shape with some of Sagittarius Jane Fonda's tapes. Dress with flair and style—it helps if you look especially good in sportswear. Sagittarius men like beautiful legs, so play up yours. And this is one of the great animal lovers, so try to get along with the dog, cat, or horse.

The Capricorn Lover

Capricorns are ambitious, even if they are the stay-at-home partner in your relationship. They will be extremely active, have a strong sense of responsibility to their partner, and take commitments seriously. However, they might look elsewhere if the relationship becomes too dutiful. They also need romance, fun, lightness, humor, and adventure!

Generation gaps are not unusual in Capricorn romances, when the older Capricorn partner works hard all through life and seeks pleasurable rewards with a young partner, or the young Capricorn gets a taste of luxury and instant status from an older lover. This is one sign that grows more interested in romance as they age! Younger Capricorns often tend to put business way ahead of pleasure.

Capricorn is impressed by those who entertain well, have "class," and can advance their status in life. Keep improving yourself and cultivate important people. Stay on the conservative side. Extravagant or frivolous loves don't last—Capricorn keeps a weather eye on the bottom line. Even the wildest Capricorns, such as Elvis Presley, Rod Stewart, or David Bowie, show a conservative streak in their personal lives. It's also important to demonstrate a strong sense of loyalty to your family, especially older members. This reassures Capricorn, who'll be happy to grow old along with you!

The Aquarius Lover

Aquarius is one of the most independent, least domestic signs. Finding time alone with this sign may be one of your greatest challenges. They are everybody's buddy, usually surrounded by people they collect—some of whom may be old lovers who are now "just friends." However, it is unlikely that old passions will be rekindled if you manage to become Aquarius's number-one best friend as well as lover, and if you get actively involved in other important aspects of Aquarius's life, such as the political or charitable causes they believe in.

Aquarius needs a supportive backup person who encourages them but is not overly possessive when their natural charisma attracts admirers by the dozen. Take a leaf from Joanne Woodward, whose marriage to perennial Aquarius heartthrob Paul Newman has lasted more than 30 years. Encourage them to develop their original ideas. Don't rain on their parade if they decide suddenly to market their spaghetti sauce and donate the proceeds to their favorite charity, or drive racing cars. Share their goals and be their fan, or you'll never see them.

You may be called on to give them grounding where needed. Aquarius needs someone who can keep track of their projects. But always remember, it's basic friendship—with the tolerance and common ideals that implies—that will hold you together.

The Pisces Lover

They are great fantasists and extremely creative lovers, so use your imagination to add drama and spice to your times together. You can let your fantasies run wild with this sign—and they'll go you one better! They enjoy variety in lovemaking, so try never to let it become routine.

To keep a Pisces hooked, don't hold the string too tight! This is a sensitive, creative sign that may appear to need someone to manage their lives or point the direction out of their Neptunian fog, but if you fall into that role, expect your Pisces to rebel against any strong-arm tactics. Pisces is more susceptible to a play for sympathy than a play for power. They are suckers for a sob story, the most empathetic sign of the zodiac. More than one Pisces has been seduced and held by someone who plays the underdog role.

Long-term relationships work best if you can bring Pisces down to earth and, at the same time, encourage their creative fantasies. Deter them from escapism into alcohol or substance abuse by helping them to get counseling, if needed. Pisces will seek a soulmate who provides positive energy, self-confidence, and a safe harbor from the storms of life.

CHAPTER 3

A User-Friendly Guide to Astrology

Astrology is like a fascinating foreign country with a language all its own and territory that's easy to get lost in. This chapter is a brief introduction to the basics of astrology, to help you find your way around in later travels. Bear in mind, as you discover the difference between signs, houses, and constellations, that the information we share so readily was in ancient times a carefully guarded secret of scholar–priests entrusted with timing sacred ceremonies. While it takes years of study and practice to become an expert, you can derive pleasure and self-knowledge by learning how astrology works. Whether you're planning a brief visit or a long study, this user-friendly guide can give you the basic lay of the land, an overview that will help you get off on the road to understanding your own horoscope.

What Do We Mean by a "Sign"?

Signs are the "real estate" of astrology. They are segments of territory located on the *zodiac,* an imaginary 360-degree belt circling the earth. This belt is divided into twelve equal 30-degree portions, which are the *signs*.

There's a lot of confusion about the difference between the *signs* and the *constellations* of the zodiac. *Constellations* are patterns of stars that originally marked the twelve divisions of the zodiac, like sign posts. Though each *sign* is named after the constellation which once marked the same area, over hundreds of years, the earth's orbit has shifted, so that from our point of view here on earth, the constellations have "moved" and are no longer valid sign posts. However the 30-degree territory that belonged to each sign remains the same. (Most Western astrologers use the 12-equal-part division of the zodiac. But some methods of astrology do still use the constellations instead of the signs.)

Most people think of themselves in terms of their sun sign. A *sun sign* refers to the sign the sun is orbiting through at a given moment (from our point of view here on earth). For instance, "I'm an Aries" means that the sun was passing through Aries when that person was born. However, there are nine other planets (plus asteroids, fixed stars, and sensitive points) which also form our total astrological personality, and some or many of these will be located in other signs. No one is completely "Aries," with all their astrological components in one sign! (Please note that in astrology, the sun and moon are usually referred to as "planets," though of course they're not.)

What Makes a Sign Special?

What makes the sign of Aries associated with go-getters and Taureans savvy with money? And Geminis talk a blue streak and Sagittarians footloose? It is important to note that characteristics associated with the signs are not accidental. They are derived from combinations of four basic components: a sign's element, quality, polarity, and place on the zodiac.

For example, take the element of fire: It's hot, passionate. Then add an active cardinal mode. Give it a jolt of positive energy and place it first in line. And doesn't that sound like the active, me-first, driving, hotheaded, energetic Aries?

Then take the element of earth, practical, sensual, the

27

place where things grow. Add the fixed, stable mode. Give it energy that reacts to its surroundings, that settles in. Put it after Aries. Now you've got a good idea of how sensual, earthy Taurus operates.

Another way to grasp the idea is to pretend you're doing a magical puzzle based on the numbers that can divide into twelve (the number of signs): 4, 3, and 2. There are four "building blocks" or elements, three ways a sign operates (qualities) and two polarities. These alternate in turn around the zodiac, with a different combination coming up for each sign. Here's how they add up.

THE FOUR ELEMENTS

These describe the physical concept of the sign. Is it fiery (dynamic), earthy (practical), airy (mental), water (emotional)? There are three zodiac signs of each of the four elements: fire (Aries, Leo, Sagittarius), earth (Taurus, Virgo, Capricorn), air (Gemini, Libra, Aquarius), water (Cancer, Scorpio, Pisces). These are the same elements that make up our planet: earth, air, fire and water. But astrology uses the elements as *symbols* that link our body and psyche to the rhythms of the planets. Fire signs spread warmth and enthusiasm. They are able to fire up or motivate others. They have hot tempers. These are people who make ideas catch fire and spring into existence. Earth signs are the builders of the zodiac who follow through after the initiative of fire signs to make things happen. These people are solid, practical realists who enjoy material things and sensual pleasures. They are interested in ideas that can be used to achieve concrete results. Air signs are mental people, great communicators. Following the consolidating earth signs, they'll reach out to inspire others through the use of words, social contacts, discussion, and debate. Water signs complete each four-sign series, adding the ingredients of emotion, compassion, and imagination. Water-sign people are nonverbal communicators who attune themselves to their surroundings and react through the medium of feelings.

A SIGN'S QUALITY

The second consideration when defining a sign is how it will operate. Will it take the initiative, or move slowly and deliberately, or adapt easily? Its *quality* (or modality) will tell. There are three qualities and four signs of each quality: cardinal, fixed, and mutable.

Cardinal signs are the start-up signs that begin each season (Aries, Cancer, Libra, Capricorn). These people love to be active, involved in projects. They are usually on the fast track to success, impatient to get things under way. *Fixed signs* (Taurus, Leo, Scorpio, Aquarius) move steadily, always in control. They happen in the middle of a season, after the initial character of the season is established. Fixed signs are naturally more centered. They tend to move more deliberately, doing things slowly but thoroughly. They govern parts of your horoscope where you take root and integrate your experiences. *Mutable signs* (Gemini, Virgo, Sagittarius, Pisces) embody the principle of distribution. These are the signs that break up the cycle, prepare the way for a change by distributing the energy to the next group. Mutables are flexible, adaptable, communicative. They can move in many directions easily, darting around obstacles.

A SIGN'S POLARITY

In addition to an element and a quality, each sign has a polarity, either a positive or negative electrical charge that generates energy around the zodiac like a giant battery. Polarity refers to opposites, which you could also define as masculine/feminine, yin/yang, active/reactive. Alternating around the zodiac, the six fire and air signs are positive, active, masculine, and yang in polarity. These signs are open, expanding outward. The six earth and water signs are reactive, negative, and yin—in other words, nurturing and receptive in polarity, which allows the energy to develop and take shape. All positive energy would be like a car without brakes. All negative energy would be like a stalled vehicle, going nowhere. Both polarities are needed in balanced proportion.

Finally we must consider the order of the signs. This

is vital to the balance of the zodiac and the transmission of energy throughout the zodiac. Each sign is quite different from its neighbors on either side. Yet each seems to grow out of its predecessor like links in a chain, transmitting a synthesis of energy gathered along the chain to the following sign, beginning with the fire-powered active positive cardinal sign of Aries and ending with watery mutable, reactive Pisces.

The Layout of a Horoscope Chart

A horoscope chart is a graphic map of the heavens at a given moment in time. It looks somewhat like a wheel divided with twelve spokes. The territory marked off by each "spoke" is a section called a *house*. The houses are extremely important in astrological interpretation because each house is associated with a different area of life and is influenced (or *ruled*) by a sign and a planet assigned to that house.

In addition, the house is colored by the sign passing over the spoke (or cusp) at the moment of the horoscope. The sequence of the houses begins at the left center spoke (or the 9 position if you were reading a clock) and follows reading counter-clockwise around the chart.

The First House—Home of Aries and Mars

This is the house of "firsts"—the first impression you make, how you initiate matters, the image you choose to project. This is your advertisement to the world. Planets that fall here will intensify the way you come across to others. Often a person's first house will project an entirely different type of personality than the sun sign. For instance, a Capricorn with Leo in the first house will come across as much more flamboyant than the average Capricorn. The sign passing over the cusp of this house at the time of your birth is known as your ascendant or rising sign.

The Second House—Home of Taurus and Venus

This is how you experience the material world—what you value. Here is your contact with the material world—your attitudes about money, possessions, finances, whatever belongs to you, and what you own, as well as your earning and spending capacity. As a Venus-ruled house, it describes your sensuality, your delight in physical pleasures. On a deeper level, this house reveals your sense of self-esteem—how you value yourself.

The Third House—Home of Gemini and Mars

This is how well you communicate with others—are you understood? This house shows how you reach out to others nearby and interact with the immediate environment. Here is how your thinking process works, how you communicate. This house shows your first relationships, your experiences with brothers and sisters, as well as how well you deal with people close to you now, such as your neighbors or pals. It's where you take short trips, write letters, or use the telephone. It shows how your mind works in terms of left-brain logical and analytical functions.

The Fourth House—Home of Cancer and the Moon

This is how you are nurtured and made to feel secure— your roots! At the bottom of the chart, the fourth house, like the home, shows the foundation of life and its psychological underpinnings. Here is where you have the deepest confrontations with who you are and how you make yourself feel secure. It shows your early home environment and the circumstances at the end of your life—your final "home"—as well as the place you call home now. Astrologers look here for information about the parental nurturers in your life.

The Fifth House—Home of Leo and the Sun

This is how you express yourself creatively—your idea of play. The Leo house is where the creative potential develops. Here you express yourself and procreate, in the sense that children are outgrowths of your creative ability. But this house most represents your inner childlike self, who delights in play. If inner security has been established by the time you reach this house, you are now free to have fun, romance, and love affairs, and to give of yourself. This is also the place astrologers look for playful love affairs, flirtations, and brief romantic encounters (rather than long-term commitments).

The Sixth House—Home of Virgo and Mercury

This is how you function in daily life. The sixth house has been called the "repair and maintenance" department. Here is where you get things done, how you look after others and fulfill responsibilities, such as taking care of pets. Here is your daily survival, your "job" routine and organization (as opposed to your career, which is the domain of the tenth house), your diet, and your health and fitness regimens. This house shows how you take care of your body and organize yourself so you can perform efficiently in the world.

The Seventh House—Home of Libra and Venus

This is how you form a partnership. Here is the way you commit to others, as well as your close, intimate, one-on-one relationships (including open enemies—those you "face off" with). This house shows your attitude toward partners and those with whom you enter commitments, contracts, or agreements. Open hostilities, lawsuits, divorces, and marriages happen here. If the first house represents the "I" in your horoscope, the seventh or opposite house is the "not-I"—the complementary partner you attract by the way you come across. If you are having trouble with partnerships, consider what you are attracting by the energies of your first and seventh houses.

The Eighth House—Home of Scorpio and Pluto (also Mars)

This is how you merge with something greater than yourself. Here is where you deal with issues of power and control, where you share with others and merge your energy with another to become something greater. Here are your attitudes toward sex, shared resources, and taxes (what you share with the government). Because this house involves what belongs to others, there can be power struggles or there can be a deep psychological transformation as you bond with another. Here you transcend yourself with the occult, dreams, drugs, or psychic experiences that reflect the collective unconscious.

The Ninth House—Home of Sagittarius and Jupiter

This is how you search for wisdom and higher knowledge. As the third house represents the "lower mind," its opposite on the wheel, the ninth house, is the "higher mind"—the abstract, intuitive, spiritual mind that asks big questions like why are we here, how everything fits together, what it all means. The ninth house shows what you believe in. After the third house explored what was close at hand, the ninth stretches out to explore more exotic territory, either by traveling, broadening mentally with higher education, or stretching spiritually with religious activity. Here is where you write a book or an extensive thesis, where you pontificate, philosophize, or preach.

The Tenth House—Home of Capricorn and Saturn

This is your public image and how you handle authority. This house is located directly overhead at the "high noon" position. This is the most "visible" house in the chart, the one where the world sees you. It deals with your public image, your career (but not your routine "job"), and your reputation. Here is where you go public and take on responsibilities (as opposed to the fourth house, where you stay home). This will affect the career you choose and your "public relations." This house is also associated with your father figure or whoever else was the authority figure in your life.

The Eleventh House—Home of Aquarius and Uranus

This is your support system, how you relate to society and your goals. This house is where you define what you really want, the kinds of friends you have, your teammates, your political affiliations, and the kind of groups you identify with as an equal. Here is where you could become a socially conscious humanitarian—or a party-going social butterfly. It's where you look to others to stimulate you and discover your kinship to the rest of humanity. The sign on this house can help you understand what you gain and lose from friendships, how concerned you are with social approval, and with what others think.

The Twelfth House—Home of Pisces and Neptune

Here is where the boundaries between yourself and others become blurred, where you become selfless. In your trip around the zodiac, you've gone from the "I" of self-assertion in the first house to the final house symbolizing the dissolution that happens before rebirth, a place where the accumulated experiences are processed in the unconscious. Spiritually oriented astrologers look to this house for your past lives and karma. Places where we go to be alone and do spiritual or reparatory work belong here, such as retreats, religious institutions, hospitals. Here is also where we withdraw from society—or are forced to withdraw because of antisocial activity. Selfless giving through charitable acts is part of this house. In your daily life, the twelfth house reveals your deepest intimacies and your best-kept secrets, especially those you hide from yourself and keep repressed deep in the unconscious. It is where we surrender a sense of a separate self to a deep feeling of wholeness, such as selfless service in religion or any activity that involves merging with the greater whole. Many sports stars have important planets in the twelfth house that enable them to find an inner, almost mystical, strength that transcends their limits.

Who's Home in Your Houses?

Houses are stronger or weaker depending on how many planets are inhabiting them and the condition of those planets. If there are many planets in a given house, it follows that the activities of that house will be especially important in your life. If the planet that rules the house is also located there, this too adds power to the house.

CHAPTER 4

The Planets—Players in Your Personal Drama

Once you understand the basic territory of astrology—what defines a sign and the layout of a horoscope chart—you're ready to meet the cast of characters who make the chart come alive. Nothing happens without the planets, which relate to each other to create the action in a chart.

The ten planets in your chart will play starring or supporting roles, depending on their position in your horoscope. A planet in the first house, particularly one that's close to your rising sign, is sure to be a featured player. Planets that are grouped together usually operate together like a team, playing off each other, rather than expressing their energy singularly. A planet that stands alone, away from the others, is usually outstanding and sometimes steals the show.

Each planet has two signs where it is especially at home. These are called its *dignities*. The most favorable place for a planet is in the sign or signs it rules; the next best place is in a sign where it is *exalted,* or especially harmonious. On the other hand, there are places in the horoscope where a planet has to work harder to play its role. These places are called the planet's *detriment* and *fall.* The sign opposite a planet's rulership, which embodies the opposite area of life, is its detriment. The sign opposite its exaltation is called its fall. Though the terms may suggest unfortunate circumstances for the planet, that is not always the case. In fact, a planet that is debilitated can actually be more complete, because it must

36

stretch itself to meet the challenges of living in a more difficult sign. Like world leaders who've had to struggle for greatness, this planet may actually develop great strength and character.

Here's a list of the best places for each planet to be, in the signs they rule. Note that, as new planets were discovered in this century, they replaced the traditional rulers of signs that best complimented their energies.

ARIES—Mars

TAURUS—Venus, in its most sensual form

GEMINI—Mercury, in its communicative role

CANCER—the moon

LEO—the sun

VIRGO—Mercury, in its critical capacity

LIBRA—Venus, in its aesthetic, judgmental form

SCORPIO—Pluto, replacing the sign's original ruler, Mars

SAGITTARIUS—Jupiter

CAPRICORN—Saturn

AQUARIUS—Uranus, replacing Saturn, its original ruler

PISCES—Neptune, replacing Jupiter, its original ruler

A person who has many planets in exalted signs is lucky indeed, for here is where the planet can accomplish the most, and be its most influential and creative.

SUN—Exalted in Aries, where its energy creates action

MOON—Exalted in Taurus, where instincts and reactions operate on a highly creative level

MERCURY—Exalted in Virgo, which it also rules, and where it can reach analytical heights

VENUS—Exalted in Pisces, a sign whose sensitivity encourages love and creativity

MARS—Exalted in Capricorn, a sign that puts energy to work

JUPITER—Exalted in Cancer, where it encourages nurturing and growth

SATURN—At home in Libra, where it steadies the scales of justice and promotes balanced, responsible judgment

URANUS—Powerful in Scorpio, where it promotes transformation

NEPTUNE—Especially favored in Cancer, where it gains the security to transcend to a higher state

PLUTO—Exalted in Pisces, where it dissolves the old cycle to make way for transition to the new

The Sun is Always Center Stage

Your sun sign is where you directly express yourself, displaying the part of you that shines brightest, even when you're accompanied by strong costars, or you're dressed modestly, or sharing a house with several other planets. When you know a person's sun sign, you already know some very useful generic qualities. Then, after you add the other planets, you'll have an accurate profile of that person and will be more able to predict how that individual will act in a given situation. The sun's just one actor on the stage, but a very powerful one—a good reason why sun-sign astrology works for so many people.

The sun rules the sign of Leo, gaining strength through the pride, dignity, and confidence of the fixed-fire personality. It is exalted in "me-first" Aries. In its detriment, Aquarius, the sun-ego is strengthened through group participation and social consciousness, rather than through self-centeredness. Note how many Aquarius people are involved in politics, social work, public life, following the demands of their sun sign to be spokesperson for a group. In its fall, Libra, the sun needs the strength of a partner—an "other"—to enhance balance and self-expression.

Like your sun sign, each of the other nine planet's personalities is colored by the sign it is passing through at the time. For example, Mercury, the planet that rules the way you communicate, will express itself in a dynamic, headstrong Aries way if it was passing through the sign of Aries when you were born. You would communicate in a much different way if it were passing through the slower, more patient sign of Taurus. Here's a rundown of the planets and how they behave in every sign.

The Moon—The Oscar Nominee

The Moon's role is to dig beneath the surface to reflect your needs, your longings, and the kind of childhood conditioning you had. In a man's chart, the moon position also describes his female, receptive, emotional side, and the woman in his life who will have the deepest effect. (Venus reveals the kind of woman who attracts him physically).

The sign the moon was passing through at your birth reflects your instinctive emotional nature and the things that appeal to you subconsciously. Since accurate moon tables are too extensive for this book, check through these descriptions to find the moon sign that feels most familiar—or better yet, have your chart calculated by a computer service to get your accurate moon placement.

The moon rules maternal Cancer and is exalted in Taurus—both comforting, home-loving signs where the natural emotional energies of the moon are easily and productively expressed. But when the moon is in the opposite signs—in its Capricorn detriment and its Scorpio fall—it leaves the comfortable nest and deals with emotional issues of power and achievement in the outside world. Those of you with the moon in these signs will find your emotional role more challenging in life.

Moon in Aries

Emotionally, you are independent and ardent. You are an idealistic, impetuous person who falls in and out of love easily. You respond to a challenge, but could cool down once your quarry is captured. To avoid continuous "treat 'em rough" situations, you should work on cultivating patience and tolerance. Be wary of responding to excitement for its own sake.

Moon in Taurus

This is a strong position for the moon, so emotional satisfaction will be an important factor in your life. You are a huggy, sentimental soul who is very fond of the good life and gravitates toward solid, secure relationships. You like frequent displays of affection and creature comforts—all the tangible trappings of a cozy atmosphere. You are sensual and steady emotionally, but very stubborn and determined. You can't be pushed and tend to protect your turf.

Moon in Gemini

You crave mental stimulation and variety in life, which you usually get through either a varied social life, the excitement of flirtation, and/or multiple professional involvements. You may marry more than once and have a rather chaotic emotional life due to your difficulty with commitment and settling down. Be sure to find a partner who is as outgoing as you are. You will have to learn at some point to focus your energies because you tend to be somewhat fragmented—you may do two things at once, or have two careers, homes, or even two lovers. If you can find a creative way to express your many-faceted nature, you'll be ahead of the game.

Moon in Cancer

This is the most powerful lunar position, which is sure to have a deep imprint on your character. Your needs are very much associated with your reaction to the needs of others. You are very sensitive and self-protective, though some of you may mask this with a hard shell. This placement also gives an excellent memory and an uncanny ability to psyche out the needs of others. All of the lunar phases will affect you, especially full moons and eclipses, so be sure to mark them on your calendar. You are happiest at home and may work at home or turn your office into a second home, where you can nurture and comfort people (you may tend to "mother the world"). This psychic, intuitive moon might draw you to occult work in some way. Or you may professionally provide food and shelter to others.

Moon in Leo

This is a warm, passionate moon that takes everything to heart. You are attracted to all that is noble, generous, and aristocratic in life and may be a bit of a snob. You have an innate ability to take command emotionally, but you need strong support, loyalty, and loud applause from those you love. You are possessive of your loved ones and your turf, and you will roar if anyone threatens to take over your territory.

Moon in Virgo

You are rather cool until you decide if others measure up. But once someone or something meets your ideal standards, you hold up your end of the arrangement perfectly. You may, in fact, drive yourself too hard to attain some notion of perfection. Try to be a bit easier on yourself and others. Don't always act the critic! You love to be the teacher and are drawn to situations where you can change others for the better. But sometimes you must learn to accept others for what they are and enjoy what you have.

Moon in Libra

This is a partnership-oriented placement—you may find it difficult to be alone or to do things alone. But you must learn to lean on yourself first. When you have learned emotional balance, you can have excellent relationships. Avoid extremes in your love life—you thrive in a rather conservative, traditional, romantic relationship, where your partner provides attention and flattery—but not possessiveness. You'll be your most charming in an elegant, harmonious atmosphere.

41

Moon in Scorpio

This is a moon that enjoys and responds to intense, passionate feelings. You may go to extremes and have a very dramatic emotional life, full of ardor, suspicion, jealousy, and obsession. It would be much healthier to channel your need for power and control into meaningful work. This is a good position for anyone in the fields of medicine, police work, research, the occult, psychoanalysis, or intuitive work, because life-and-death situations are not as likely to faze you. However, you do take personal disappointments very hard.

Moon in Sagittarius

You take life's ups and downs with good humor and the proverbial grain of salt. You'll love 'em and leave 'em, and take off on a great adventure at a moment's notice. "Born free" could be your slogan, for you can't stand to be possessed emotionally by anyone. Attracted by the exotic, you have wanderlust mentally and physically. You may be too much in search of new mental and spiritual stimulation to ever settle down.

Moon in Capricorn

Are you ever accused of being too cool and calculating? You have an earthy side, but you take prestige and position very seriously. Your strong drive to succeed extends to your romantic life, where you will be devoted to improving your lifestyle and rising to the top. A structured situation where you can advance methodically makes you feel wonderfully secure. You may be attracted to someone older or very much younger or from a different social world. It may be difficult to look at the lighter side of emotional relationships, but the "up" side of this moon in its detriment is that you tend to be very dutiful and responsible to those you care for.

Moon in Aquarius

You are a people collector with many friends of all backgrounds. You are happiest surrounded by people and may feel slightly uneasy when left alone. Though intense emotions could be unsettling, you usually stay friends with those with whom you get involved. You're tolerant and understanding, but sometimes you can be emotionally unpredictable. You don't like anything to be too rigid and you may resist working on schedule. You may even have a very unconventional love life. With plenty of space, you will be able to sustain relationships, but you'll blow away from possessive demanding types.

Moon in Pisces

You are very responsive and empathetic to others, especially if they have problems, but be on guard against attracting too many people with sob stories. You'll be happiest if you can find a way to express your creative imagination in the arts or in the spiritual or healing professions. You may tend to escape to a fantasy world or be attracted to exotic places or people. You need an emotional anchor, as you are very sensitive to the moods of others. You are happiest near water, working in a field that gives you emotional variety. But steer clear of too much escapism (especially in alcohol) or reclusiveness. Keep a firm foothold in reality.

Mercury—The Scriptwriter

Mercury shows how you think and speak, and how logically your mind works. It stays close to the sun—never more than a sign away—and very often it shares the same sign as the sun, reinforcing the sun's communicative talents. Mercury functions easily in the naturally analytical signs Gemini and Virgo, which it rules. Yet Mercury in Sagittarius and Pisces, where logic often takes second place to visionary ideas, and where Mercury is debilitated, can provide visionary thinking and poetic expression. But this planet must be properly harnessed. Check your sun sign and the signs preceding and following it to see which Mercury position most applies to you.

Mercury in Aries

Your mind is very active and assertive. You never hesitate to say what you think; you never shy away from a battle. In fact, you may relish a verbal confrontation. Tact is not your strong point, so you may have to learn not to trip over your tongue.

Mercury in Taurus

You may be a slow learner, but you have good concentration and mental stamina. You want to make your ideas really happen. You'll attack a problem methodically and consider every angle thoroughly, never jumping to conclusions. You'll stick with a subject until you master it.

Mercury in Gemini

You are a wonderful communicator with great facility for expressing yourself both verbally and in writing. You talk and talk, and you love gathering all kinds of information. You probably finish other people's sentences and talk with hand gestures. You can talk to anybody anytime—and you probably have the phone bills to prove it. You read anything from sci-fi to Shakespeare, and you might need an extra room just for your book collection. Though you learn fast, you may lack focus and discipline. Watch a tendency to jump from subject to subject.

Mercury in Cancer

You rely on intuition more than logic. Your mental processes are usually colored by your emotions, so you may seem shy or hesitant to voice your opinions. But this placement gives you the advantage of great imagination and empathy in the way you communicate with others.

Mercury in Leo

You are enthusiastic and very dramatic in the way you express yourself. You like to hold the attention of groups and could be a great public speaker. You think big, preferring to deal with the overall picture rather than the details.

Mercury in Virgo

This is one of the best places for Mercury. It should give you the ability to think critically, pay attention to details, and analyze thoroughly. Your mind focuses on the practical side of things, making you well suited to teaching or editing.

Mercury in Libra

You are a born diplomat who smoothes over ruffled feathers. You may be a talented debater or lawyer, but constantly weighing the pros and cons of situations makes you vacillate when making decisions.

Mercury in Scorpio

Yours is an investigative mind that stops at nothing to get the answers. You may have a sarcastic, stinging wit, and a gift for the cutting remark. But there's always a grain of truth to your verbal sallies, thanks to your penetrating insight.

Mercury in Sagittarius

You are a super salesman with a tendency to expound. Though you are very broad minded, you can be dogmatic when it comes to telling others what's good for them. You won't hesitate to tell the truth as you see it, so watch a tendency toward tactlessness. On the plus side, you have a great sense of humor. This position of Mercury is often considered by astrologers to be at a disadvantage because Sagittarius opposes Gemini, the sign Mercury rules, and squares off with Virgo, another Mercury-ruled sign. What often happens is that Mercury in Sagittarius oversteps its bounds and loses sight of the facts in a situation. Do a reality check before making promises that you may not be able to deliver.

Mercury in Capricorn

This placement endows good mental discipline. You have a love of learning and a very orderly approach to your subjects. You will patiently plod through the facts and figures until you have mastered the tasks. You grasp structured situations easily, but may be short on creativity.

Mercury in Aquarius

With Uranus and Neptune in Aquarius now energizing your Mercury, you're sure to be on the cutting edge of new ideas. An independent, original thinker, you'll have more far-out ideas than the average person and be quick to check out any unusual opportunities. Your opinions are so well researched and grounded in fact that once your mind is made up, it is difficult to change.

Mercury in Pisces

You have the psychic intuitive mind of a natural poet. You should learn to make use of your creative imagination. You think in terms of helping others, but check a tendency to be vague and forgetful of details.

Venus—The Romantic Heroine

Venus is the planet of romantic love, pleasure, and artistry. It shows what you react to, your tastes, and what (or who) turns you on. It is naturally at home in Libra, the sign of partnerships, or Taurus, the sign of physical pleasures, both of which it rules. Yet in Aries, its detriment, Venus, daring and full of energy, is negatively self-serving. In Pisces, where Venus is exalted, this planet can go overboard, loving to the point of self-sacrifice. While Venus in Virgo, its fall, can be the perfectionist in love, it can also offer affectionate service and true support.

You can find your Venus placement on the charts in this book. Look for the year of your birth in the left-hand column, then follow the line across the page until you read the time period of your birthday. The sign heading that column will be your Venus. If you were born on a day when Venus was changing signs, check the signs preceding or following that day. Here are the roles your Venus plays—and the songs it sings.

Venus in Aries

Scarlett O'Hara could embody this placement. You can't stand to be bored, confined, or ordered around. But a good challenge—maybe even a rousing row—turns you on. Confess—don't you pick a fight now and then just to get someone stirred up? You're attracted by the chase, not the catch, which could cause some problems in your love life if the object of your affection becomes too attainable. You like to wear red and be first with the latest fashion. You'll spot a trend before anyone else.

Venus in Taurus

All your senses work in high gear, making this the perfect placement for a "Material Girl." You love to be surrounded by glorious tastes, smells, textures, sounds, and sights—austerity is not for you. Neither is being rushed, for you like time to enjoy your pleasures. Soothing surroundings with plenty of creature comforts are your cup of tea. You like to feel secure in your nest, with no sudden jolts or surprises. You like familiar objects—in fact, you may hate to let anything or anyone go.

Venus in Gemini

You are a lively, sparkling personality who "Loves the Night Life," thriving in constant variety and a frequent change of scenery. A varied social life is important to you, with plenty of stimulation and a chance to engage in some light flirtation. Commitment may be difficult because playing the field is so much fun.

Venus in Cancer

An atmosphere where you feel protected, coddled, and mothered is best for you. You'd love to be surrounded by children in a cozy, homelike situation. You are attracted to those who are tender and nurturing, who make you feel secure and well provided for—your "Heart Belongs to Daddy" (or Mommy). You may be secretive about your emotional life or attracted to clandestine relationships.

Venus in Leo

You're an "Uptown Girl" or boy who loves "Puttin' on the Ritz" to consort with elegant people, dress up, and be the center of attraction. First-class attention in large doses turns you on, and so does the glitter of real gold and the flash of mirrors. You like to feel like a star at all times, surrounded by your admiring audience. But you may be attracted to flatterers and tinsel, while the real gold requires some digging.

Venus in Virgo

Everything neatly in its place? On the surface, you are attracted to an atmosphere where everything is in perfect order, but underneath are some basic, earthy urges. You are attracted to those who appeal to your need to teach, serve, or play out a Pygmalion fantasy. You are at your best when you are busy doing something useful.

Venus in Libra

"I Feel Pretty" could be your theme song. Elegance and harmony are your key words—you can't abide an atmosphere of contention. Your taste tends toward the classic, with light harmonies of color—nothing clashing, trendy, or outrageous. You love doing things with a partner and should be careful to pick one who is decisive, but patient enough to let you weigh the pros and cons. Steer clear of argumentative types.

Venus in Scorpio

Hidden mysteries intrigue you—in fact, anything that is too open and above board is a bit of a bore. You surely have a stack of whodunits by the bed, along with an erotic magazine or two. You like to solve puzzles, and you may also be fascinated with the occult, crime, or scientific research. Intense, "All or Nothing at All" situations add spice to your life, and you love to ferret out the secrets of others. But you could get burned by your flair for living on the edge. The color black, spicy food, dark wood furniture, and heady perfume all get you in the right mood.

Venus in Sagittarius

"Like a Rolling Stone" sums up your Venus personality. If you are not actually a world traveler, your surroundings are sure to reflect your love of faraway places. You like a casual outdoor atmosphere and a dog or two to pet. There should be plenty of room for athletic equipment and suitcases. You're attracted to kindred souls who love to travel and who share your freedom-loving philosophy of life. Athletics, as well as spiritual or New Age pursuits, could be your other interests.

Venus in Capricorn

"Diamonds Are a Girl's Best Friend" could be the theme song of this ambitious Venus. You want substance in life and you are attracted to whatever will help you get where you are going. Status objects turn you on, and so do those who have a serious, responsible, businesslike approach, or who remind you of a beloved parent. It is characteristic of this placement to be attracted to someone of a different generation. Antiques, traditional clothing, and dignified behavior favor you.

Venus in Aquarius

"Just Friends, Lovers No More" is often what happens to this Venus. You like to be in a group, particularly one pushing a worthy cause. You feel quite at home surrounded by people, remaining detached from any intense commitment. Original ideas and unpredictable people fascinate you. You don't like everything to be planned out in advance, preferring spontaneity and delightful surprises.

Venus in Pisces

"Why Not Take all of Me?" pleads this Venus, who loves to give of yourself—and you find plenty of takers. Stray animals and people appeal to your heart and your pocketbook, but be careful to look at their motives realistically once in a while. You are extremely vulnerable to sob stories of all kinds. Fantasy, theater, and psychic or spiritual activities also speak to you.

Mars—The Conquering Hero

Mars is the mover and shaker in your life. It shows how you pursue your goals and whether you have energy to burn or proceed in a slow, steady pace. Or perhaps you are nervous, restless, and unable to sit still. Your Mars placement will also show how you get angry: Do you explode, do a slow burn, or hold everything inside, then get revenge later?

In Aries, which it rules, and Scorpio, which it corules, Mars is at its most powerful. Yet this drive can be self-serving and impetuous. In Libra, the sign of its detriment, Mars demands cooperation in a relationship. In Capricorn, where it is exalted, Mars becomes an ambitious achiever headed for the top. But in Cancer, the sign of its fall, Mars's aggression becomes tempered by feelings, especially those involving self-protection and security, which are always considered first. The end can never justify the means for Mars in Cancer.

To find your Mars, turn to the chart on page 86. Find your birth year in the left-hand column and trace the line across horizontally until you come to the column headed by the month of your birth. There you will find an abbreviation of your Mars sign. If the description of your Mars sign doesn't ring true, read the description of the sign preceding and following it. You may have been born on a day when Mars was changing signs, and your Mars would then be in the adjacent sign.

Mars in Aries

In the sign it rules, Mars shows its brilliant, fiery nature. You have an explosive temper and can be quite impatient, but on the other hand you have tremendous courage, energy, and drive. You'll let nothing stand in your way as you race to be first! Obstacles are met head on and broken through by force. However, those that require patience and persistence can have you exploding in rage. You're a great starter, but not necessarily around for the finish.

Mars in Taurus

Slow, steady, concentrated energy gives you the power. You've great stamina and you never give up, as you wear away obstacles with your persistence. Often you come out a winner because you've had the patience to hang in there. When angered, you do a slow burn.

Mars in Gemini

You can't sit still for long; this Mars craves variety. You often have two or more things going on at once—it's all an amusing game to you. Your life can get very complicated, but that only adds spice and stimulation. What drives you into a nervous, hyper state? Boredom, sameness, routine, and confinement. You can do wonderful things with your hands and you have a way with words.

Mars in Cancer

You rarely attack head on—instead, you'll keep things to yourself, make plans in secret, and always cover your actions. This might be interpreted by some as manipulative, but you are only being self-protective. You get furious when anyone knows too much about you, but you do like to know all about others. Your mothering and feeding instincts can be put to good use if you work in the food, hotel, or child-care industry. You may have to overcome your fragile sense of security, which prompts you not to take risks and to get physically upset when criticized. Don't take things so personally!

Mars in Leo

You have a very dominant personality that takes center stage—modesty is not one of your traits, nor is taking a back seat. You prefer giving the orders and have been known to make a dramatic scene if they are not obeyed. Properly used, this Mars confers leadership ability, endurance, and courage.

Mars in Virgo

You are the fault finder of the zodiac, who notices every little detail. Mistakes of any kind make you very nervous. You may worry even if everything is going smoothly. You may not express your anger directly, but you sure can nag. You have definite likes and dislikes and you are sure you can do the job better than anyone else. You are certainly more industrious and detail oriented than other signs. Your Mars energy is often most positively expressed in some kind of teaching role.

Mars in Libra

This Mars will have a passion for beauty, justice, and art. Generally, you will avoid confrontations at all costs, preferring to spend your energy finding a diplomatic solution or weighing the pros and cons. Your other techniques are using passive aggression or charm to get people to do what you want.

Mars in Scorpio

This is a powerful placement, so intense that it demands careful channeling into worthwhile activities. Otherwise, you could become obsessed with your sexuality or might use your need for power and control to manipulate others. You are strong willed, shrewd, and very private about your affairs, and you'll usually have a secret agenda behind your actions. Your great stamina, focus, and discipline would be excellent assets for careers in the military or medical fields, especially research or surgery. When angry, you don't get mad—you get even!

Mars in Sagittarius

This expansive Mars often propels people into sales, travel, athletics, or philosophy. Your energies function well when you are on the move. You have a hot temper and are inclined to say what you think before you consider the consequences. You shoot for high goals—and talk endlessly about them—but you may be weak on groundwork. This Mars needs a solid foundation. Watch a tendency to take unnecessary risks.

Mars in Capricorn

This is an ambitious Mars with an excellent sense of timing. You have the drive for success and the discipline to achieve it. You have an eye for those who can be of use to you, and you may dismiss people ruthlessly when you're angry. But you drive yourself hard and deliver full value. This is a good placement for an executive. You'll aim for status and a high material position in life, and keep climbing despite the odds. A great Mars to have!

Mars in Aquarius

This is the most rebellious Mars. You seem to have a drive to assert yourself against the status quo. You may enjoy provoking people, shocking them out of traditional views. Or this placement could express itself in an off-beat sex life—somehow you often find yourself in unconventional situations. You enjoy being a leader of an active group that pursues forward-looking studies, politics, or goals.

Mars in Pisces

This Mars is a good actor who knows just how to appeal to the sympathies of others. You create and project wonderful fantasies or use your sensitive antennae to crusade for those less fortunate. You get what you want through creating a veil of illusion and glamour. This is a good Mars for someone in the creative fields—a dancer, performer, or photographer—or for someone in the motion-picture industry. Many famous film stars have this placement. Watch a tendency to manipulate by making others feel sorry for you.

Jupiter—The Jolly Giant

Jupiter is often viewed as the "Santa Claus" of the horoscope, a jolly happy planet that brings good luck, gifts, success, and opportunities. Jupiter also embodies the functions of the higher mind, where you do complex, expansive thinking and deal with the big overall picture rather than the specifics (the role of Mercury). This big, bright, swirling mass of gases is associated with the kind of windfall you get without too much hard work. You're optimistic under Jupiter's influence—anything seems possible. You'll travel, expand your mind with higher education, and publish to share your knowledge widely. But a strong Jupiter has its down side, too. Jupiter's influence is neither discriminating nor disciplined. It represents the principle of growth without judgment, and could result in extravagance, weight gain, laziness, and carelessness if not kept in check.

Be sure to look up your Jupiter in the tables in this book. When the current position of Jupiter is favorable, you may get that lucky break. At any rate, it's a great time to try new things, take risks, travel, or get more education. Opportunities seem to open up at this time, so take advantage of them. Once a year, Jupiter changes signs. That means you are due for an expansive time every twelve years, when Jupiter travels through your sun sign. You'll also have "up" periods every four years, when Jupiter is in the same element as your sun sign.

Jupiter in Aries

You are the soul of enthusiasm and optimism. Your luckiest times are when you are getting started on an exciting project or selling an ideal that you really believe in, but don't be arrogant with those who do not share your enthusiasm. You follow your impulses, often ignoring budget or other common sense limitations. To produce real, solid benefits, you'll need patience and follow-through wherever this Jupiter falls in your horoscope.

Jupiter in Taurus

You'll spend on beautiful material things, especially items made of natural materials, such as rare woods, pure fabrics, or precious gems. You can't have too much comfort or too many sensual pleasures. Watch a tendency to overindulge in good food, or to overpamper yourself with nothing but the best. Spartan living is not for you! You may be especially lucky in matters of real estate.

Jupiter in Gemini

You are the great talker of the zodiac, and you may be a great writer, too. But restlessness could be your weak point. You jump around, talk too much, and could be a jack of all trades. Keeping a secret is especially difficult, so you'll also have to watch a tendency to spill the beans. Since you love to be at the center of a beehive of activity, you'll have a vibrant social life. Your best opportunities will come through your talent for language—speaking, writing, communicating, and selling.

Jupiter in Cancer

You are luckiest in situations where you can find emotional closeness or deal with basic security needs, such as food, nurturing, or shelter. You may be a great collector and you may simply love to accumulate things—you are the one who stashed things away for a rainy day. You probably have a very good memory and love children—in fact, you may have many children to care for. The food, hotel, child-care, or shipping business hold good opportunities for you.

Jupiter in Leo

You are a natural showman who loves to live in a larger-than-life way. Yours is a personality full of color that always find its way into the limelight. You can't have too much attention or applause. Show biz is a natural place for you, and so is any area where you can play to a crowd. Exercising your flair for drama, your natural playfulness, and your romantic nature brings you good fortune. But watch a tendency to be overly extravagant or to monopolize center stage.

Jupiter in Virgo

You actually love those minute details others find boring. To you, they make all the difference between the perfect and the ordinary. You are the fine craftsman who spots every flaw. You expand your awareness by finding the most efficient methods and by being of service to others. Many will be drawn to medical or teaching fields. You'll also have luck in publishing, crafts, nutrition, and service professions. Watch out for a tendency to overwork.

Jupiter in Libra

This is an other-directed Jupiter that develops best with a partner, for the stimulation of others helps you grow.

You are also most comfortable in harmonious, beautiful situations, and you work well with artistic people. You have a great sense of fair play and an ability to evaluate the pros and cons of a situation. You usually prefer to play the role of diplomat rather than adversary.

Jupiter in Scorpio

You love the feeling of power and control, of taking things to their limit. You can't resist a mystery, and your shrewd, penetrating mind sees right through to the heart of most situations and people. You have luck in work that provides for solutions to matters of life and death. You may be drawn to undercover work, behind-the-scenes intrigue, psychotherapy, the occult, and sex-related ventures. Your challenge will be to develop a sense of moderation and tolerance for other beliefs—this Jupiter can be fanatical. You may have luck in handling other people's money—insurance, taxes, and inheritance can bring you a windfall.

Jupiter in Sagittarius

Independent, outgoing, and idealistic, you'll shoot for the stars. This Jupiter compels you to travel far and wide, both physically and mentally, via higher education. You may have luck while traveling in an exotic place. You also have luck with outdoor ventures, exercise, and animals, particularly horses. Since you tend to be very open about your opinions, watch a tendency to be tactless and to exaggerate. Instead, use your wonderful sense of humor to make your point.

Jupiter in Capricorn

Jupiter is much more restrained in Capricorn, the sign of rules and authority. Here, Jupiter can make you overwork and heighten your ambition or sense of duty. You'll expand in areas that advance your position, putting you farther up the social or corporate ladder. You are lucky working within the establishment in a very structured situation, where you can show off your ability to organize and reap rewards for your hard work.

Jupiter in Aquarius

This is another freedom-loving Jupiter, with great tolerance and originality. You are at your best when you are working for a humanitarian cause and in the company of many supporters. This is a good Jupiter for a political career, for you'll relate to all kinds of people on all social levels. You have an abundance of original ideas, but you are best off away from routine and any situation that imposes rigid rules. You need mental stimulation!

Jupiter in Pisces

You are a giver whose feelings and pocketbook are easily touched by others, so choose your companions with care. You could be the original sucker for a hard-luck story—better find a worthy hospital or charity to appreciate your selfless support. You have a great creative imagination and may attract good fortune in fields related to oil, perfume, pharmaceuticals, petroleum, dance, footwear, and alcohol. But beware of overindulgence in alcohol—focus on a creative outlet instead.

Saturn—The "Heavy"

Jupiter speeds you up with lucky breaks, then along comes Saturn to slow you down with the disciplinary brakes. Saturn has unfairly been called a malefic planet, one of the bad guys of the zodiac. On the contrary, Saturn is one of our best friends, the kind who tells you what's wrong with you for your own good. Under a Saturn transit, we grow up, take responsibility for our lives, and emerge from whatever test this planet has in store, far wiser, more capable, and mature.

When Saturn hits a critical point in your horoscope, you can count on an experience that will make you slow down, pull back, and reexamine your life. It is a call to eliminate what is not working and to shape up. By the end of its 28-year trip around the zodiac, Saturn will have tested you in all areas of your life. The major tests usually happen in seven-year cycles, when Saturn passes over the angles of your chart—your rising sun, midheaven, descendant, and nadir. This is when the real life-changing experiences happen. But you are also in for a testing period whenever Saturn passes a planet in your chart or stresses that planet from a distance. Therefore it is useful to check your planetary positions with the travel schedule of Saturn in order to prepare in advance, or at least to brace yourself.

When Saturn returns to its location at the time of your birth, at approximately age 28, you'll have your first Saturn return. At this time, a person usually takes stock or settles down to find his mission in life and assume full adult duties and responsibilities.

Another way Saturn helps us is to reveal the karmic lessons from previous lives and give us the chance to overcome them. So look at Saturn's challenges as much-needed opportunities for self-improvement. Under a Jupiter influence, you'll have more fun, but Saturn gives you solid, long-lasting results.

Look up your natal Saturn in the tables in this book for clues on where you need work.

Saturn in Aries

Saturn here puts the brakes on Aries' natural drive and enthusiasm. You don't let anyone push you around and you know what's best for yourself. Following orders is not your strong point, and neither is diplomacy. You tend to be quick to go on the offensive in relationships, attacking first, before anyone attacks you. Because no one quite lives up to your standards, you often wind up doing everything yourself. You'll have to learn to cooperate and tone down self-centeredness.

Saturn in Taurus

A big issue is getting control of the cash flow. There will be lean periods that can be frightening, but you have the patience and endurance to stick them out and the methodical drive to prosper in the end. Learn to take a philosophical attitude like Ben Franklin, who also had this placement and who said, "A penny saved is a penny earned."

Saturn in Gemini

You are a serious student of life who may have difficulty communicating or sharing your knowledge. You may be shy, speak slowly, or have fears about communicating, like Eleanor Roosevelt. You dwell in the realms of science, theory, or abstract analysis, even when you are dealing with the emotions, like Sigmund Freud, who also had this placement.

Saturn in Cancer

Your tests come with establishing a secure emotional base. In doing so, you may have to deal with some very basic fears centering on your early home environment. Most of your Saturn tests will have emotional roots in those early childhood experiences. You may have difficulty remaining objective in terms of what you try to achieve, so it will be especially important for you to deal with negative feelings such as guilt, paranoia, jealousy, resentment, and suspicion. Galileo and Michelangelo also navigated these murky waters.

Saturn in Leo

This is an authoritarian Saturn, a strict, demanding parent who may deny the pleasure principle in your zeal to see that rules are followed. Though you may feel guilty about taking the spotlight, you are very ambitious and loyal. You have to watch a tendency toward rigidity, as well as a leaning toward overwork and holding back affection. Joseph Kennedy and Billy Graham share this placement.

Saturn in Virgo

This is a cautious, exacting Saturn, intensely hard on yourself. Most of all, you give yourself the roughest time with your constant worries about every little detail, often making yourself sick. You may have difficulties setting priorities and getting the job done. Your tests will come in learning tolerance and understanding of others. Charles de Gaulle and Nathaniel Hawthorne had this meticulous Saturn.

Saturn in Libra

Saturn is exalted here, which makes this planet an ally. You may choose very serious, older partners in life, perhaps stemming from a fear of dependency. You need to learn to stand solidly on your own before you commit to another. You are extremely cautious as you deliberate every involvement—with good reason. It is best that you find an occupation that makes good use of your sense of duty and honor. Steer clear of fly-by-night situations. Khrushchev and Mao Tse-tung had this placement, too.

Saturn in Scorpio

You have great staying power. This Saturn tests you in situations involving the control of others. You may feel drawn to some kind of intrigue or undercover work, like J. Edgar Hoover. Or there may be an air of mystery surrounding your life and death, like Marilyn Monroe and Robert Kennedy, who had this placement. There are lessons to be learned from your sexual involvements—often sex is used for manipulation or is somehow out of the ordinary. The Roman emperor Caligula and the transvestite Christine Jorgensen are extreme cases.

Saturn in Sagittarius

Your challenges and lessons will come from tests of your spiritual and philosophical values, as happened to Martin Luther King and Gandhi. You are high minded and sincere with the reflective, moral placement. Uncompromising in your ethical standards, you could become a benevolent despot.

Saturn in Capricorn

With the help of Saturn at maximum strength, your judgment will improve with age. And, like Spencer Tracy's screen image, you'll be the gray-haired hero with a strong sense of responsibility. You advance in life slowly but steadily, always with a strong hand at the helm and an eye for the advantageous situation. Negatively, you may be a loner, prone to periods of melancholy.

Saturn in Aquarius

Do you care too much about what others think? Do you feel like an outsider, as Greta Garbo did? You may fear being different from others and therefore slight your own unique, forward-looking gifts, or, like Lord Byron and Howard Hughes, you may take the opposite tack and rebel in the extreme. You can apply discipline to accomplish great humanitarian goals, as Albert Schweitzer did.

Saturn in Pisces

Your fear of the unknown and the irrational may lead you to the safety and protection of an established institution. Some of you may avoid looking too deeply inside at all costs. Jesse James, who had this placement, spent his life on the run. Or you might go in the opposite, more positive direction by developing a discipline that puts you more in control of your feelings. Some of you will take refuge in work with hospitals, charities, or religious institutions.

Queen Victoria, who had this placement, symbolized an era when charitable institutions of all kinds were founded. Discipline applied to artistic work, especially poetry and dance, or spiritual work, such as yoga or meditation, might be helpful.

Uranus, Neptune, and Pluto— The Character Roles

These three outer planets are slow moving but powerful forces in your life. Since they stay in a sign at least seven years, you'll share the sign placement with everyone you went to school with and perhaps your brothers and sisters. However, the area of life (house) where the planet operates in your chart is what makes its influence unique to you. When one of these distant planets changes signs, there is a definite shift in the atmosphere, bringing the feeling of the end of an era.

Since these planets are so far away from the sun—too distant to be seen by the naked eye—they pick up signals from the universe at large. These planetary receivers literally link the sun with distant energies, and then perform a similar function in your horoscope by linking your central character with intuitive, spiritual, transformative forces from the cosmos. Each planet has a special domain and will reflect this in the area of your life where it falls.

Uranus—The Revolutionary, the Techie

Uranus is the brilliant, highly unpredictable genius who shakes us out of our rut and propels us forward. There is nothing ordinary about this quirky green planet that seems to be traveling on its side, surrounded by a swarm of at least fifteen moons. Is it any wonder that astrologers assigned it to Aquarius, the most eccentric and gregarious sign? Uranus seems to wend its way around the sun, marching to its own tune.

Uranus energy is electrical, happening in sudden flashes. It is not influenced by karma or past events, nor does it regard tradition, sex, or sentiment. The Uranian key words are "surprise" and "awakening." Suddenly, there's that flash of inspiration, that bright idea, that totally new approach that turns around whatever scheme you were undertaking. The Uranus place in your life is where you awaken and become your own person, and it is probably the most unconventional place in your chart.

Look up the sign of Uranus at the time of your birth and see where you follow your own tune.

Uranus in Aries

BIRTH DATES:
March 30, 1927–November 4, 1927
January 13, 1928—June 6, 1934
October 10, 1934—March 28, 1935

Your generation is original, creative, and pioneering. It developed the computer, the airplane, and the cyclotron. You let nothing hold you back from exploring the unknown and you have a powerful mixture of fire and electricity behind you. Women of your generation were among the first to be liberated. You are the unforgettable style setters, with a surprise in store for everyone. Like Yoko Ono, Grace Kelly, and Jacqueline Onassis, your life may be jolted by sudden and violent changes.

Uranus in Taurus

BIRTH DATES:
June 6, 1934–October 10, 1934
March 28, 1935–August 7, 1941
October 5, 1941–May 15, 1942

You are probably self-employed or would like to be. You have original ideas about making money, and you brace yourself for sudden changes of fortune. This Uranus can cause shakeups, particularly in finances, but it can also make you a born entrepreneur.

Uranus in Gemini

BIRTH DATES:
August 7, 1941–October 5, 1941
May 15, 1942–August 30, 1948
November 12, 1948–June 10, 1949

You were the first children to be influenced by television and in your adult years, your generation stocks up on answering machines, cordless phones, car phones, computers, and fax machines—any new way you can communicate. You have an inquiring mind, but your interests are rather short lived. This Uranus can be easily fragmented if there is no structure and focus.

Uranus in Cancer

BIRTH DATES:
August 30, 1948–November 12, 1948
June 10, 1949–August 24, 1955
January 28, 1956–June 10, 1956

This generation came at a time when divorce was becoming commonplace, so your home image is unconventional. You may have an unusual relationship with your parents; you may have come from a broken home or an unconventional one. You'll have unorthodox ideas about parenting, intimacy, food, and shelter. You may also be interested in dreams, psychic phenomena, and memory work.

Uranus in Leo

BIRTH DATES:
August 24, 1955–January 28, 1956
June 10, 1956–November 1, 1961
January 10, 1962–August 10, 1962

This generation understood how to use electronic media. Many of your group are now leaders in the high-tech industries, and you also understand how to use the new media to promote yourself. Like Isadora Duncan, you may have a very eccentric kind of charisma and a life that is sparked by unusual love affairs. Your children, too, may have traits that are out of the ordinary. Where this planet falls in your chart, you'll have a love of freedom, be a bit of an egomaniac, and show the full force of your personality in a unique way, like tennis great Martina Navratilova.

Uranus in Virgo

BIRTH DATES:
November 1, 1961–January 10, 1962
August 10, 1962–September 28, 1968
May 20, 1969–June 24, 1969

You'll have highly individual work methods, and many of you will be finding newer, more practical ways to use computers. Like Einstein, who had this placement, you'll break the rules brilliantly. Your generation came at a time of student rebellions, the civil rights movement, and the general acceptance of health foods. Chances are, you're concerned about pollution and cleaning up the environment. You may also be involved with nontraditional healing methods. Heavyweight champ Mike Tyson has this placement.

Uranus in Libra

BIRTH DATES:
September 28, 1968–May 20, 1969
June 24, 1969–November 21, 1974
May 1, 1975–September 8, 1975.

Your generation is likely to have unconventional relationships. Born during the time when women's liberation was a major issue, many of your generation came from broken homes and have no clear image of what a committed relationship entails. There may be sudden splits and experiments before you settle down. Your generation will be much involved in legal and political reforms and in changing artistic and fashion looks.

Uranus in Scorpio

BIRTH DATES:
November 21, 1974–May 1, 1975
September 8, 1975–February 17, 1981
March 20, 1981–November 16, 1981

Interest in transformation, meditation, and life after death signaled the beginning of New Age consciousness. Your generation recognizes no boundaries, no limits, and no external controls. You'll have new attitudes toward death and dying, psychic phenomena, and the occult. Like Mae West and Casanova, you'll shock 'em sexually, too.

Uranus in Sagittarius

BIRTH DATES:
February 17, 1981–March 20, 1981
November 16, 1981–February 15, 1988
Mary 27, 1988–December 2, 1988

Could this generation be the first to travel in outer space? The last generation with this placement included Charles Lindbergh—at that time, the first Zeppelins and the Wright Brothers were conquering the skies. Uranus here forecasts great discoveries, mind expansion, and long-distance travel. Like Galileo and Martin Luther, this generation will generate new theories about the cosmos and man's relation to it.

Uranus in Capricorn

BIRTH DATES:
December 20, 1903–January 30, 1912
September 4, 1912–November 12, 1912

February 15, 1988–May 27, 1988
December 2, 1988–April 1, 1995
June 9, 1995–January 12, 1996

This generation will challenge traditions with the help of electronic gadgets. In these years, we got organized with the help of technology put to practical use. Great leaders, movers and shakers of history like Julius Caesar and Henry VIII, were born under this placement.

Uranus in Aquarius

BIRTH DATES:
January 30, 1912–September 4, 1912
November 12, 1912–April 1, 1919
August 16, 1919–January 22, 1920
April 1, 1995–June 9, 1995
January 12, 1996–March 10, 2003

The last generation with this placement produced great innovative minds such as Leonard Bernstein and Orson Welles. The next will become another radical breakthrough generation, much concerned with global issues that involve all humanity. Intuition, innovation, and sudden changes will surprise everyone when Uranus is in its home sign. This will be a time of experimentation on every level.

Uranus in Pisces

BIRTH DATES:
April 1, 1919–August 16, 1919
January 22, 1920–March 31, 1927
November 4, 1927–January 12, 1928

In this century, Uranus in Pisces focused attention on the rise of electronic entertainment—radio and the cinema, and the secretiveness of Prohibition. This produced a generation of idealists exemplified by Judy Garland's theme, "Somewhere Over the Rainbow."

Neptune—The Glamour Girl

Under Neptune's influence, you see what you want to see. Neptune is the planet of illusion, dissolution (it dissolves hard reality), and makeup. Neptune is not interested in the world at face value—it dons tinted glasses or blurs the facts with the haze of an intoxicating substance.

But Neptune also encourages you to create, to let your fantasies and daydreams run free, to break through your ordinary perceptions and go to another level of reality, where you can experience either confusion or ecstasy. Neptune's force can pull you off course, like this planet affects its neighbor, Uranus, but only if you allow this to happen. Those who use Neptune wisely can translate their daydreams into poetry, theater, design, or inspired moves in the business world, avoiding the tricky "con artist" side of this planet.

Find your Neptune listed here:

Neptune in Cancer

BIRTH DATES:
July 19, 1901–December 25, 1901
May 21, 1902–September 23, 1914
December 14, 1914–July 19, 1915
March 19, 1916–May 2, 1916

Dreams of the homeland, idealistic patriotism, and glamorization of the nurturing assets of women characterized this time. You who were born here have unusual psychic ability and deep insights into the basic needs of others.

Neptune in Leo

BIRTH DATES:
September 23, 1914–December 14, 1914
July 19, 1915–March 19, 1916

May 2, 1916–September 21, 1928
February 19, 1929–July 24, 1929

Neptune here brought us the glamour and high living of the 1920s and the big spenders of that time, when Neptunian temptations of gambling, seduction, theater, and lavish entertaining distracted from the realities of the age. Those born in that generation also made great advances in the arts.

Neptune in Virgo

BIRTH DATES:

September 21, 1928–February 19, 1929
July 24, 1929–October 3, 1942
April 17, 1943–August 2, 1943

Neptune in Virgo encompassed the Great Depression and World War II, while those born at this time later spread the gospel of health and fitness. This generation's devotion to spending hours at the office inspired the term "workaholic." Health-care concerns of the elderly will come to the forefront of national consciousness as this generation ages, changing the way we think about growing old.

Neptune in Libra

BIRTH DATES:

October 3, 1942–April 17, 1943
August 2, 1943–December 24, 1955
March 12, 1956–October 19, 1956
June 15, 1957–August 6, 1957

Neptune in Libra was the romantic generation who would later be concerned with relating. As this generation matured, there was a new trend toward marriage and commitment. Racial and sexual equality became important issues, as they redesigned traditional male and female roles to suit modern times.

Neptune in Scorpio

BIRTH DATES:
December 24, 1955–March 12, 1956
October 19, 1956–June 15, 1957
August 6, 1957–January 4, 1970
May 3, 1970–November 6, 1970

Neptune in Scorpio brought in a generation that would become interested in transformative power. Born in an era that glamorized sex, drugs, rock and roll, and Eastern religion, they matured in a more sobering time of AIDS, cocaine abuse, and New Age spirituality. As they evolve, they will become active in healing the planet from the results of the abuse of power.

Neptune in Sagittarius

BIRTH DATES:
January 4, 1970–May 3, 1970
November 6, 1970–January 19, 1984
June 23, 1984–November 21, 1984

Neptune in Sagittarius was the time when space travel became a reality. The Neptune influence glamorized new approaches to mysticism, religion, and mind expansion. This generation will take a new approach to spiritual life, with emphasis on visions, mysticism, and clairvoyance.

Neptune in Capricorn

BIRTH DATES:
January 19, 1984–June 23, 1984
November 21, 1984–January 29, 1998

Neptune in Capricorn, which began in 1984 and would stay until 1998, brought a time when delusions about material power were first glamorized, then dashed on the rocks of reality. It was also a time when the psychic and occult worlds spawned a new category of business enterprise and sold services on television.

Neptune in Aquarius

BIRTH DATES:
Starting January 29, 1998 through the end of the century

This should be a time of breakthroughs, when the creative influence of Neptune reaches a universal audience. This is a time of dissolving barriers, when we truly become one world.

Pluto—The Private Eye

Pluto deals with the underworld of our personality, digging out our secrets to effect a total transformation as it brings deep subconscious feelings to the surface. Nothing escapes—or is sacred—with Pluto. When this tiny planet zaps a strategic point in your horoscope, your life changes so dramatically that there's no going back.

While Mars governs the visible power, Pluto is the power behind the scenes, where you can transform, heal, and affect the unconscious needs of the masses. Pluto governs your need to control, as well as your attitudes toward death and immortality. Much of the strength of your Pluto will depend on its position in your chart and the aspects it makes to other planets.

Because Pluto was discovered only recently, the signs of its exaltation and fall are debated. However, it was given the rulership of Scorpio. As it passed through Scorpio from 1984 to 1995 under the rule of Pluto, we were able to witness this planet's fullest effect. Because of its eccentric path, the length of time Pluto stays in any given sign can vary from 13 to 32 years.

Pluto in Gemini

BIRTH DATES:
Late 1800s–May 28, 1914

This was a time of mass suggestion and breakthroughs in communications, when many brilliant writers, such as Ernest Hemingway and F. Scott Fitzgerald, were born. Henry Miller, D. H. Lawrence, and James Joyce scandalized society by using explicit sexual images and language in their literature. "Muckraking" journalists exposed corruption. Pluto-ruled Scorpio President Theodore Roosevelt said, "Speak softly, but carry a big stick." This generation had an intense need to communicate and made major breakthroughs in knowledge. A compulsive restlessness and a thirst for a variety of experiences characterizes many of this generation.

Pluto in Cancer

BIRTH DATES:
May 28, 1914–June 14, 1939

Pluto in Cancer suggests great emotional (Cancer) power. During this time period dictators and mass media arose to manipulate the emotions of the masses. Women's rights were obtained as Pluto transited this lunar-ruled sign, transforming the position of women in society. Deep sentimental feelings, acquisitiveness, and possessiveness characterize these times and the people who were born then.

Pluto in Leo

BIRTH DATES:
June 14, 1939–August 19, 1957

The performing arts, under Leo's rule, never wielded more power over the masses than during this era. Pluto in Leo transforms via creative self-expression, exemplified by the almost shamanistic rock and roll stars such as Mick Jagger and John Lennon, who were born at this time. (So were Bill and Hillary Clinton.) People born with Pluto in Leo often tend to be self-centered and love to "do their own thing"—for better or for worse.

Pluto in Virgo

BIRTH DATES:
August 19, 1957–October 5, 1971
April 17, 1972–July 30, 1972

This became the "yuppie" generation that sparked a mass clean-up shape-up movement toward fitness, health, and obsessive careerism. It's a much more sober, serious, driven generation than the fun-loving Pluto in Leos. During this time, inventions took on a practical turn, as answering machines, fax machines, car phones, and home office equipment have all transformed the workplace.

Pluto in Libra

BIRTH DATES:
October 5, 1971–April 17, 1972
July 30, 1972–August 28, 1984

A mellower generation, people born at this time are concerned with partnerships, working together, and finding diplomatic solutions to problems. Marriage is important to this generation, who redefine it along more traditional, but equal-partnership lines. This was a time of women's liberation, gay rights, ERA, and legal battles over abortion, all of which transformed our ideas about relationships.

Pluto in Scorpio

BIRTH DATES:
August 28, 1984–January 17, 1995

Pluto was in its ruling sign for a comparatively short period of time. In 1989, it was at its perihelion, or the closest point to the sun and Earth. We have all felt this transforming power somewhere in our lives. This was a time of record achievements, destructive sexually transmitted diseases, nuclear power controversies, and explosive political issues. Pluto destroys in order to create new understanding—think of it as a phoenix rising from the ashes, which should be some consolation for those of you who have felt Pluto's force before 1995. Sexual shockers were par for the course during these intense years, when black clothing, transvestites, body piercing, tattoos, and sexually explicit advertising pushed the boundaries of good taste.

Pluto in Sagittarius

BIRTH DATES:
January 17, 1995–January 27, 2008

During our current Pluto transit through Sagittarius, we are being pushed to expand our horizons and find deeper meaning in life. For many of us, this will mean traveling the globe via our modems as we explore the vastness of the Internet. It signals a time of spiritual transformation and religion will exert much power in politics as well. Since Sagittarius is the sign that rules travel, there's a good possibility that Pluto, the planet of extremes, will make space travel a reality for some of us. Discovery of life on Mars, traveling here as minute life forms on meteors, could transform our ideas about where we came from. At this writing, a giant telescope in Puerto Rico has been reactivated to search the faraway galaxies for pulsing hints of life.

New dimensions in electronic publishing, concern with animal rights and the environment, and an increasing emphasis on extreme forms of religion are signs of Pluto in Sagittarius. Look for charismatic religious leaders to arise now. We'll also be developing far-reaching philosophies designed to elevate our lives with a new sense of purpose.

Look Up Your Planets

The following tables are provided so that you can look up the signs of seven major planets—Venus, Mars, Saturn, Jupiter, Uranus, Neptune, and Pluto. We do not have room for tables for the moon and Mercury, which change signs often.

How to Use the Venus Table

Find the year of your birth in the vertical column on the left, then follow across the page until you find the correct date. Your Venus sign is at the top of that column.

VENUS SIGNS 1901–2000

	Aries	Taurus	Gemini	Cancer	Leo	Virgo
1901	3/29–4/22	4/22–5/17	5/17–6/10	6/10–7/5	7/5–7/29	7/29–8/23
1902	5/7–6/3	6/3–6/30	6/30–7/25	7/25–8/19	8/19–9/13	9/13–10/7
1903	2/28–3/24	3/24–4/18	4/18–5/13	5/13–6/9	6/9–7/7	7/7–8/17
						9/6–11/8
1904	3/13–5/7	5/7–6/1	6/1–6/25	6/25–7/19	7/19–8/13	8/13–9/6
1905	2/3–3/6	3/6–4/9	7/8–8/6	8/6–9/1	9/1–9/27	9/27–10/21
	4/9–5/28	5/28–7/8				
1906	3/1–4/7	4/7–5/2	5/2–5/26	5/26–6/20	6/20–7/16	7/16–8/11
1907	4/27–5/22	5/22–6/16	6/16–7/11	7/11–8/4	8/4–8/29	8/29–9/22
1908	2/14–3/10	3/10–4/5	4/5–5/5	5/5–9/8	9/8–10/8	10/8–11/3
1909	3/29–4/22	4/22–5/16	5/16–6/10	6/10–7/4	7/4–7/29	7/29–8/23
1910	5/7–6/3	6/4–6/29	6/30–7/24	7/25–8/18	8/19–9/12	9/13–10/6
1911	2/28–3/23	3/24–4/17	4/18–5/12	5/13–6/8	6/9–7/7	7/8–11/8
1912	4/13–5/6	5/7–5/31	6/1–6/24	6/24–7/18	7/19–8/12	8/13–9/5
1913	2/3–3/6	3/7–5/1	7/8–8/5	8/6–8/31	9/1–9/26	9/27–10/20
	5/2–5/30	5/31–7/7				
1914	3/14–4/6	4/7–5/1	5/2–5/25	5/26–6/19	6/20–7/15	7/16–8/10
1915	4/27–5/21	5/22–6/15	6/16–7/10	7/11–8/3	8/4–8/28	8/29–9/21
1916	2/14–3/9	3/10–4/5	4/6–5/5	5/6–9/8	9/9–10/7	10/8–11/2
1917	3/29–4/21	4/22–5/15	5/16–6/9	6/10–7/3	7/4–7/28	7/29–8/21
1918	5/7–6/2	6/3–6/28	6/29–7/24	7/25–8/18	8/19–9/11	9/12–10/5
1919	2/27–3/22	3/23–4/16	4/17–5/12	5/13–6/7	6/8–///	7/8–11/8
1920	4/12–5/6	5/7–5/30	5/31–6/23	6/24–7/18	7/19–8/11	8/12–9/4
1921	2/3–3/6	3/7–4/25	7/8–8/5	8/6–8/31	9/1–9/25	9/26–10/20
	4/26–6/1	6/2–7/7				
1922	3/13–4/6	4/7–4/30	5/1–5/25	5/26–6/19	6/20–7/14	7/15–8/9
1923	4/27–5/21	5/22–6/14	6/15–7/9	7/10–8/3	8/4–8/27	8/28–9/20
1924	2/13–3/8	3/9–4/4	4/5–5/5	5/6–9/8	9/9–10/7	10/8–11/12
1925	3/28–4/20	4/21–5/15	5/16–6/8	6/9–7/3	7/4–7/27	7/28–8/21

78

Libra	Scorpio	Sagittarius	Capricorn	Aquarius	Pisces
8/23–9/17	9/17–10/12	10/12–1/16	1/16–2/9 11/7–12/5	2/9–3/5 12/5–1/11	3/5–3/29
10/7–10/31	10/31–11/24	11/24–12/18	12/18–1/11	2/6–4/4	1/11–2/6 4/4–5/7
8/17–9/6 11/8–12/9	12/9–1/5			1/11–2/4	2/4–2/28
9/6–9/30	9/30–10/25	1/5–1/30 10/25–11/18	1/30–2/24 11/18–12/13	2/24–3/19 12/13–1/7	3/19–4/13
10/21–11/14	11/14–12/8	12/8–1/1/06			1/7–2/3
8/11–9/7	9/7–10/9 12/15–12/25	10/9–12/15 12/25–2/6	1/1–1/25	1/25–2/18	2/18–3/14
9/22–10/16	10/16–11/9	11/9–12/3	2/6–3/6 12/3–12/27	3/6–4/2 12/27–1/20	4/2–4/27
11/3–11/28	11/28–12/22	12/22–1/15			1/20–2/4
8/23–9/17	9/17–10/12	10/12–11/17	1/15–2/9 11/17–12/5	2/9–3/5 12/5–1/15	3/5–3/29
10/7–10/30	10/31–11/23	11/24–12/17	12/18–12/31	1/1–1/15 1/29–4/4	1/16–1/28 4/5–5/6
11/19–12/8	12/9–12/31		1/1–1/10	1/11–2/2	2/3–2/27
9/6–9/30	1/1–1/4 10/1–10/24	1/5–1/29 10/25–11/17	1/30–2/23 11/18–12/12	2/24–3/18 12/13–12/31	3/19–4/12
10/21–11/13	11/14–12/7	12/8–12/31		1/1–1/6	1/7–2/2
8/11–9/6	9/7–10/9 12/6–12/30	10/10–12/5 12/31	1/1–1/24	1/25–2/17	2/18–3/13
9/22–10/15	10/16–11/8	1/1–2/6 11/9–12/2	2/7–3/6 12/3–12/26	3/7–4/1 12/27–12/31	4/2–4/26
11/3–11/27	11/28–12/21	12/22–12/31		1/1–1/19	1/20–2/13
8/22–9/16	9/17–10/11	1/1–1/14 10/12–11/6	1/15–2/7 11/7–12/5	2/8–3/4 12/6–12/31	3/5–3/28
10/6–10/29	10/30–11/22	11/23–12/16	12/17–12/31	1/1–4/5	4/6–5/6
11/9–12/8	12/9–12/31		1/1–1/9	1/10–2/2	2/3–2/26
9/5–9/30	1/1–1/3 9/31–10/23	1/4–1/28 10/24–11/17	1/29–2/22 11/18–12/11	2/23–3/18 12/12–12/31	3/19–4/11
10/21–11/13	11/14–12/7	12/8–12/31		1/1–1/6	1/7–2/2
8/10–9/6	9/7–10/10 11/29–12/31	10/11–11/28	1/1–1/24	1/25–2/16	2/17–3/12
9/21–10/14	1/1 10/15–11/7	1/2–2/6 11/8–12/1	2/7–3/5 12/2–12/25	3/6–3/31 12/26–12/31	4/1–4/26
11/13–11/26	11/27–12/21	12/22–12/31		1/1–1/19	1/20–2/12
8/22–9/15	9/16–10/11	1/1–1/14 10/12–11/6	1/15–2/7 11/7–12/5	2/8–3/3 12/6–12/31	3/4–3/27

VENUS SIGNS 1901–2000

	Aries	Taurus	Gemini	Cancer	Leo	Virgo
1926	5/7–6/2	6/3–6/28	6/29–7/23	7/24–8/17	8/18–9/11	9/12–10/5
1927	2/27–3/22	3/23–4/16	4/17–5/11	5/12–6/7	6/8–7/7	7/8–11/9
1928	4/12–5/5	5/6–5/29	5/30–6/23	6/24–7/17	7/18–8/11	8/12–9/4
1929	2/3–3/7 4/20–6/2	3/8–4/19 6/3–7/7	7/8–8/4	8/5–8/30	8/31–9/25	9/26–10/19
1930	3/13–4/5	4/6–4/30	5/1–5/24	5/25–6/18	6/19–7/14	7/15–8/9
1931	4/26–5/20	5/21–6/13	6/14–7/8	7/9–8/2	8/3–8/26	8/27–9/19
1932	2/12–3/8	3/9–4/3	4/4–5/5 7/13–7/27	5/6–7/12 7/28–9/8	9/9–10/6	10/7–11/1
1933	3/27–4/19	4/20–5/28	5/29–6/8	6/9–7/2	7/3–7/26	7/27–8/20
1934	5/6–6/1	6/2–6/27	6/28–7/22	7/23–8/16	8/17–9/10	9/11–10/4
1935	2/26–3/21	3/22–4/15	4/16–5/10	5/11–6/6	6/7–7/6	7/7–11/8
1936	4/11–5/4	5/5–5/28	5/29–6/22	6/23–7/16	7/17–8/10	8/11–9/4
1937	2/2–3/8 4/14–6/3	3/9–4/13 6/4–7/6	7/7–8/3	8/4–8/29	8/30–9/24	9/25–10/18
1938	3/12–4/4	4/5–4/28	4/29–5/23	5/24–6/18	6/19–7/13	7/14–8/8
1939	4/25–5/19	5/20–6/13	6/14–7/8	7/9–8/1	8/2–8/25	8/26–9/19
1940	2/12–3/7	3/8–4/3	4/4–5/5 7/5–7/31	5/6–7/4 8/1–9/8	9/9–10/5	10/6–10/31
1941	3/27–4/19	4/20–5/13	5/14–6/6	6/7–7/1	7/2–7/26	7/27–8/20
1942	5/6–6/1	6/2–6/26	6/27–7/22	7/23–8/16	8/17–9/9	9/10–10/3
1943	2/25–3/20	3/21–4/14	4/15–5/10	5/11–6/6	6/7–7/6	7/7–11/8
1944	4/10–5/3	5/4–5/28	5/29–6/21	6/22–7/16	7/17–8/9	8/10–9/2
1945	2/2–3/10 4/7–6/3	3/11–4/6 6/4–7/6	7/7–8/3	8/4–8/29	8/30–9/23	9/24–10/18
1946	3/11–4/4	4/5–4/28	4/29–5/23	5/24–6/17	6/18–7/12	7/13–8/8
1947	4/25–5/19	5/20–6/12	6/13–7/7	7/8–8/1	8/2–8/25	8/26–9/18
1948	2/11–3/7	3/8–4/3	4/4–5/6 6/29–8/2	5/7–6/28 8/3–9/7	9/8–10/5	10/6–10/31
1949	3/26–4/19	4/20–5/13	5/14–6/6	6/7–6/30	7/1–7/25	7/26–8/19
1950	5/5–5/31	6/1–6/26	6/27–7/21	7/22–8/15	8/16–9/9	9/10–10/3
1951	2/25–3/21	3/22–4/15	4/16–5/10	5/11–6/6	6/7–7/7	7/8–11/9

Libra	Scorpio	Sagittarius	Capricorn	Aquarius	Pisces
10/6–10/29	10/30–11/22	11/23–12/16	12/17–12/31	1/1–4/5	4/6–5/6
11/10–12/8	12/9–12/31	1/1–1/7	1/8	1/9–2/1	2/2–2/26
9/5–9/28	1/1–1/3	1/4–1/28	1/29–2/22	2/23–3/17	3/18–4/11
	9/29–10/23	10/24–11/16	11/17–12/11	12/12–12/31	
10/20–11/12	11/13–12/6	12/7–12/30	12/31	1/1–1/5	1/6–2/2
8/10–9/6	9/7–10/11	10/12–11/21	1/1–1/23	1/24–2/16	2/17–3/12
	11/22–12/31				
9/20–10/13	1/1–1/3	1/4–2/6	2/7–3/4	3/5–3/31	4/1–4/25
	10/14–11/6	11/7–11/30	12/1–12/24	12/25–12/31	
11/2–11/25	11/26–12/20	12/21–12/31		1/1–1/18	1/19–2/11
8/21–9/14	9/15–10/10	1/1–1/13	1/14–2/6	2/7–3/2	3/3–3/26
		10/11–11/5	11/6–12/4	12/5–12/31	
10/5–10/28	10/29–11/21	11/22–12/15	12/16–12/31	1/1–4/5	4/6–5/5
11/9–12/7	12/8–12/31		1/1–1/7	1/8–1/31	2/1–2/25
9/5–9/27	1/1–1/2	1/3–1/27	1/28–2/21	2/22–3/16	3/17–4/10
	9/28–10/22	10/23–11/15	11/16–12/10	12/11–12/31	
10/19–11/11	11/12–12/5	12/6–12/29	12/30–12/31	1/1–1/5	1/6–2/1
8/9–9/6	9/7–10/13	10/14–11/14	1/1–1/22	1/23–2/15	2/16–3/11
	11/15–12/31				
9/20–10/13	1/1–1/3	1/4–2/5	2/6–3/4	3/5–3/30	3/31–4/24
	10/14–11/6	11/7–11/30	12/1–12/24	12/25–12/31	
11/1–11/25	11/26–12/19	12/20–12/31		1/1–1/18	1/19–2/11
8/21–9/14	9/15–10/9	1/1–1/12	1/13–2/5	2/6–3/1	3/2–3/26
		10/10–11/5	11/6–12/4	12/5–12/31	
10/4–10/27	10/28–11/20	11/21–12/14	12/15–12/31	1/1–4/4	4/6–5/5
11/9–12/7	12/8–12/31		1/1–1/7	1/8–1/31	2/1–2/24
9/3–9/27	1/1–1/2	1/3–1/27	1/28–2/20	2/21–3/16	3/17–4/9
	9/28–10/21	10/22–11/15	11/16–12/10	12/11–12/31	
10/19–11/11	11/12–12/5	12/6–12/29	12/30–12/31	1/1–1/4	1/5–2/1
8/9–9/6	9/7–10/15	10/16–11/7	1/1–1/21	1/22–2/14	2/15–3/10
	11/8–12/31				
9/19–10/12	1/1–1/4	1/5–2/5	2/6–3/4	3/5–3/29	3/30–4/24
	10/13–11/5	11/6–11/29	11/30–12/23	12/24–12/31	
11/1–11/25	11/26–12/19	12/20–12/31		1/1–1/17	1/18–2/10
8/20–9/14	9/15–10/9	1/1–1/12	1/13–2/5	2/6–3/1	3/2–3/25
		10/10–11/5	11/6–12/5	12/6–12/31	
10/4–10/27	10/28–11/20	11/21–12/13	12/14–12/31	1/1–4/5	4/6–5/4
11/10–12/7	12/8–12/31		1/1–1/7	1/8–1/31	2/1–2/24

VENUS SIGNS 1901–2000

	Aries	Taurus	Gemini	Cancer	Leo	Virgo
1952	4/10–5/4	5/5–5/28	5/29–6/21	6/22–7/16	7/17–8/9	8/10–9/3
1953	2/2–3/3	3/4–3/31	7/8–8/3	8/4–8/29	8/30–9/24	9/25–10/18
	4/1–6/5	6/6–7/7				
1954	3/12–4/4	4/5–4/28	4/29–5/23	5/24–6/17	6/18–7/13	7/14–8/8
1955	4/25–5/19	5/20–6/13	6/14–7/7	7/8–8/1	8/2–8/25	8/26–9/18
1956	2/12–3/7	3/8–4/4	4/5–5/7	5/8–6/23	9/9–10/5	10/6–10/31
			6/24–8/4	8/5–9/8		
1957	3/26–4/19	4/20–5/13	5/14–6/6	6/7–7/1	7/2–7/26	7/27–8/19
1958	5/6–5/31	6/1–6/26	6/27–7/22	7/23–8/15	8/16–9/9	9/10–10/3
1959	2/25–3/20	3/21–4/14	4/15–5/10	5/11–6/6	6/7–7/8	7/9–9/20
					9/21–9/24	9/25–11/9
1960	4/10–5/3	5/4–5/28	5/29–6/21	6/22–7/15	7/16–8/9	8/10–9/2
1961	2/3–6/5	6/6–7/7	7/8–8/3	8/4–8/29	8/30–9/23	9/24–10/17
1962	3/11–4/3	4/4–4/28	4/29–5/22	5/23–6/17	6/18–7/12	7/13–8/8
1963	4/24–5/18	5/19–6/12	6/13–7/7	7/8–7/31	8/1–8/25	8/26–9/18
1964	2/11–3/7	3/8–4/4	4/5–5/9	5/10–6/17	9/9–10/5	10/6–10/31
			6/18–8/5	8/6–9/8		
1965	3/26–4/18	4/19–5/12	5/13–6/6	6/7–6/30	7/1–7/25	7/26–8/19
1966	5/6–6/31	6/1–6/26	6/27–7/21	7/22–8/15	8/16–9/8	9/9–10/2
1967	2/24–3/20	3/21–4/14	4/15–5/10	5/11–6/6	6/7–7/8	7/9–9/9
					9/10–10/1	10/2–11/9
1968	4/9–5/3	5/4–5/27	5/28–6/20	6/21–7/15	7/16–8/8	8/9–9/2
1969	2/3–6/6	6/7–7/6	7/7–8/3	8/4–8/28	8/29–9/22	9/23–10/17
1970	3/11–4/3	4/4–4/27	4/28–5/22	5/23–6/16	6/17–7/12	7/13–8/8
1971	4/24–5/18	5/19–6/12	6/13–7/6	7/7–7/31	8/1–8/24	8/25–9/17
1972	2/11–3/7	3/8–4/3	4/4–5/10	5/11–6/11	9/9–10/5	10/6–10/30
			6/12–8/6	8/7–9/8		
1973	3/25–4/18	4/18–5/12	5/13–6/5	6/6–6/29	7/1–7/25	7/26–8/19
1974						
	5/5–5/31	6/1–6/25	6/26–7/21	7/22–8/14	8/15–9/8	9/9–10/2
1975	2/24–3/20	3/21–4/13	4/14–5/9	5/10–6/6	6/7–7/9	7/10–9/2
					9/3–10/4	10/5–11/9

82

Libra	Scorpio	Sagittarius	Capricorn	Aquarius	Pisces
9/4–9/27	1/1–1/2	1/3–1/27	1/28–2/20	2/21–3/16	3/17–4/9
	9/28–10/21	10/22–11/15	11/16–12/10	12/11–12/31	
10/19–11/11	11/12–12/5	12/6–12/29	12/30–12/31	1/1–1/5	1/6–2/1
8/9–9/6	9/7–10/22	10/23–10/27	1/1–1/22	1/23–2/15	2/16–3/11
	10/28–12/31				
9/19–10/13	1/1–1/6	1/7–2/5	2/6–3/4	3/5–3/30	3/31–4/24
	10/14–11/5	11/6–11/30	12/1–12/24	12/25–12/31	
11/1–11/25	11/26–12/19	12/20–12/31		1/1–1/17	1/18–2/11
8/20–9/14	9/15–10/9	1/1–1/12	1/13–2/5	2/6–3/1	3/2–3/25
		10/10–11/5	11/6–12/6	12/7–12/31	
10/4–10/27	10/28–11/20	11/21–12/14	12/15–12/31	1/1–4/6	4/7–5/5
11/10–12/7	12/8–12/31		1/1–1/7	1/8–1/31	2/1–2/24
9/3–9/26	1/1–1/2	1/3–1/27	1/28–2/20	2/21–3/15	3/16–4/9
	9/27–10/21	10/22–11/15	11/16–12/10	12/11–12/31	
10/18–11/11	11/12–12/4	12/5–12/28	12/29–12/31	1/1–1/5	1/6–2/2
8/9–9/6	9/7–12/31		1/1–1/21	1/22–2/14	2/15–3/10
9/19–10/12	1/1–1/6	1/7–2/5	2/6–3/4	3/5–3/29	3/30–4/23
	10/13–11/5	11/6–11/29	11/30–12/23	12/24–12/31	
11/1–11/24	11/25–12/19	12/20–12/31		1/1–1/16	1/17–2/10
8/20–9/13	9/14–10/9	1/1–1/12	1/13–2/5	2/6–3/1	3/2–3/25
		10/10–11/5	11/6–12/7	12/8–12/31	
10/3–10/26	10/27–11/19	11/20–12/13	2/7–2/25	1/1–2/6	4/7–5/5
			12/14–12/31	2/26–4/6	
11/10–12/7	12/8–12/31		1/1–1/6	1/7–1/30	1/31–2/23
9/3–9/26	1/1	1/2–1/26	1/27–2/20	2/21–3/15	3/16–4/8
	9/27–10/21	10/22–11/14	11/15–12/9	12/10–12/31	
10/18–11/10	11/11–12/4	12/5–12/28	12/29–12/31	1/1–1/4	1/5–2/2
8/9–9/7	9/8–12/31		1/1–1/21	1/22–2/14	2/15–3/10
9/18–10/11	1/1–1/7	1/8–2/5	2/6–3/4	3/5–3/29	3/30–4/23
	10/12–11/5	11/6–11/29	11/30–12/23	12/24–12/31	
	11/25–12/18	12/19–12/31		1/1–1/16	1/17–2/10
10/31–11/24					
8/20–9/13	9/14–10/8	1/1–1/12	1/13–2/4	2/5–2/28	3/1–3/24
		10/9–11/5	11/6–12/7	12/8–12/31	
			1/30–2/28	1/1–1/29	
10/3–10/26	10/27–11/19	11/20–12/13	12/14–12/31	3/1–4/6	4/7–5/4
			1/1–1/6	1/7–1/30	1/31–2/23
11/10–12/7	12/8–12/31				

VENUS SIGNS 1901–2000

	Aries	Taurus	Gemini	Cancer	Leo	Virgo
1976	4/8–5/2	5/2–5/27	5/27–6/20	6/20–7/14	7/14–8/8	8/8–9/1
1977	2/2–6/6	6/6–7/6	7/6–8/2	8/2–8/28	8/28–9/22	9/22–10/17
1978	3/9–4/2	4/2–4/27	4/27–5/22	5/22–6/16	6/16–7/12	7/12–8/6
1979	4/23–5/18	5/18–6/11	6/11–7/6	7/6–7/30	7/30–8/24	8/24–9/17
1980	2/9–3/6	3/6–4/3	4/3–5/12 6/5–8/6	5/12–6/5 8/6–9/7	9/7–10/4	10/4–10/30
1981	3/24–4/17	4/17–5/11	5/11–6/5	6/5–6/29	6/29–7/24	7/24–8/18
1982	5/4–5/30	5/30–6/25	6/25–7/20	7/20–8/14	8/14–9/7	9/7–10/2
1983	2/22–3/19	3/19–4/13	4/13–5/9	5/9–6/6	6/6–7/10 8/27–10/5	7/10–8/27 10/5–11/9
1984	4/7–5/2	5/2–5/26	5/26–6/20	6/20–7/14	7/14–8/7	8/7–9/1
1985	2/2–6/6	6/7–7/6	7/6–8/2	8/2–8/28	8/28–9/22	9/22–10/16
1986	3/9–4/2	4/2–4/26	4/26–5/21	5/21–6/15	6/15–7/11	7/11–8/7
1987	4/22–5/17	5/17–6/11	6/11–7/5	7/5–7/30	7/30–8/23	8/23–9/16
1988	2/9–3/6	3/6–4/3	4/3–5/17 5/27–8/6	5/17–5/27 8/28–9/22	9/7–10/4 9/22–10/16	10/4–10/29
1989	3/23–4/16	4/16–5/11	5/11–6/4	6/4–6/29	6/29–7/24	7/24–8/18
1990	5/4–5/30	5/30–6/25	6/25–7/20	7/20–8/13	8/13–9/7	9/7–10/1
1991	2/22–3/18	3/18–4/13	4/13–5/9	5/9–6/6	6/6–7/11 8/21–10/6	7/11–8/21 10/6–11/9
1992	4/7–5/1	5/1–5/26	5/26–6/19	6/19–7/13	7/13–8/7	8/7–8/31
1993	2/2–6/6	6/6–7/6	7/6–8/1	8/1–8/27	8/27–9/21	9/21–10/16
1994	3/8–4/1	4/1–4/26	4/26–5/21	5/21–6/15	6/15–7/11	7/11–8/7
1995	4/22–5/16	5/16–6/10	6/10–7/5	7/5 7/29	7/29–8/23	8/23–9/16
1996	2/9–3/6	3/6–4/3	4/3–8/7	8/7–9/7	9/7–10/4	10/4–10/29
1997	3/23–4/16	4/16–5/10	5/10–6/4	6/4–6/28	6/28–7/23	7/23–8/17
1998	5/3–5/29	5/29–6/24	6/24–7/19	7/19–8/13	8/13–9/6	9/6–9/30
1999	2/21–3/18	3/18–4/12	4/12–5/8	5/8–6/5	6/5–7/12 8/15–10/7	7/12–8/15 10/7–11/9
2000	4/6–5/1	5/1–5/25	5/25–6/13	6/13–7/13	7/13–8/6	8/6–8/31

Libra	Scorpio	Sagittarius	Capricorn	Aquarius	Pisces
9/1–9/26	9/26–10/20	1/1–1/26	1/26–2/19	2/19–3/15	3/15–4/8
		10/20–11/14	11/14–12/8	12/9–1/4	
10/17–11/10	11/10–12/4	12/4–12/27	12/27–1/20/78		1/4–2/2
8/6–9/7	9/7–1/7			1/20–2/13	2/13–3/9
9/17–10/11	10/11–11/4	1/7–2/5	2/5–3/3	3/3–3/29	3/29–4/23
		11/4–11/28	11/28–12/22	12/22–1/16/80	
10/30–11/24	11/24–12/18	12/18–1/11/81			1/16–2/9
8/18–9/12	9/12–10/9	10/9–11/5	1/11–2/4	2/4–2/28	2/28–3/24
			11/5–12/8	12/8–1/23/82	
10/2–10/26	10/26–11/18	11/18–12/12	1/23–3/2	3/2–4/6	4/6–5/4
			12/12–1/5/83		
11/9–12/6	12/6–1/1/84			1/5–1/29	1/29–2/22
9/1–9/25	9/25–10/20	1/1–1/25	1/25–2/19	2/19–3/14	3/14–4/7
		10/20–11/13	11/13–12/9	12/10–1/4	
10/16–11/9	11/9–12/3	12/3–12/27	12/28–1/19		1/4–2/2
8/7–9/7	9/7–1/7			1/20–2/13	2/13–3/9
9/16–10/10	10/10–11/3	1/7–2/5	2/5–3/3	3/3–3/28	3/28–4/22
		11/3–11/28	11/28–12/22	12/22–1/15	
10/29–11/23	11/23–12/17	12/17–1/10			1/15–2/9
8/18–9/12	9/12–10/8	10/8–11/5	1/10–2/3	2/3–2/27	2/27–3/23
			11/5–12/10	12/10–1/16/90	
10/1–10/25	10/25–11/18	11/18–12/12	1/16–3/3	3/3–4/6	4/6–5/4
			12/12–1/5		
11/9–12/6	12/6–12/31	12/31–1/25/92		1/5–1/29	1/29–2/22
8/31–9/25	9/25–10/19	10/19–11/13	1/25–2/18	2/18–3/13	3/13–4/7
			11/13–12/8	12/8–1/3/93	
10/16–11/9	11/9–12/2	12/2–12/26	12/26–1/19		1/3–2/2
8/7–9/7	9/7–1/7			1/19–2/12	2/12–3/8
9/16–10/10	10/10–11/13	1/7–2/4	2/4–3/2	3/2–3/28	3/28–4/22
		11/3–11/27	11/27–12/21	12/21–1/15	
10/29–11/23	11/23–12/17	12/17–1/10/97			1/15–2/9
8/17–9/12	9/12–10/8	10/8–11/5	1/10–2/3	2/3–2/27	2/27–3/23
			11/5–12/12	12/12–1/9	
9/30–10/24	10/24–11/17	11/17–12/11	1/9–3/4	3/4–4/6	4/6–5/3
11/9–12/5	12/5–12/31	12/31–1/24		1/4–1/28	1/28–2/21
8/31–9/24	9/24–10/19	10/19–11/13	1/24–2/18	2/18–3/12	3/13–4/6
			11/13–12/8	12/8	

How to Use the Mars, Jupiter, and Saturn Tables

Find the year of your birth on the left side of each column. The dates when the planet entered each sign are listed on the right side of each column. (Signs are abbreviated to the first three letters.) Your birthday should fall on or between each date listed, and your planetary placement should correspond to the earlier sign of that period.

MARS SIGN 1901–2000

Year	Month	Day	Sign		Year	Month	Day	Sign
1901	MAR	1	Leo		1905	JAN	13	Scp
	MAY	11	Vir			AUG	21	Sag
	JUL	13	Lib			OCT	8	Cap
	AUG	31	Scp			NOV	18	Aqu
	OCT	14	Sag			DEC	27	Pic
	NOV	24	Cap		1906	FEB	4	Ari
1902	JAN	1	Aqu			MAR	17	Tau
	FEB	8	Pic			APR	28	Gem
	MAR	19	Ari			JUN	11	Can
	APR	27	Tau			JUL	27	Leo
	JUN	7	Gem			SEP	12	Vir
	JUL	20	Can			OCT	30	Lib
	SEP	4	Leo			DEC	17	Scp
	OCT	23	Vir		1907	FEB	5	Sag
	DEC	20	Lib			APR	1	Cap
1903	APR	19	Vir			OCT	13	Aqu
	MAY	30	Lib			NOV	29	Pic
	AUG	6	Scp		1908	JAN	11	Ari
	SEP	22	Sag			FEB	23	Tau
	NOV	3	Cap			APR	7	Gem
	DEC	12	Aqu			MAY	22	Can
1904	JAN	19	Pic			JUL	8	Leo
	FEB	27	Ari			AUG	24	Vir
	APR	6	Tau			OCT	10	Lib
	MAY	18	Gem			NOV	25	Scp
	JUN	30	Can		1909	JAN	10	Sag
	AUG	15	Leo			FEB	24	Cap
	OCT	1	Vir			APR	9	Aqu
	NOV	20	Lib			MAY	25	Pic

	JUL	21	Ari		AUG	19	Can
	SEP	26	Pic		OCT	7	Leo
	NOV	20	Ari	1916	MAY	28	Vir
1910	JAN	23	Tau		JUL	23	Lib
	MAR	14	Gem		SEP	8	Scp
	MAY	1	Can		OCT	22	Sag
	JUN	19	Leo		DEC	1	Cap
	AUG	6	Vir	1917	JAN	9	Aqu
	SEP	22	Lib		FEB	16	Pic
	NOV	6	Scp		MAR	26	Ari
	DEC	20	Sag		MAY	4	Tau
1911	JAN	31	Cap		JUN	14	Gem
	MAR	14	Aqu		JUL	28	Can
	APR	23	Pic		SEP	12	Leo
	JUN	2	Ari		NOV	2	Vir
	JUL	15	Tau	1918	JAN	11	Lib
	SEP	5	Gem		FEB	25	Vir
	NOV	30	Tau		JUN	23	Lib
1912	JAN	30	Gem		AUG	17	Scp
	APR	5	Can		OCT	1	Sag
	MAY	28	Leo		NOV	11	Cap
	JUL	17	Vir		DEC	20	Aqu
	SEP	2	Lib	1919	JAN	27	Pic
	OCT	18	Scp		MAR	6	Ari
	NOV	30	Sag		APR	15	Tau
1913	JAN	10	Cap		MAY	26	Gem
	FEB	19	Aqu		JUL	8	Can
	MAR	30	Pic		AUG	23	Leo
	MAY	8	Ari		OCT	10	Vir
	JUN	17	Tau		NOV	30	Lib
	JUL	29	Gem	1920	JAN	31	Scp
	SEP	15	Can		APR	23	Lib
1914	MAY	1	Leo		JUL	10	Scp
	JUN	26	Vir		SEP	4	Sag
	AUG	14	Lib		OCT	18	Cap
	SEP	29	Scp		NOV	27	Aqu
	NOV	11	Sag	1921	JAN	5	Pic
	DEC	22	Cap		FEB	13	Ari
1915	JAN	30	Aqu		MAR	25	Tau
	MAR	9	Pic		MAY	6	Gem
	APR	16	Ari		JUN	18	Can
	MAY	26	Tau		AUG	3	Leo
	JUL	6	Gem		SEP	19	Vir

	NOV	6	Lib		APR	7	Pic
	DEC	26	Scp		MAY	16	Ari
1922	FEB	18	Sag		JUN	26	Tau
	SEP	13	Cap		AUG	9	Gem
	OCT	30	Aqu		OCT	3	Can
	DEC	11	Pic		DEC	20	Gem
1923	JAN	21	Ari	1929	MAR	10	Can
	MAR	4	Tau		MAY	13	Leo
	APR	16	Gem		JUL	4	Vir
	MAY	30	Can		AUG	21	Lib
	JUL	16	Leo		OCT	6	Scp
	SEP	1	Vir		NOV	18	Sag
	OCT	18	Lib		DEC	29	Cap
	DEC	4	Scp	1930	FEB	6	Aqu
1924	JAN	19	Sag		MAR	17	Pic
	MAR	6	Cap		APR	24	Ari
	APR	24	Aqu		JUN	3	Tau
	JUN	24	Pic		JUL	14	Gem
	AUG	24	Aqu		AUG	28	Can
	OCT	19	Pic		OCT	20	Leo
	DEC	19	Ari	1931	FEB	16	Can
1925	FEB	5	Tau		MAR	30	Leo
	MAR	24	Gem		JUN	10	Vir
	MAY	9	Can		AUG	1	Lib
	JUN	26	Leo		SEP	17	Scp
	AUG	12	Vir		OCT	30	Sag
	SEP	28	Lib		DEC	10	Cap
	NOV	13	Scp	1932	JAN	18	Aqu
	DEC	28	Sag		FEB	25	Pic
1926	FEB	9	Cap		APR	3	Ari
	MAR	23	Aqu		MAY	12	Tau
	MAY	3	Pic		JUN	22	Gem
	JUN	15	Ari		AUG	4	Can
	AUG	1	Tau		SEP	20	Leo
1927	FEB	22	Gem		NOV	13	Vir
	APR	17	Can	1933	JUL	6	Lib
	JUN	6	Leo		AUG	26	Scp
	JUL	25	Vir		OCT	9	Sag
	SEP	10	Lib		NOV	19	Cap
	OCT	26	Scp		DEC	28	Aqu
	DEC	8	Sag	1934	FEB	4	Pic
1928	JAN	19	Cap		MAR	14	Ari
	FEB	28	Aqu		APR	22	Tau

	JUN	2	Gem		AUG	19	Vir
	JUL	15	Can		OCT	5	Lib
	AUG	30	Leo		NOV	20	Scp
	OCT	18	Vir	1941	JAN	4	Sag
	DEC	11	Lib		FEB	17	Cap
1935	JUL	29	Scp		APR	2	Aqu
	SEP	16	Sag		MAY	16	Pic
	OCT	28	Cap		JUL	2	Ari
	DEC	7	Aqu	1942	JAN	11	Tau
1936	JAN	14	Pic		MAR	7	Gem
	FEB	22	Ari		APR	26	Can
	APR	1	Tau		JUN	14	Leo
	MAY	13	Gem		AUG	1	Vir
	JUN	25	Can		SEP	17	Lib
	AUG	10	Leo		NOV	1	Scp
	SEP	26	Vir		DEC	15	Sag
	NOV	14	Lib	1943	JAN	26	Cap
1937	JAN	5	Scp		MAR	8	Aqu
	MAR	13	Sag		APR	17	Pic
	MAY	14	Scp		MAY	27	Ari
	AUG	8	Sag		JUL	7	Tau
	SEP	30	Cap		AUG	23	Gem
	NOV	11	Aqu	1944	MAR	28	Can
	DEC	21	Pic		MAY	22	Leo
1938	JAN	30	Ari		JUL	12	Vir
	MAR	12	Tau		AUG	29	Lib
	APR	23	Gem		OCT	13	Scp
	JUN	7	Can		NOV	25	Sag
	JUL	22	Leo	1945	JAN	5	Cap
	SEP	7	Vir		FEB	14	Aqu
	OCT	25	Lib		MAR	25	Pic
	DEC	11	Scp		MAY	2	Ari
1939	JAN	29	Sag		JUN	11	Tau
	MAR	21	Cap		JUL	23	Gem
	MAY	25	Aqu		SEP	7	Can
	JUL	21	Cap		NOV	11	Leo
	SEP	24	Aqu		DEC	26	Can
	NOV	19	Pic	1946	APR	22	Leo
1940	JAN	4	Ari		JUN	20	Vir
	FEB	17	Tau		AUG	9	Lib
	APR	1	Gem		SEP	24	Scp
	MAY	17	Can		NOV	6	Sag
	JUL	3	Leo		DEC	17	Cap

1947	JAN	25	Aqu		MAR	20	Tau
	MAR	4	Pic		MAY	1	Gem
	APR	11	Ari		JUN	14	Can
	MAY	21	Tau		JUL	29	Leo
	JUL	1	Gem		SEP	14	Vir
	AUG	13	Can		NOV	1	Lib
	OCT	1	Leo		DEC	20	Scp
	DEC	1	Vir	1954	FEB	9	Sag
1948	FEB	12	Leo		APR	12	Cap
	MAY	18	Vir		JUL	3	Sag
	JUL	17	Lib		AUG	24	Cap
	SEP	3	Scp		OCT	21	Aqu
	OCT	17	Sag		DEC	4	Pic
	NOV	26	Cap	1955	JAN	15	Ari
1949	JAN	4	Aqu		FEB	26	Tau
	FEB	11	Pic		APR	10	Gem
	MAR	21	Ari		MAY	26	Can
	APR	30	Tau		JUL	11	Leo
	JUN	10	Gem		AUG	27	Vir
	JUL	23	Can		OCT	13	Lib
	SEP	7	Leo		NOV	29	Scp
	OCT	27	Vir	1956	JAN	14	Sag
	DEC	26	Lib		FEB	28	Cap
1950	MAR	28	Vir		APR	14	Aqu
	JUN	11	Lib		JUN	3	Pic
	AUG	10	Scp		DEC	6	Ari
	SEP	25	Sag	1957	JAN	28	Tau
	NOV	6	Cap		MAR	17	Gem
	DEC	15	Aqu		MAY	4	Can
1951	JAN	22	Pic		JUN	21	Leo
	MAR	1	Ari		AUG	8	Vir
	APR	10	Tau		SEP	24	Lib
	MAY	21	Gem		NOV	8	Scp
	JUL	3	Can		DEC	23	Sag
	AUG	18	Leo	1958	FEB	3	Cap
	OCT	5	Vir		MAR	17	Aqu
	NOV	24	Lib		APR	27	Pic
1952	JAN	20	Scp		JUN	7	Ari
	AUG	27	Sag		JUL	21	Tau
	OCT	12	Cap		SEP	21	Gem
	NOV	21	Aqu		OCT	29	Tau
	DEC	30	Pic	1959	FEB	10	Gem
1953	FEB	8	Ari		APR	10	Can

	JUN	1	Leo		NOV	14	Cap
	JUL	20	Vir		DEC	23	Aqu
	SEP	5	Lib	1966	JAN	30	Pic
	OCT	21	Scp		MAR	9	Ari
	DEC	3	Sag		APR	17	Tau
1960	JAN	14	Cap		MAY	28	Gem
	FEB	23	Aqu		JUL	11	Can
	APR	2	Pic		AUG	25	Leo
	MAY	11	Ari		OCT	12	Vir
	JUN	20	Tau		DEC	4	Lib
	AUG	2	Gem	1967	FEB	12	Scp
	SEP	21	Can		MAR	31	Lib
1961	FEB	5	Gem		JUL	19	Scp
	FEB	7	Can		SEP	10	Sag
	MAY	6	Leo		OCT	23	Cap
	JUN	28	Vir		DEC	1	Aqu
	AUG	17	Lib	1968	JAN	9	Pic
	OCT	1	Scp		FEB	17	Ari
	NOV	13	Sag		MAR	27	Tau
	DEC	24	Cap		MAY	8	Gem
1962	FEB	1	Aqu		JUN	21	Can
	MAR	12	Pic		AUG	5	Leo
	APR	19	Ari		SEP	21	Vir
	MAY	28	Tau		NOV	9	Lib
	JUL	9	Gem		DEC	29	Scp
	AUG	22	Can	1969	FEB	25	Sag
	OCT	11	Leo		SEP	21	Cap
1963	JUN	3	Vir		NOV	4	Aqu
	JUL	27	Lib		DEC	15	Pic
	SEP	12	Scp	1970	JAN	24	Ari
	OCT	25	Sag		MAR	7	Tau
	DEC	5	Cap		APR	18	Gem
1964	JAN	13	Aqu		JUN	2	Can
	FEB	20	Pic		JUL	18	Leo
	MAR	29	Ari		SEP	3	Vir
	MAY	7	Tau		OCT	20	Lib
	JUN	17	Gem		DEC	6	Scp
	JUL	30	Can	1971	JAN	23	Sag
	SEP	15	Leo		MAR	12	Cap
	NOV	6	Vir		MAY	3	Aqu
1965	JUN	29	Lib		NOV	6	Pic
	AUG	20	Scp		DEC	26	Ari
	OCT	4	Sag	1972	FEB	10	Tau

	MAR	27	Gem	1978	JAN	26	Can
	MAY	12	Can		APR	10	Leo
	JUN	28	Leo		JUN	14	Vir
	AUG	15	Vir		AUG	4	Lib
	SEP	30	Lib		SEP	19	Scp
	NOV	15	Scp		NOV	2	Sag
	DEC	30	Sag		DEC	12	Cap
1973	FEB	12	Cap	1979	JAN	20	Aqu
	MAR	26	Aqu		FEB	27	Pic
	MAY	8	Pic		APR	7	Ari
	JUN	20	Ari		MAY	16	Tau
	AUG	12	Tau		JUN	26	Gem
	OCT	29	Ari		AUG	8	Can
	DEC	24	Tau		SEP	24	Leo
1974	FEB	27	Gem		NOV	19	Vir
	APR	20	Can	1980	MAR	11	Leo
	JUN	9	Leo		MAY	4	Vir
	JUL	27	Vir		JUL	10	Lib
	SEP	12	Lib		AUG	29	Scp
	OCT	28	Scp		OCT	12	Sag
	DEC	10	Sag		NOV	22	Cap
1975	JAN	21	Cap		DEC	30	Aqu
	MAR	3	Aqu	1981	FEB	6	Pic
	APR	11	Pic		MAR	17	Ari
	MAY	21	Ari		APR	25	Tau
	JUL	1	Tau		JUN	5	Gem
	AUG	14	Gem		JUL	18	Can
	OCT	17	Can		SEP	2	Leo
	NOV	25	Gem		OCT	21	Vir
1976	MAR	18	Can		DEC	16	Lib
	MAY	16	Leo	1982	AUG	3	Scp
	JUL	6	Vir		SEP	20	Sag
	AUG	24	Lib		OCT	31	Cap
	OCT	8	Scp		DEC	10	Aqu
	NOV	20	Sag	1983	JAN	17	Pic
1977	JAN	1	Cap		FEB	25	Ari
	FEB	9	Aqu		APR	5	Tau
	MAR	20	Pic		MAY	16	Gem
	APR	27	Ari		JUN	29	Can
	JUN	6	Tau		AUG	13	Leo
	JUL	17	Gem		SEP	30	Vir
	SEP	1	Can		NOV	18	Lib
	OCT	26	Leo	1984	JAN	11	Scp

	AUG	17	Sag		JUL	12	Tau
	OCT	5	Cap		AUG	31	Gem
	NOV	15	Aqu		DEC	14	Tau
	DEC	25	Pic	1991	JAN	21	Gem
1985	FEB	2	Ari		APR	3	Can
	MAR	15	Tau		MAY	26	Leo
	APR	26	Gem		JUL	15	Vir
	JUN	9	Can		SEP	1	Lib
	JUL	25	Leo		OCT	16	Scp
	SEP	10	Vir		NOV	29	Sag
	OCT	27	Lib	1992	JAN	9	Cap
	DEC	14	Scp		FEB	18	Aqu
1986	FEB	2	Sag		MAR	28	Pic
	MAR	28	Cap		MAY	5	Ari
	OCT	9	Aqu		JUN	14	Tau
	NOV	26	Pic		JUL	26	Gem
1987	JAN	8	Ari		SEP	12	Can
	FEB	20	Tau	1993	APR	27	Leo
	APR	5	Gem		JUN	23	Vir
	MAY	21	Can		AUG	12	Lib
	JUL	6	Leo		SEP	27	Scp
	AUG	22	Vir		NOV	9	Sag
	OCT	8	Lib		DEC	20	Cap
	NOV	24	Scp	1994	JAN	28	Aqu
1988	JAN	8	Sag		MAR	7	Pic
	FEB	22	Cap		APR	14	Ari
	APR	6	Aqu		MAY	23	Tau
	MAY	22	Pic		JUL	3	Gem
	JUL	13	Ari		AUG	16	Can
	OCT	23	Pic		OCT	4	Leo
	NOV	1	Ari		DEC	12	Vir
1989	JAN	19	Tau	1995	JAN	22	Leo
	MAR	11	Gem		MAY	25	Vir
	APR	29	Can		JUL	21	Lib
	JUN	16	Leo		SEP	7	Scp
	AUG	3	Vir		OCT	20	Sag
	SEP	19	Lib		NOV	30	Cap
	NOV	4	Scp	1996	JAN	8	Aqu
	DEC	18	Sag		FEB	15	Pic
1990	JAN	29	Cap		MAR	24	Ari
	MAR	11	Aqu		MAY	2	Tau
	APR	20	Pic		JUN	12	Gem
	MAY	31	Ari		JUL	25	Can

	SEP	9	Leo		NOV	27	Lib
	OCT	30	Vir	1999	JAN	26	Scp
1997	JAN	3	Lib		MAY	5	Lib
	MAR	8	Vir		JUL	5	Scp
	JUN	19	Lib		SEP	2	Sag
	AUG	14	Scp		OCT	17	Cap
	SEP	28	Sag		NOV	26	Aqu
	NOV	9	Cap	2000	JAN	4	Pic
	DEC	18	Aqu		FEB	12	Ari
1998	JAN	25	Pic		MAR	23	Tau
	MAR	4	Ari		MAY	3	Gem
	APR	13	Tau		JUN	16	Can
	MAY	24	Gem		AUG	1	Leo
	JUL	6	Can		SEP	17	Vir
	AUG	20	Leo		NOV	4	Lib
	OCT	7	Vir		DEC	23	Scp

JUPITER SIGN 1901–2000

1901	JAN	19	Cap		OCT	26	Ari
1902	FEB	6	Aqu	1917	FEB	12	Tau
1903	FEB	20	Pic		JUN	29	Gem
1904	MAR	1	Ari	1918	JUL	13	Can
	AUG	8	Tau	1919	AUG	2	Leo
	AUG	31	Ari	1920	AUG	27	Vir
1905	MAR	7	Tau	1921	SEP	25	Lib
	JUL	21	Gem	1922	OCT	26	Scp
	DEC	4	Tau	1923	NOV	24	Sag
1906	MAR	9	Gem	1924	DEC	18	Cap
	JUL	30	Can	1926	JAN	6	Aqu
1907	AUG	18	Leo	1927	JAN	18	Pic
1908	SEP	12	Vir		JUN	6	Ari
1909	OCT	11	Lib		SEP	11	Pic
1910	NOV	11	Scp	1928	JAN	23	Ari
1911	DEC	10	Sag		JUN	4	Tau
1913	JAN	2	Cap	1929	JUN	12	Gem
1914	JAN	21	Aqu	1930	JUN	26	Can
1915	FEB	4	Pic	1931	JUL	17	Leo
1916	FEB	12	Ari	1932	AUG	11	Vir
	JUN	26	Tau	1933	SEP	10	Lib

1934	OCT	11	Scp		OCT	5	Sag
1935	NOV	9	Sag	1960	MAR	1	Cap
1936	DEC	2	Cap		JUN	10	Sag
1937	DEC	20	Aqu		OCT	26	Cap
1938	MAY	14	Pic	1961	MAR	15	Aqu
	JUL	30	Aqu		AUG	12	Cap
	DEC	29	Pic		NOV	4	Aqu
1939	MAY	11	Ari	1962	MAR	25	Pic
	OCT	30	Pic	1963	APR	4	Ari
	DEC	20	Ari	1964	APR	12	Tau
1940	MAY	16	Tau	1965	APR	22	Gem
1941	MAY	26	Gem		SEP	21	Can
1942	JUN	10	Can		NOV	17	Gem
1943	JUN	30	Leo	1966	MAY	5	Can
1944	JUL	26	Vir		SEP	27	Leo
1945	AUG	25	Lib	1967	JAN	16	Can
1946	SEP	25	Scp		MAY	23	Leo
1947	OCT	24	Sag		OCT	19	Vir
1948	NOV	15	Cap	1968	FEB	27	Leo
1949	APR	12	Aqu		JUN	15	Vir
	JUN	27	Cap		NOV	15	Lib
	NOV	30	Aqu	1969	MAR	30	Vir
1950	APR	15	Pic		JUL	15	Lib
	SEP	15	Aqu		DEC	16	Scp
	DEC	1	Pic	1970	APR	30	Lib
1951	APR	21	Ari		AUG	15	Scp
1952	APR	28	Tau	1971	JAN	14	Sag
1953	MAY	9	Gem		JUN	5	Sc
1954	MAY	24	Can		SEP	11	Sag
1955	JUN	13	Leo	1972	FEB	6	Cap
	NOV	17	Vir		JUL	24	Sag
1956	JAN	18	Leo		SEP	25	Cap
	JUL	7	Vir	1973	FEB	23	Aqu
	DEC	13	Lib	1974	MAR	8	Pic
1957	FEB	19	Vir	1975	MAR	18	Ari
	AUG	7	Lib	1976	MAR	26	Tau
1958	JAN	13	Scp		AUG	23	Gem
	MAR	20	Lib		OCT	16	Tau
	SEP	7	Scp	1977	APR	3	Gem
1959	FEB	10	Sag		AUG	20	Can
	APR	24	Scp		DEC	30	Gem

1978	APR	12	Can
	SEP	5	Leo
1979	FEB	28	Can
	APR	20	Leo
	SEP	29	Vir
1980	OCT	27	Lib
1981	NOV	27	Scp
1982	DEC	26	Sag
1984	JAN	19	Cap
1985	FEB	6	Aqu
1986	FEB	20	Pic
1987	MAR	2	Ari
1988	MAR	8	Tau
	JUL	22	Gem
	NOV	30	Tau

1989	MAR	11	Gem
	JUL	30	Can
1990	AUG	18	Leo
1991	SEP	12	Vir
1992	OCT	10	Lib
1993	NOV	10	Scp
1994	DEC	9	Sag
1996	JAN	3	Cap
1997	JAN	21	Aqu
1998	FEB	4	Pic
1999	FEB	13	Ari
	JUN	28	Tau
	OCT	23	Ari
2000	FEB	14	Tau
	JUN	30	Gem

SATURN SIGN 1903–2000

1903	JAN	19	Aqu
1905	APR	13	Pic
	AUG	17	Aqu
1906	JAN	8	Pic
1908	MAR	19	Ari
1910	MAY	17	Tau
	DEC	14	Ari
1911	JAN	20	Tau
1912	JUL	7	Gem
	NOV	30	Tau
1913	MAR	26	Gem
1914	AUG	24	Can
	DEC	7	Gem
1915	MAY	11	Can
1916	OCT	17	Leo
	DEC	7	Can
1917	JUN	24	Leo
1919	AUG	12	Vir
1921	OCT	7	Lib
1923	DEC	20	Scp
1924	APR	6	Lib

	SEP	13	Scp
1926	DEC	2	Sag
1929	MAR	15	Cap
	MAY	5	Sag
	NOV	30	Cap
1932	FEB	24	Aqu
	AUG	13	Cap
	NOV	20	Aqu
1935	FEB	14	Pic
1937	APR	25	Ari
	OCT	18	Pic
1938	JAN	14	Ari
1939	JUL	6	Tau
	SEP	22	Ari
1940	MAR	20	Tau
1942	MAY	8	Gem
1944	JUN	20	Can
1946	AUG	2	Leo
1948	SEP	19	Vir
1949	APR	3	Leo
	MAY	29	Vir

Year	Month	Day	Sign		Year	Month	Day	Sign
1950	NOV	20	Lib			JUN	5	Leo
1951	MAR	7	Vir		1977	NOV	17	Vir
	AUG	13	Lib		1978	JAN	5	Leo
1953	OCT	22	Scp			JUL	26	Vir
1956	JAN	12	Sag		1980	SEP	21	Lib
	MAY	14	Scp		1982	NOV	29	Scp
	OCT	10	Sag		1983	MAY	6	Lib
1959	JAN	5	Cap			AUG	24	Scp
1962	JAN	3	Aqu		1985	NOV	17	Sag
1964	MAR	24	Pic		1988	FEB	13	Cap
	SEP	16	Aqu			JUN	10	Sag
	DEC	16	Pic			NOV	12	Cap
1967	MAR	3	Ari		1991	FEB	6	Aqu
1969	APR	29	Tau		1993	MAY	21	Pic
1971	JUN	18	Gem			JUN	30	Aqu
1972	JAN	10	Tau		1994	JAN	28	Pic
	FEB	21	Gem		1996	APR	7	Ari
1973	AUG	1	Can		1998	JUN	9	Tau
1974	JAN	7	Gem			OCT	25	Ari
	APR	18	Can		1999	MAR	1	Tau
1975	SEP	17	Leo		2000	AUG	10	Gem
1976	JAN	14	Can			OCT	16	Tau

CHAPTER 5

How to Decode the Symbols (Glyphs) on Your Chart

Astrology has its own special symbolic language, which has evolved over thousands of years. For beginners, it looks like a mysterious code . . . and it is! When you first try to decipher your chart, you may recognize the tiny moon and the symbol for your sign. Perhaps you'll also recognize Mars and Venus, since they are often used as male and female gender symbols outside of astrology. But the other marks could look as strange as Japanese to the uninitiated. Those little characters, called glyphs (or sigils) were created centuries ago, and any astrologer from Russia to Argentina could read your chart and know what it means. So a chart set up in Moscow can be interpreted by an astrologer in New York. And, since there are only 12 signs and 10 planets (not counting a few asteroids and other space creatures some astrologers use), it's a lot easier than learning to read Japanese!

You may well ask why you should bother to put in the effort at all. There are several good reasons. First, it's interesting. The glyphs are much more than little drawings—they are magical codes that contain within them keys to the meanings of the planets. Cracking the code can teach you immediately, in a visual way, much about the deeper meaning of a planet or sign.

If you ever get your horoscope chart done by computer, the printout will be written in glyphs. Though many charts have a list of the planets in plain English, many do not, leaving you mystified if you can't read the glyphs. You might pick out the symbol for the sun and the trident of Neptune . . . but then there's Jupiter (is that a number 4?) and Mercury, who looks like Venus wearing a hat.

Here's a code-cracker for the glyphs, beginning with the glyphs for the planets. To those who already know their glyphs . . . don't just skim over the chapter! There are hidden meanings to discover, so test your glyph-ese.

The Glyphs for the Planets

Almost all the glyphs of the planets are combinations of the most basic forms: the circle, the half-circle or arc, and the cross. Artists and glyph designers have stylized these forms over the years, but the basic concept is always visible. Each component of the glyph has a special meaning in relation to the others, which combines to create the meaning of the completed symbol.

For instance, the circle, which has no beginning or end, is one of the oldest symbols of spirit or spiritual forces. All of the early diagrams of the heavens—the spiritual territory—are shown in circular form. The semicircle or arc symbolizes the receptive, finite soul, which contains spiritual potential in the curving line. The vertical line symbolizes movement from heaven to earth. The horizontal line describes temporal movement, here and now, in time and space. Superimposed together, the vertical and horizontal planes symbolize manifestation in the material world.

The Sun Glyph ☉

The sun is always shown by this powerful solar symbol, a circle with a point in the center. It is you, your spiritual center, your infinite personality incarnating the point into the finite cycles of birth and death.

This symbol was brought into common use in the 16th century, after a German occultist and scholar, Cornelius Agrippa (1486–1535) wrote a book called *Die Occulta*

Philosophia, which became accepted as the standard work in its field. Agrippa collected many medieval astrological and magical symbols in this book, which astrologers later copied and continued to use.

The Moon Glyph ☽

This is surely the easiest symbol to spot on a chart. The moon glyph is a left-facing arc stylized into the crescent moon, which perfectly captures the reactive, receptive, emotional nature of the moon. As part of a circle, the arc symbolizes the potential fulfillment of the entire circle. It is the life force that is still incomplete.

The Mercury Glyph ☿

This is the "Venus with a hat" glyph. With another stretch of the imagination, can't you see the winged cap of Mercury the messenger? The upturned crescent could be antennae that tune in and transmit messages from the sun, signifying that Mercury is the way you communicate, the way your mind works. The upturned arc is receiving energy into the spirit or solar circle, which will later be translated into action on the material plane, symbolized by the cross. All the elements are equally sized because Mercury is neutral—it doesn't play favorites! This planet symbolizes objective, detached, unemotional thinking.

The Venus Glyph ♀

Here the relationship is between two elements—the circle, or spirit, above the cross of matter. Spirit is elevated over matter, pulling it upward. Venus asks, "What is beautiful? What do you like best, what do you love to have done to you?" Venus determines both your ideal of beauty and what feels good sensually. It governs your own allure and power to attract, as well as what attracts and pleases you.

The Mars Glyph ♂

In this glyph, the cross of matter is stylized into an arrowhead pointed up and outward, propelled by the circle of spirit. You can deduce that Mars embodies your spiritual energy projected into the outer world. It's your assertiveness, your initiative, your aggressive drive; it's what you like to do to others; it's your temper. If you know someone's Mars, you know whether they'll blow up when angry or do a slow burn. Your task is to use your outgoing Mars energy wisely and well.

The Jupiter Glyph ♃

Jupiter is the basic cross of the matter, with a large stylized crescent perched on the left side of the horizontal, temporal plane. You might think of the crescent as an open hand—one meaning of Jupiter is "luck," or what's handed to you. You don't work for what you get from Jupiter—it comes to you if you're open to it.

The Jupiter glyph might also remind you of a jumbo jet with a huge tail fin, about to take off. This is the planet of travel, mental and spiritual, and of expanding your horizons via new ideas, new spiritual dimensions, and new places. Jupiter embodies the optimism and enthusiasm of the traveler about to embark on an exciting adventure.

The Saturn Glyph ♄

Flip Jupiter over and you've got Saturn. (This might not be immediately apparent, because Saturn is usually stylized into an "h" form like the one shown here.) But the principle it expresses is the opposite of Jupiter's expansive tendencies. Saturn pulls you back to earth—the receptive arc is pushed down underneath the cross of matter. Before there are any rewards or expansion, the duties and obligations of the material world must be considered. Saturn says, "Stop, wait, and finish your chores before you take off!"

Saturn's glyph also resembles the sickle of old Father Time. Saturn was first known as Chronos, the Greek god of time, for time brings all matter to an end. When it was thought to be the most distant planet (before the discovery of Uranus), Saturn was believed to be the place where time stopped. After the soul, having departed from earth, journeyed back to the outer reaches of the universe, it finally stopped at Saturn, at "the end of time."

The Uranus Glyph ♅

The glyph for Uranus is often stylized to form a capital "H" after Sir William Herschel, the planet's discoverer. But the more esoteric version curves the two pillars of the H into crescent antennae, or ears, or like satellite discs receiving signals from space. These are perched on the horizontal material line of the cross (matter) and pushed from below by the circle of the spirit. To many sci-fi fans, Uranus looks like an orbiting satellite.

Uranus channels the highest energy of all, the white electrical light of the universal spiritual sun, the force that holds the cosmos together. This pure electrical energy is gathered from all over the universe. Because it doesn't follow an ordinary celestial drumbeat, it can't be controlled or predicted, which is also true of those who are strongly influenced by this eccentric planet. In the symbol, this energy is manifested through the balance of polarities (the two opposite arms of the glyph) like the two polarized wires of a lightbulb.

The Neptune Glyph ♆

Neptune's glyph is usually stylized to look like a trident, the weapon of the Roman god Neptune. However, on a more esoteric level, it shows the large upturned crescent of the soul pierced through by the cross of matter. Neptune nails down, or materializes, soul energy, bringing impulses from the soul level into manifestation. That is why Neptune is associated with imagination or "imagining in," making an image of the soul. Neptune works through feeling, sensitivity, and mystical capacity to bring the divine into the earthly realm.

The Pluto Glyph ♀

Pluto is written two ways. One is a composite of the letters "PL," the first two letters of the word Pluto and coincidentally the initials of Percival Lowell, one of the planet's discoverers. The other, more esoteric symbol is a small circle above a large open crescent that surmounts the cross of matter. This depicts Pluto's power to regenerate—you might imagine from this glyph a new little spirit emerging from the sheltering cup of the soul. Pluto rules the forces of life and death—after a Pluto experience, you are transformed or reborn in some way.

Sci-fi fans might visualize this glyph as a small satellite (the circle) being launched. It was shortly after Pluto's discovery that we learned how to harness the nuclear forces that made space exploration possible. Pluto rules the transformative power of atomic energy, which totally changed our lives and from which there was no turning back.

The Glyphs for the Signs

On an astrological chart, the glyph for the sign will appear after that of the planet. When you see the moon glyph followed by a number and the glyph for the sign, this means that the moon was passing over a certain degree of an astrological sign at the time of the chart. On the dividing points between the segments, or "houses," on your chart, you'll find the symbol for the sign that rules the house.

Since sun-sign symbols do not always bring together the same basic components of the planetary glyphs, where do their meanings come from? Many have been passed down from ancient Egyptian and Chaldean civilizations with few modifications. Others have been adapted over the centuries. In deciphering many of the glyphs, you'll often find that many symbols reveal a dual nature of the sign, which is not always apparent in sun-sign descriptions. For instance, the Gemini glyph is similar to the Roman numeral for two, and reveals this sign's longing to discover a twin soul. The Cancer glyph may be interpreted as resembling either nurturing breasts or the self-protective claws of the crab. Libra's glyph embodies the duality of the spirit balanced with material reality. The Sagittarius glyph shows that the aspirant must also carry along the earthly animal nature in his quest. The Capricorn sea goat is another symbol with dual emphasis. The goat climbs high yet is always pulled back by the deep waters of the unconscious. Aquarius embodies the double waves of mental detachment, balanced by the desire for connection with others in a friendly way. And finally, the two fishes of Pisces, which are forever tied together, show the duality of the soul and the spirit that must be reconciled.

The Aries Glyph ♈

Since the symbol for Aries is the ram, this glyph's most obvious association is with a ram's horns, which characterize one aspect of the Aries personality—an aggressive, me-first, leaping-head-first attitude. But the symbol may have other meanings for you, too. Some astrologers liken it to a fountain of energy, which Aries people also embody. The first sign of the zodiac bursts on the scene eagerly, ready to go. Another analogy is to the eyebrows and nose of the human head, which Aries rules, and the thinking power that is initiated in the brain. Another interesting theory is that the symbol represents spirit descending from a higher realm into the mind of man, which would be the point of the V shape in the Aries glyph.

The origin of this symbol links it to the Egyptian god Amun, represented by a ram. As Amon-Ra, this god was believed to embody the creator of the universe, the leader of all the other gods. This relates easily to the position of Aries as the leader (or first sign) of the zodiac, which begins at the spring equinox, a time of the year when nature is renewed.

The Taurus Glyph ♉

This is another easy glyph to draw and identify. It takes little imagination to decipher the bull's head with long, curving horns. Like the bull, the archetypal Taurus is slow to anger but ferocious when provoked, as well as stubborn, steady, and sensual. Another association is the Taurus-ruled larynx (and thyroid) of the throat area and the Eustachian tubes (the "horns" of the glyph) running up to the ears, which coincide with the relationship of Taurus to the voice, song, and music. Many famous singers, musicians, and composers have prominent Taurus influences.

Many ancient religions involved a bull as the central figure in fertility rites or initiations, usually symbolizing the victory of man over his animal nature. Another possible origin is in the sacred bull of Egypt, who embodied the incarnate form of Osiris, god of death and resurrection. In early Christian imagery, the Taurean bull, representing St. Luke, appears in many art forms along with the Lion (Leo and St. Mark), the Man (Aquarius and St. Matthew) and the Eagle (Scorpio and St. John).

The Gemini Glyph ♊

The standard glyph immediately calls to mind the Roman numeral for two and the symbol for Gemini, the "twins." In almost all images for this sign, the relationship between two persons is emphasized. This is the sign of communication and human contact, and it manifests the desire to share. Many of the figurative images for Gemini show twins with their arms around each other, emphasizing that they are sharing the same ideas and the same ground. In the glyph, the top line indicates mental communication, while the bottom line indicates shared physical space.

The most famous Gemini legend is that of the twin sons, Castor and Pollux, one of whom had a mortal father, while the other was the son of Zeus, king of the gods. When it came time for the mortal twin to die, his grief-stricken brother pleaded with Zeus, who agreed to let them spend half the year on earth, in mortal form, and half in immortal life, with the gods on Mt. Olympus. This reflects a basic concept of humankind, which possesses an immortal soul yet is also subject to the limits of mortality.

The Cancer Glyph ♋

Two convenient images relate to the Cancer glyph. The easiest to picture is the curving claws of the Cancer symbol, the crab. Like the crab, Cancer's element is water. This sensitive sign also has a hard protective shell to protect its tender interior. It must be wily to escape predators, scampering sideways and hiding shyly under the rocks. The crab also responds to the cycles of the moon, as do all shellfish. The other image is that of two female breasts, which Cancer rules, showing that this is a sign that nurtures and protects others as well as itself. In ancient Egypt, Cancer was also represented by the scarab beetle, a symbol of regeneration and eternal life.

The Leo Glyph ♌

Lions have belonged to the sign of Leo since earliest times and it is not difficult to imagine the king of beasts with his sweeping mane and curling tail from this glyph. The upward sweep of the glyph easily describes the positive energy of Leos—the flourishing tail and the flamboyant qualities. Another analogy, which is a stretch, is that of a heart leaping up with joy and enthusiasm, also very typical of Leo. Notice that the Leo glyph seems to be an extension of Cancer's glyph, with a significant difference. In the Cancer glyph, the figures are folding inward, protectively, while the Leo glyph expresses energy outwardly, with no duality in the symbol (or in

Leo). In early Christian imagery, the Leo lion represented St. Mark.

The Virgo Glyph ♍

You can read much into this mysterious glyph. For instance, it could represent the initials of "Mary Virgin," or a young woman holding a staff of wheat, or stylized female genitalia, all common interpretations. The "M" shape might also remind you that Virgo is ruled by Mercury. The cross beneath the symbol could indicate the grounded, practical nature of this earth sign.

The earliest zodiacs link Virgo with the Egyptian goddess Isis, who gave birth to the god Horus after her husband Osiris had been killed, in the archetype of a miraculous conception. There are many statues of Isis nursing her baby son, which are reminiscent of medieval Virgin and Child motifs. This sign has also been associated with the image of the Holy Grail, where the Virgo symbol was substituted with a chalice.

The Libra Glyph ♎

It is not difficult to read the standard image for Libra, the scales, into this glyph. There is another meaning, however, that is equally relevant: the setting sun as it descends over the horizon. Libra's natural position on the zodiac wheel is the descendent or sunset position (as Aries' natural position is the ascendant, or rising sign). Both images relate to Libra's personality. Libra is always weighing pros and cons for a balanced decision. In the sunset image, the sun (male) hovers over the horizontal Earth (female) before setting. Libra is the space between these lines, harmonizing yin and yang, spiritual and material, the ideal and real worlds. The glyph has also been linked to the kidneys, which are ruled by Libra.

The Scorpio Glyph ♏

With its barbed tail, this glyph is easy to identify with the sign of the Scorpion. It also represents the male sexual parts, over which the sign rules. However, some earlier symbols for Scorpio, such as the Egyptian, represent it as an erect serpent. You can also draw the conclusion that Mars is ruled by the arrowhead.

Another image for Scorpio, not identifiable in this glyph, is the eagle. Scorpios can go to extremes, soaring like the eagle or self-destructing like the Scorpion. In early Christian imagery, which often used zodiacal symbols, the Scorpio eagle was chosen to symbolize the intense apostle St. John the Evangelist.

The Sagittarius Glyph ♐

This glyph is one of the easiest to spot and draw—an upward pointing arrow lifting up a cross. The arrow is pointing skyward, while the cross represents the four elements of the material world, which the arrow must convey. Elevating materiality into spirituality is an important Sagittarius quality, which explains why this sign is associated with higher learning, religion, philosophy, and travel—the aspiring professions. Sagittarius can also send barbed arrows of frankness in the pursuit of truth. (This is also the sign of the super-salesman.)

Sagittarius is symbolically represented by the centaur, a mythological creature who is half-man, half horse, aiming his arrow toward the skies. Though Sagittarius is motivated by spiritual aspiration, it also must balance the powerful appetites of the animal nature. The centaur Chiron, a figure in Greek mythology, became a wise teacher after many adventures and world travels.

The Capricorn Glyph ♑

One of the most difficult symbols to draw, this glyph may take some practice. It is a representation of the seagoat: a mythical animal that is a goat with a curving fish's tail. The goat part of Capricorn wants to leave the waters of the emotions and climb to the elevated areas of life. But the first part is the unconscious, the deep chaotic psychic level that draws the goat back. Capricorn is often trying to escape the deep, feeling part of life by submerging himself in work, steadily climbing to the top. To some people, the glyph represents a seated figure with a bent knee, a reminder that Capricorn governs the knee area of the body.

An interesting aspect of this figure is how the sharp pointed horns of the symbol, which represent the penetrating, shrewd, conscious side of Capricorn, contrast with the swishing tail, which represents its serpentine, unconscious, emotional force. One Capricorn legend, which dates from Roman times, tells of the earthy fertility god, Pan, who tried to save himself from uncontrollable sexual desires by jumping into the Nile. His upper body then turned into a goat, while the lower part became a fish. Later, Jupiter gave him a safe haven in the skies, as a constellation.

The Aquarius Glyph ≈

This ancient water symbol can be traced back to an Egyptian hieroglyph representing streams of life force. Symbolized by the water bearer, Aquarius is distributor of the waters of life—the magic liquid of regeneration. The two waves can also be linked to the positive and negative charges of the electrical energy that Aquarius rules, a sort of universal wavelength. Aquarius is tuned in intuitively to higher forces via this electrical force. The duality of the glyph could also refer to the dual nature of Aquarius, a sign that runs hot and cold, is friendly but also detached in the mental world of air signs.

In Greek legends, Aquarius is represented by Ganymede, who was carried to heaven by an eagle in order to become the cup bearer of Zeus, and to supervise the annual flooding of the Nile. The sign became associated with aviation and notions of flight.

The Pisces Glyph)(

Here is an abstraction of the familiar image of Pisces, two fishes swimming in opposite directions, bound together by a cord. The fishes represent spirit, which yearns for the freedom of heaven, while the soul remains attached to the desires of the temporal world. During life on earth, the spirit and the soul are bound together and when they complement each other, instead of pulling in opposite directions, this facilitates the creative expression for which Pisceans are known. The ancient version of this glyph, taken from the Egyptians, had no connecting line, which was added in the fourteenth century.

Another interpretation is that the left fish indicates the direction of involution or the beginning of the cycle; the right-hand fish, the direction of evolution, the way to completion of a cycle. It's an appropriate meaning for Pisces, the last sign of the zodiac.

CHAPTER 6

Answers to Your Questions

Here are the answers to some questions frequently asked by regular readers of this book. You may have been wondering about them, too.

QUESTION: *Why don't other stars in the cosmos influence our horoscopes?*
Most astrologers find that ten planets—considering the sun and moon as "planets"—give us quite enough information to delineate a horoscope. However, a growing number of astrologers are finding that other celestial bodies, such as asteroids and certain fixed stars, add an extra dimension and special nuances to the horoscope. Certain stars are said to bring specific lessons on life's journey when they are also linked with one of the key planets in a horoscope. These lessons are expressed by the mythology the star represents.

The fixed stars were used by the ancient astrologers and now are enjoying a renaissance thanks to a group of scholars dedicated to reinterpreting their mythology and adapting ancient techniques for modern times. Those interested in fixed stars will find much fascinating information in *Brady's Book of Fixed Stars* by Bernadette Brady (Samuel Weiser, 1998).

QUESTION: *If I was born on a Mercury retrograde, does it make a difference?*
Many highly original and creative thinkers were born with Mercury in retrograde, or apparent backward motion, such as Oscar Wilde, Norman Mailer, Dylan

Thomas, Bruce Springsteen, Hillary Clinton, Harry S. Truman, and Mae West. You might find the three Mercury retrograde periods each year easier to cope with than other people. However, it is the whole chart and the aspects to your natal Mercury that must be considered before drawing any conclusions.

QUESTION: *I'm very different from my twin brother. Since we were born only twenty minutes apart, how do you account for that?*

If you have your exact time of birth, you might be able to find out for yourself by having an accurate horoscope chart made. Even a few minutes difference in time of birth can change the emphasis in a chart because of the movement of the earth. A different rising sign, which sets up the "houses" of your chart, moves over the horizon every two hours. And the moon moves about 13 degrees in a day. A change of degree or a rising sign can make a big difference.

If you have the exact degree of your moon and rising sign and your brother's moon and rising sign, you might be interested in comparing Sabian Symbols, which are symbolic meanings for each degree; they can be quite enlightening. There are several books on the Sabian Symbols, such as *The Sabian Symbols as an Oracle* by Lynda and Richard Hill (White Horse Books, 1995), a very readable recent addition to these interpretations.

Another possible reason for your differences is that you may each operate on a different level of your similar horoscopes. Or because you react to each other, you may each choose to manifest other facets of your charts. For example, one twin with a Cancer sun sign may manifest the creative, perceptive facets of her chart and become a child psychologist. Her sister may become a sharp businesswoman, running a hotel or real estate business, choosing the more practical side of her chart.

QUESTION: *If you were born on a day when the sun was changing signs, does that mean that you*

have characteristics of the preceding or following sign?

If you were born on a day when the Sun or moon was changing signs, then it is very important to get your exact time of birth and to have an accurate horoscope chart cast. When there is a sign change, there are many shifts in energy. Between one sign and the next, there is a difference in element, modality, and polarity. Therefore, you are not likely to be partly one sign and partly another. If you do manifest characteristics of the adjacent sign, it may be due to other planets in that sign or to your rising sign.

QUESTION: *How do I answer my religious friends and family who disapprove of my interest in astrology?*

Astrology has a long history of being attacked by religious and scientific skeptics, most of whom know little about real astrology. (There's even an Internet mailing list especially for those who wish to ventilate their anti-astrology feelings.) Point out that there has never been any conflict between astrology and religion; there are no anti-astrology writings in the Bible. In fact, the three Wise Men or Magi were astrologers. In medieval times, astrology was integrated with religion. Many famous European cathedrals, such as Chartres and Canterbury, have astrology motifs, and there's a very ancient zodiac from the floor of a synagogue in New York's Jewish Museum. There is no dogma to astrology that might counter religious beliefs—astrology is not a belief system, it is a technique. In other words, you are not getting into anything dangerous with astrology, which may be what your friends fear.

Many religious people feel threatened by astrologers because they confuse modern-day astrology with that practiced by charlatans of the past or because they feel that someone interested in astrology will turn away from religion. However, as anyone who has delved seriously into astrology can attest, the study of astrology tends to bring one closer to a spiritual understanding of the interchange between a universal design, the material world, and man's place in it. Astrology can, in a very practical way, help man keep in balance with the forces of the universe.

QUESTION: *Can I find the answer to a question based on a horoscope for the time it is asked?*

This belongs to a specific discipline within astrology called *horary astrology*. It works according to specific rules and is practiced by specialists within the field. If you would like to find an answer this way, be sure to consult an astrologer who specializes in horary techniques. There is also an astrology program called "Nostradamus" (by Air Software; see our resource list in the Internet chapter), which was created for horary work.

CHAPTER 7

Your Daily Agenda:
Make the Most of the Millennium!

Set your schedule on a successful course by letting astrology help you coordinate your activities with the most beneficial times. For instance, if you know the dates that the tricky planet Mercury will be creating havoc with communications, you'll be sure to back up the hard drive on your computer, keep duplicates of your correspondence, record those messages, and read between the lines of contracts. When Venus is in your sign, you'll get a new hairstyle, entertain a VIP client, and circulate where you'll be seen and admired.

To find out for yourself if there's truth to the saying "timing is everything," mark your own calendar for love, career moves, vacations, and important events by using the following information and the tables in this chapter and the one titled "Look Up Your Planets," as well as the moon sign listings under your daily forecast. Here are the happenings to note on your agenda:

- Dates of your sun sign (high-energy period)
- The month previous to your sun sign (love energy period)
- Dates of planets in your sign this year
- Full and new moons (pay special attention when these fall in your sun sign)
- Eclipses

- Moon in your sun sign every month, as well as moon in the opposite sign (listed in daily forecast)
- Mercury retrogrades
- Other retrograde periods

When to Switch on the Power!

Every birthday starts a cycle of solar energy for you. You should feel a new surge of vitality as the powerful sun enters your sign. This is the time when predominant energies are most favorable to you—so go for it! Start new projects, make your big moves. You'll get the recognition you deserve now, because your sun sign is most prominent. Look in the tables in this book to see if other planets will also be passing through your sun sign at this time. Venus (love, beauty), Mars (energy, drive), or Mercury (communication, mental sharpness) reinforce the sun and give an extra boost to your life in the areas they affect. Venus will rev up your social and love life, making you seem especially attractive. Mars gives you extra energy and drive, while Mercury fuels your brain power and helps you communicate. Jupiter signals an especially lucky period of expansion.

There are two "down" times related to the sun. During the month before your birthday period, when you are winding up your annual cycle, you could be feeling especially vulnerable and depleted, so get extra rest, watch your diet, and don't overstress yourself. Use this time to gear up for a big "push" when the sun enters your sign.

Another "down" time is when the sun is the opposite sign (six months from your birthday) and the prevailing energies are very different from yours. You may feel at odds with the world and things might not come easily. You'll have to work harder for recognition, because people are not on your wavelength. However, this could be a good time to work on a team, in cooperation with others, or behind the scenes.

Phase in and Phase out with the Moon

Working with the phases of the moon is as easy as looking up at the night sky. At the new moon, when both sun and moon are in the same sign, it's the best time to begin new ventures, especially the activities that are favored by that sign. You'll have powerful energies pulling you in the same direction. You'll be focused outward, toward action. Postpone breaking off, terminating, deliberating, or reflecting, activities that require introspection and passive work.

Get your project under way during the first quarter, then go public at the full moon, a time of high intensity, when feelings come out into the open. This is your time to shine—to express yourself. Be aware, however, that because pressures are being released, other people are also letting off steam and confrontations are possible. So try to avoid arguments. Traditionally, astrologers often advise against surgery at this time, for it could produce heavier bleeding.

From the last quarter to the new moon is a winding-down phase, a time to cut off unproductive relationships, do serious thinking, and perform inwardly directed activities.

You'll feel some new and full moons more strongly than others, especially the new moons that fall in your sun sign and the full moons in your opposite sign. Because that particular full moon happens at your low-energy time of year, it is likely to be an especially stressful time in a relationship, when hidden problems or unexpressed emotions could surface.

The Year 2000 Full and New Moons

New Moon in Capricorn—January 6
Full Moon in Leo—January 20 (eclipse 11:45 p.m. EST)
New Moon in Aquarius—February 5 (eclipse 8:03 a.m. EST)
Full Moon in Virgo—February 19

New Moon in Pisces—March 6
Full Moon in Virgo—March 20
New Moon in Aries—April 4
Full Moon in Libra—April 18
New Moon in Taurus—May 4
Full Moon in Scorpio—May 18
New Moon in Gemini—June 2
Full Moon in Sagittarius—June 16
New Moon in Cancer—July 1 (eclipse 3:34 p.m. EDT)
Full Moon in Capricorn—July 16 (eclipse 9:55 a.m. EDT)
New Moon in Leo—July 30 (eclipse 10:25 p.m. EDT)
Full Moon in Aquarius—August 15
New Moon in Virgo—August 29
Full Moon in Pisces—September 13
New Moon in Libra—September 27
Full Moon in Aries—October 13
New Moon in Scorpio—October 27
Full Moon in Taurus—November 11
New Moon in Sagittarius—November 25
Full Moon in Gemini—December 11
New Moon in Capricorn—December 25 (eclipse 12:22 p.m. EST)

Six Eclipses this Year!

There are six eclipses this year (last year, there were only four), which means you can expect changes that will be sure to influence your life, especially if you are a Capricorn, Cancer, Leo, or Aquarius. Both solar and lunar eclipses are times when our natural rhythms are altered, depending on where the eclipse falls in your horoscope and how many planets you have in the sign of the eclipse. If it falls on or close to your birthday, you're going to have important changes in your life, perhaps a turning point.

Lunar eclipses happen when the earth is on a level plane with the sun and moon and moves exactly between them during the time of the full moon, breaking the powerful monthly cycle of opposition of these two forces. We might say the earth "short circuits" the connection between them. The effect can be either confusion or clarity, as our subconscious energies, which normally react to the pull of opposing sun and moon, are turned off. As we are temporarily freed from the subconscious attachments, we might have objective insights that could help us change any destructive emotional patterns, such as addictions, which normally occur at this time. This momentary "turn off" could help us turn our lives around. On the other hand, this break in the normal cycle could cause a bewildering disorientation that intensifies our insecurities.

The solar eclipse occurs at the new moon and this time the moon blocks the sun's energies as it passes exactly between the sun and the earth. This means the objective, conscious force, represented by the sun, will be temporarily darkened. Subconscious lunar forces, activating our deepest emotions, will now dominate, putting us in a highly subjective state. Emotional truths can be revealed or emotions can run wild, as our objectivity is cut off and hidden patterns surface. If your sign is affected, you may find yourself beginning a period of work on a deep inner level; you may have psychic experiences or a surfacing of deep feelings.

You'll start feeling the energies of an upcoming eclipse a few days after the previous new or full moon. The energy continues to intensify until the actual eclipse, then disperses for three or four days. So plan ahead at least a week or more before an eclipse and allow several days afterward for the natural rhythms to return. Try not to make major moves during this period (it's not a great time to get married, change jobs, or buy a home).

Eclipses in 2000

Lunar Eclipse in Leo—January 20 (11:45 p.m. EST)
Solar Eclipse in Aquarius—February 5 (8:03 a.m. EST)
Solar Eclipse in Cancer—July 1 (3:34 p.m. EDT)

Lunar Eclipse in Capricorn—July 16 (9:55 a.m. EDT)
Solar Eclipse in Leo—July 30 (10:25 p.m. EDT)
Solar Eclipse in Capricorn—December 25 (12:22 p.m. EST)

Moon Sign Timing

You can forecast the daily emotional "weather" to determine your monthly high and low days, or to synchronize your activities with the cycles and the sign of the moon. Take note of the moon's daily sign under your daily forecast at the end of the book. Here are some of the activities favored and moods you are likely to encounter under each sign.

Moon in Aries

Get moving! The new moon in Aries is an ideal time to start new projects. Everyone is pushy and raring to go, rather impatient and short tempered. Leave details and follow-up for later. Competitive sports or martial arts are great ways to let off steam. Quiet types could use some assertiveness, but it's a great day for dynamos. Be careful not to step on too many toes.

Moon in Taurus

It's time to do solid, methodical tasks. This is the time to tackle follow-through or backup work, laying the foundations for success. Make investments, buy real estate, do appraisals, make some hard bargains. Attend to your property—get out in the country or spend some time in your garden. Enjoy creature comforts, music, a good dinner, and sensual lovemaking. Forget about starting a diet.

Moon in Gemini

Talk means action today. Telephone, write letters, fax! Make new contacts, and be sure to stay in touch with steady customers as well. You can handle lots of tasks at once. It's a great day for mental activity of any kind. Don't try to pin people down—they too are feeling restless, so keep it light. Flirtations and socializing are good. Watch gossip—and don't give away secrets.

Moon in Cancer

This is a moody, sensitive, emotional time. People respond to personal attention and mothering. Stay at home, have a family dinner, call your mother. Nostalgia, memories, and psychic powers are heightened. You'll want to hang on to people and things—don't clean out your closets now. You could have some shrewd insights into what others really need and want, so pay attention to dreams, intuition, and gut reactions.

Moon in Leo

Everybody is in a much more confident, enthusiastic, generous mood. It's a good day to ask for a raise, show what you can do, and dress like a star. People will respond to flattery, and are sure to enjoy a bit of drama and theater. You may be feeling extravagant, so treat yourself royally and show off a bit—but don't break the bank! Be careful that you don't promise more than you can deliver!

Moon in Virgo

Do practical, down-to-earth chores, such as reviewing your budget and making repairs. Be an efficiency expert. This is not a day to ask for a raise. Have a health checkup, revamp your diet, buy vitamins or health food. Make your home spotless, taking care of details and piled-up chores. Reorganize your work and life so they run more smoothly, efficiently, and inexpensively. Be prepared for others to be in a critical, fault-finding mood.

Moon in Libra

Relationships of all kinds are favored. Attend to legal matters, negotiate contracts, and arbitrate. Do things with your favorite partner—socialize, be romantic, or buy a special gift or a beautiful object. Decorate yourself or your surroundings, buying new clothes, throwing a party, or having an elegant, romantic evening. Smooth over any ruffled feathers as you avoid confrontations and stick to civilized discussions.

Moon in Scorpio

This is a day to do things with passion. You'll have excellent concentration and focus, but try not to get too intense emotionally, and avoid sharp exchanges with loved ones. Others may tend to go to extremes, get jealous, and overreact. Today is great for troubleshooting, problem-solving, research, scientific work—and making love. Pay attention to psychic vibes.

Moon in Sagittarius

It's a great time for travel and for having philosophical discussions. Set long-range career goals, work out, do sports, or buy athletic equipment. Others will be feeling upbeat, exuberant, and adventurous. Risk taking is favored today—you may feel like taking a gamble, betting on the horses, visiting a local casino, or buying a lottery ticket. Teaching, writing, and spiritual activities also get the green light. Relax outdoors; take care of animals.

Moon in Capricorn

You can accomplish a lot today, so get on the ball! Issues concerning your basic responsibilities, duties, family, and parents could crop up. You'll be expected to deliver on your promises and stick to your schedule now, so weed out the deadwood from your life and attack chores systematically. Get a dental checkup or attend to your aching knees.

Moon in Aquarius

It's a great day for doing things in groups—so take part in clubs, meetings, outings, politics, or parties. Campaign for your candidate, work for a worthy cause, or deal with larger issues that affect the welfare of humanity. Buy a computer or electronic gadget. Watch TV. Wear something outrageous or try something you've never done before. Present an original idea. Don't stick to a rigid schedule—go with the flow. Take a class in meditation, mind control, or yoga.

Moon in Pisces

This can be a very creative day, so let your imagination work overtime. Film, theater, music, or ballet could inspire you. Spend some time alone, resting and reflecting, reading, watching a favorite film, or writing poetry. Daydreams can also be profitable. Help those less fortunate or lend a listening ear to someone who may be feeling blue. Don't overindulge in self-pity or escapism via alcohol, however, for people are especially vulnerable to substance abuse now. Turn your thoughts to romance and someone special.

When the Planets Go Backward

All the planets, except for the sun and moon, have times when they appear to move backward—or retrograde—in the sky, or so it seems from our point of view on earth. At these times, planets do not work as they usually do, so it's best to take a break from that planet's energies in our life and do some work on an inner level.

How to Outwit Mercury Mischief

Mercury goes retrograde most often, and its effects can be especially irritating. When it reaches a short distance ahead of the sun three times a year, it seems to move backward from our point of view. Astrologers often compare retrograde motion to the optical illusion that occurs when we ride on a train that passes another train traveling at a different speed—the second train appears to be moving in reverse.

What this means to you is that the Mercury-ruled areas of your life—analytical thought processes, communications, scheduling, and such—are subject to all kinds of confusion. So be prepared as people change their minds and renege on commitments. Communications equipment can break down, schedules must be changed on short notice, and people are late for appointments or don't show up at all. Traffic is terrible, and major purchases malfunction, don't work out, or get delivered in the wrong color. Letters don't arrive or are delivered to the wrong address. Employees will make errors that have to be corrected later. Contracts don't work out or must be renegotiated.

Since most of us can't put our lives on hold for nine weeks every year (three Mercury retrograde periods), we should learn to tame the trickster and make it work for us. The key is in the prefix "re." This is the time to go back over things in your life. Reflect on what you've done during the previous months, looking for deeper insights, spotting errors you've missed, and taking time to review and reevaluate what has happened. This time is very good for inner spiritual work and meditations. REst and REward yourself—it's a good time to take a vacation, especially if you REvisit a favorite place. REorganize your work and finish up projects that are backed up, or clean out your desk and closets, throwing away what you can't REcycle. If you must sign contracts or agreements, do so with a contingency clause that lets you REevaluate the terms later.

Postpone major purchases or commitments. Don't get married (unless you're remarrying the same person). Try not to rely on other people keeping appointments, contracts or agreements to the letter—it's best to have several alternatives. Double-check and read between the lines. Don't buy anything connected with communications or transportation—and if you must, be sure to cover yourself. Mercury retrograding through your sun sign will intensify its effect on your life.

If Mercury was retrograde when you were born, you may be one of the lucky people who don't suffer the frustrations of this period. If so, your mind probably works in a very intuitive, insightful way.

The sign Mercury is retrograding through can give you an idea of what's in store—as well as the sun signs that will be especially challenged.

Mercury Retrograde Periods in 2000
February 21–March 14
June 23–July 17
October 18–November 8
Fortunately, there are no Venus or Mars retrograde periods this year; however, both planes were retrograde in 1999, so it might be useful to reexamine what to do during these times.

Venus Retrograde—Make Peace!

Retrograding Venus can cause relationships to take a backward step or it can make you extravagant and impractical. It's *not* a good time to redecorate—you'll hate the color of the walls later. Postpone getting a new hairstyle and try not to fall in love either. But if you wish to make amends in an already-troubled relationship, make peaceful overtures then.

There is no Venus retrograde period in the year 2000.

Mars Tips—When to Push and When to Hold Back!

Mars shows how and when to get where you want to go, so timing your moves with Mars on your side can give you a big push. On the other hand, pushing Mars the wrong way can guarantee that you'll run into frustrations in every corner. Your best times to forge ahead are during the weeks when Mars is traveling through your sun sign or your Mars sign (look these up in the chapter on how to find your planets). Also consider times when Mars is in a compatible sign (fire with air signs, or earth with water signs). You'll be sure to have planetary power on your side.

Hold your fire when Mars retrogrades (fortunately this is a "go-ahead" year, when Mars moves forward all year long). This is the time to exercise patience, so let someone else run with the ball, especially if it's the opposing team. You may feel that you're not accomplishing much, but that's the right idea. Slow down and work off any frustrations at the gym. It's also best to postpone buying mechanical devices, which are Mars ruled, and to take extra care when handling sharp objects. Sports, especially those requiring excellent balance, should be played with care—be sure to use the appropriate protective gear and don't take unnecessary chances. This is not the time for daredevil moves! Pace yourself and pay extra attention to your health, since you may be especially vulnerable at this time.

When Other Planets Retrograde

The slower-moving planets, (Saturn, Jupiter, Neptune, Uranus, and Pluto) stay retrograde for months at a time. When Saturn is retrograde, you may feel more like hanging out at the beach than getting things done—it's an uphill battle with self-discipline at this time. Neptune retrograde promotes a dreamy escapism from reality, whereas Uranus retrograde may mean setbacks in areas where there have been sudden changes. Think of this as an adjustment period, a time to think things over and allow new ideas to develop. Pluto retrograde is a time to work on establishing proportion and balance in areas where there have been recent dramatic transformations.

When the planets start moving forward again, there's a shift in the atmosphere. Activities connected with each planet start moving ahead; planets that were stalled get rolling. Make a special note of those days on your calendar and proceed accordingly.

Other Retrogrades in 2000

Pluto turns retrograde in Sagittarius—March 15
Neptune turns retrograde in Aquarius—May 8
Uranus turns retrograde in Aquarius—May 25
Pluto turns direct in Sagittarius—August 20
Saturn turns retrograde in Taurus—September 12
Jupiter turns retrograde in Taurus—September 29
Neptune turns direct in Aquarius—October 15
Uranus turns direct in Aquarius—October 26

CHAPTER 8

What Makes Your Horoscope Special—Your Rising Sign

At the moment you were born, when you assumed an independent physical body, one of the signs of the zodiac (that is, a 30-degree slice of the sky) was just passing over the eastern horizon. In astrology, this is called the rising sign or ascendant, and it is one of the most important factors in your horoscope because it determines the uniqueness of your chart. Other babies who were born later or earlier in the day, in the same hospital as you were born, might have planets in the same signs as you do, but would have a different rising sign because as the earth turns, a different sign rises over the horizon every two hours. Therefore the planets would be in a different place in their horoscopes, emphasizing different areas of their lives.

In a horoscope, the other signs follow the rising sings in sequence, rotating counterclockwise. Therefore, the rising sign sets up the pathway of your chart. It rules the first house, which is your physical body and your appearance, and it also influences your style, tastes, health, and physical environment—where you are most comfortable working and living. The rising sign is one of the most important factors in your chart because it not only shows how you appear outwardly, but it also sets up the path you are to follow through the horoscope. After the rising sign is determined, then each house or area of your chart will be influenced by the signs following in sequence.

When we know the rising sign of a chart, we know where to put each planet—in which area of life it will operate. Without a valid rising sign, your collection of planets would have no "homes." Once the rising sign is established, it becomes possible to analyze a chart accurately. That is why many astrologers insist on knowing the exact time of a client's birth before they analyze a chart.

Your rising sign has an important relationship with your sun sign. Some complement the sun sign; others hide the sun under a totally different mask, as if playing an entirely different role. So it is often difficult to guess the person's sun sign from outer appearances. For example, a Leo with a conservative Capricorn ascendant would come across as much less flamboyant than a Leo with an Aries or Sagittarius ascendant. If the sun sign is reinforced by other planets in the same sign, it can also assert its personality much more strongly. A Leo with Venus and Jupiter also in Leo might counteract the conservative image of the Capricorn ascendant, in the preceding example. However, it is usually the ascendant that is reflected in the first impression.

Rising signs change every two hours with the earth's rotation. Those born early in the morning when the sun was on the horizon, will be most likely to project the image of the sun sign. These people are often called a "double Aries" or a "double Virgo," because the same sun sign and ascendant reinforce each other.

Look up your rising sign on the chart at the end of this chapter. Since rising signs change rapidly, it is important to know your birth time as close to the minute as possible. Even a few minutes' difference could change the rising sign and the setup of your chart. If you are unsure about the exact time, but know within a few hours, check the following descriptions to see which is most like the personality you project.

Aries Rising—Fiery Emotions

You are the most aggressive version of your sun sign, with boundless energy that can be used productively. Watch a tendency to overreact emotionally and blow your top. You come across as openly competitive, a positive asset in business or sports, but be on guard against impatience, which could lead to head injuries. Your walk and bearing could have the telltale head-forward Aries posture. You may wear more bright colors, especially red, than others of your sign. You may also have a tendency to drive your car faster.

Taurus Rising—The Earth Mother

You'll exude a protective nurturing quality, even if you're male, which draws those in need of TLC and support. You're slow moving, with a beautiful (or distinctive) speaking or singing voice that can be especially soothing or melodious. You probably surround yourself with comfort, good food, luxurious surroundings, and sensual pleasures, and you prefer welcoming others into your home to gadding about. You may have a talent for business, especially in trading, appraising, or real estate. This ascendant gives a well-padded physique that gains weight easily.

Gemini Rising—Expressive Talents

You're naturally sociable, with a lighter, more ethereal look than others of your sign, especially if you're female. You love to be with people and you express your ideas and feelings easily; you may have writing or speaking talent. You thrive on variety and a constantly changing scenario, with many different characters, though you may relate at a deeper level than might be suspected and you will be far more sympathetic and caring than you might project. You will probably travel widely and change partners and jobs several times (or juggle two at once). Physically, you should try to cultivate tranquility and create a calmer atmosphere, because your nerves are quite sensitive.

Cancer Rising—Sensitive Antenna

You easily pick up others' needs and feelings—a great gift in business, the arts, and personal relationships—but guard against overreacting or taking things too personally, especially during full-moon periods. Find creative outlets for your natural nurturing gifts, such as helping the less fortunate, particularly children. Your insights would be useful in psychology; your desire to feed and care for others in the restaurant, hotel, or child-care industry. You may be especially fond of wearing romantic old clothes, collecting antiques, and, of course, good food. Since your body will retain fluids, you should pay attention to your diet. Escape to places near water for relaxation.

Leo Rising—Scene Player

You may come across as more poised than you really feel, but you play it to the hilt, projecting a proud royal presence. This ascendant gives you a natural flair for drama, as you project a much more outgoing, optimistic, sunny personality than others of your sign. You take care to please your public by always projecting your best star quality, probably tossing a luxuriant mane of hair or, if you're female, dazzling with a spectacular jewelry collection. Since you may have a strong parental nature, you could well be the regal family matriarch or patriarch.

Virgo Rising—Cool and Calculating

Virgo rising masks your inner nature with a practical, analytical outer image. You seem very neat, orderly, and more particular, than others of your sign. Others in your life may feel they must live up to your high standards. Though at times you may be openly critical, this masks a well-meaning desire to have only the best for your loved ones. Your sharp eye for details could be used in the financial world, or your literary skills could draw you to teaching or publishing. The healing arts, health care, and other service-oriented professions attract many with this Virgo emphasis in their chart. Physically, you may have a very sensitive digestive system.

Libra Rising—The Charmer

Libra rising makes you appear a charmer—a more social, public person than others of your sign. Your private life will extend beyond your home and family to include an active social life. You may tend to avoid confrontations in relationships, preferring to smooth the way or negotiate diplomatically than give in to an emotional reaction. Because you are interested in all aspects of a situation, you may be slow to reach decisions. Physically, you'll have good proportions and pleasing symmetry. You're likely to have pleasing, if not beautiful, facial features. You move gracefully, and you have a winning smile and good taste in your clothes and home decor. Legal, diplomatic, or public relations professions could draw your interest.

Scorpio Rising—Magnetic Power

You project an intriguing air of mystery when Scorpio's secretiveness and sense of underlying power combines with your sign. You can project the image of a master manipulator, always in control and moving comfortably in the world of power. Your physical look comes across as intense and many of you have remarkable eyes, with a direct, penetrating gaze. But you'll never reveal your private agenda and you tend to keep your true feelings under wraps (watch a tendency toward paranoia). You may have an interesting romantic history with secret love affairs. Many of you heighten your air of mystery by wearing black. You're happiest near water and should provide yourself with a seaside retreat.

Sagittarius Rising—The Wanderer

You travel with this ascendant. You may also be a more outdoor, sportive type, with an athletic, casual, outgoing air. Your moods are camouflaged with cheerful optimism or a philosophical attitude. Though you don't hesitate to speak your mind, you can also laugh at your troubles or crack a joke more easily than others of your sign. This ascendant can also draw you to the field of higher education or to a spiritual life. You'll seem to have less attachment to things and people and you may travel widely. Your strong, fast legs are a physical bonus.

Capricorn Rising—Serious Business

This rising sign makes you come across as serious, goal oriented, disciplined, and careful with cash. You are not one of the zodiac's big spenders, though you might splurge occasionally on items with good investment value. You're the traditional, conservative type in dress and environment, and you might come across as quite formal and businesslike. You'll function well in a structured or corporate environment where you can climb to the top (you are always aware of who's the boss). In your personal life, you could be a loner or a single parent who is "father and mother" to your children.

Aquarius Rising—One of a Kind

You come across as less concerned about what others think and could even be a bit eccentric. You're more at ease with groups of people than others in your sign, and you may be attracted to public life. Your appearance may be unique—either unconventional or unimportant to you. Those with the sun in a water sign (Cancer, Scorpio, Pisces) may exercise your nurturing qualities with a large group, an extended family, or a day-care or community center.

Pisces Rising—Romantic Roles

Your creative, nurturing talents are heightened, and so is your ability to project emotional drama. And your dreamy eyes and poetic air bring out the protective instinct in others. You could be attracted to the arts, especially theater, dance, film, or photography, or to psychology or spiritual or charity work. Since you are vulnerable to up-and-down mood swings, it is especially important for you to find interesting, creative work where you can express your talents and boost your self-esteem. Accentuate the positive and be wary of escapist tendencies, particularly involving alcohol or drugs, to which you are supersensitive.

RISING SIGNS—A.M. BIRTHS

	1 AM	2 AM	3 AM	4 AM	5 AM	6 AM	7 AM	8 AM	9 AM	10 AM	11 AM	12 NOON
Jan 1	Lib	Sc	Sc	Sc	Sag	Sag	Cap	Cap	Aq	Aq	Pis	Ar
Jan 9	Lib	Sc	Sc	Sag	Sag	Sag	Cap	Cap	Aq	Pis	Ar	Tau
Jan 17	Sc	Sc	Sc	Sag	Sag	Cap	Cap	Aq	Aq	Pis	Ar	Tau
Jan 25	Sc	Sc	Sag	Sag	Sag	Cap	Cap	Aq	Pis	Ar	Tau	Tau
Feb 2	Sc	Sc	Sag	Sag	Cap	Cap	Aq	Pis	Pis	Ar	Tau	Gem
Feb 10	Sc	Sag	Sag	Sag	Cap	Cap	Aq	Pis	Ar	Tau	Tau	Gem
Feb 18	Sc	Sag	Sag	Cap	Cap	Aq	Pis	Pis	Ar	Tau	Gem	Gem
Feb 26	Sag	Sag	Sag	Cap	Aq	Aq	Pis	Ar	Tau	Tau	Gem	Gem
Mar 6	Sag	Sag	Cap	Cap	Aq	Pis	Pis	Ar	Tau	Gem	Gem	Can
Mar 14	Sag	Cap	Cap	Aq	Aq	Pis	Ar	Tau	Tau	Gem	Gem	Can
Mar 22	Sag	Cap	Cap	Aq	Pis	Ar	Ar	Tau	Gem	Gem	Can	Can
Mar 30	Cap	Cap	Aq	Pis	Pis	Ar	Tau	Tau	Gem	Can	Can	Can
Apr 7	Cap	Cap	Aq	Pis	Ar	Ar	Tau	Gem	Gem	Can	Can	Leo
Apr 14	Cap	Aq	Aq	Pis	Ar	Tau	Tau	Gem	Gem	Can	Can	Leo
Apr 22	Cap	Aq	Pis	Ar	Ar	Tau	Gem	Gem	Gem	Can	Leo	Leo
Apr 30	Aq	Aq	Pis	Ar	Tau	Tau	Gem	Can	Can	Can	Leo	Leo
May 8	Aq	Pis	Ar	Ar	Tau	Gem	Gem	Can	Can	Leo	Leo	Leo
May 16	Aq	Pis	Ar	Tau	Gem	Gem	Can	Can	Can	Leo	Leo	Vir
May 24	Pis	Ar	Ar	Tau	Gem	Gem	Can	Can	Leo	Leo	Leo	Vir
June 1	Pis	Ar	Tau	Gem	Gem	Can	Can	Can	Leo	Leo	Vir	Vir
June 9	Ar	Ar	Tau	Gem	Gem	Can	Can	Leo	Leo	Leo	Vir	Vir
June 17	Ar	Tau	Gem	Gem	Can	Can	Can	Leo	Leo	Vir	Vir	Vir
June 25	Tau	Tau	Gem	Gem	Can	Can	Leo	Leo	Leo	Vir	Vir	Lib
July 3	Tau	Gem	Gem	Can	Can	Can	Leo	Leo	Vir	Vir	Vir	Lib
July 11	Tau	Gem	Gem	Can	Can	Leo	Leo	Leo	Vir	Vir	Lib	Lib
July 18	Gem	Gem	Can	Can	Can	Leo	Leo	Vir	Vir	Vir	Lib	Lib
July 26	Gem	Gem	Can	Can	Leo	Leo	Vir	Vir	Vir	Lib	Lib	Lib
Aug 3	Gem	Can	Can	Can	Leo	Leo	Vir	Vir	Vir	Lib	Lib	Sc
Aug 11	Gem	Can	Can	Leo	Leo	Leo	Vir	Vir	Lib	Lib	Lib	Sc
Aug 18	Can	Can	Can	Leo	Leo	Vir	Vir	Vir	Lib	Lib	Sc	Sc
Aug 27	Can	Can	Leo	Leo	Leo	Vir	Vir	Lib	Lib	Lib	Sc	Sc
Sept 4	Can	Can	Leo	Leo	Leo	Vir	Vir	Vir	Lib	Lib	Sc	Sc
Sept 12	Can	Leo	Leo	Leo	Vir	Vir	Lib	Lib	Lib	Sc	Sc	Sag
Sept 20	Leo	Leo	Leo	Vir	Vir	Vir	Lib	Lib	Sc	Sc	Sc	Sag
Sept 28	Leo	Leo	Leo	Vir	Vir	Lib	Lib	Lib	Sc	Sc	Sag	Sag
Oct 6	Leo	Leo	Vir	Vir	Vir	Lib	Lib	Sc	Sc	Sc	Sag	Sag
Oct 14	Leo	Leo	Vir	Vir	Lib	Lib	Lib	Sc	Sc	Sag	Sag	Cap
Oct 22	Leo	Vir	Vir	Lib	Lib	Lib	Sc	Sc	Sc	Sag	Sag	Cap
Oct 30	Vir	Vir	Vir	Lib	Lib	Sc	Sc	Sc	Sag	Sag	Cap	Cap
Nov 7	Vir	Vir	Lib	Lib	Lib	Sc	Sc	Sc	Sag	Sag	Cap	Cap
Nov 15	Vir	Vir	Lib	Lib	Sc	Sc	Sc	Sag	Sag	Cap	Cap	Aq
Nov 23	Vir	Lib	Lib	Lib	Sc	Sc	Sag	Sag	Sag	Cap	Cap	Aq
Dec 1	Vir	Lib	Lib	Sc	Sc	Sc	Sag	Sag	Cap	Cap	Aq	Aq
Dec 9	Lib	Lib	Lib	Sc	Sc	Sag	Sag	Sag	Cap	Cap	Aq	Pis
Dec 18	Lib	Lib	Sc	Sc	Sc	Sag	Sag	Cap	Cap	Aq	Aq	Pis
Dec 28	Lib	Lib	Sc	Sc	Sag	Sag	Sag	Cap	Aq	Aq	Pis	Ar

RISING SIGNS—P.M. BIRTHS

	1 PM	2 PM	3 PM	4 PM	5 PM	6 PM	7 PM	8 PM	9 PM	10 PM	11 PM	12 MID-NIGHT
Jan 1	Tau	Gem	Gem	Can	Can	Can	Leo	Leo	Vir	Vir	Vir	Lib
Jan 9	Tau	Gem	Gem	Can	Can	Leo	Leo	Leo	Vir	Vir	Vir	Lib
Jan 17	Gem	Gem	Can	Can	Can	Leo	Leo	Vir	Vir	Vir	Lib	Lib
Jan 25	Gem	Gem	Can	Can	Leo	Leo	Leo	Vir	Vir	Lib	Lib	Lib
Feb 2	Gem	Can	Can	Can	Leo	Leo	Vir	Vir	Vir	Lib	Lib	Sc
Feb 10	Gem	Can	Can	Leo	Leo	Leo	Vir	Vir	Lib	Lib	Lib	Sc
Feb 18	Can	Can	Can	Leo	Leo	Vir	Vir	Vir	Lib	Lib	Sc	Sc
Feb 26	Can	Can	Leo	Leo	Leo	Vir	Vir	Lib	Lib	Lib	Sc	Sc
Mar 6	Can	Leo	Leo	Leo	Vir	Vir	Vir	Lib	Lib	Sc	Sc	Sc
Mar 14	Can	Leo	Leo	Vir	Vir	Vir	Lib	Lib	Lib	Sc	Sc	Sag
Mar 22	Leo	Leo	Leo	Vir	Vir	Lib	Lib	Lib	Sc	Sc	Sc	Sag
Mar 30	Leo	Leo	Vir	Vir	Vir	Lib	Lib	Sc	Sc	Sc	Sag	Sag
Apr 7	Leo	Leo	Vir	Vir	Lib	Lib	Lib	Sc	Sc	Sc	Sag	Sag
Apr 14	Leo	Vir	Vir	Vir	Lib	Lib	Sc	Sc	Sc	Sag	Sag	Cap
Apr 22	Leo	Vir	Vir	Lib	Lib	Lib	Sc	Sc	Sc	Sag	Sag	Cap
Apr 30	Vir	Vir	Vir	Lib	Lib	Sc	Sc	Sc	Sag	Sag	Cap	Cap
May 8	Vir	Vir	Lib	Lib	Lib	Sc	Sc	Sag	Sag	Sag	Cap	Cap
May 16	Vir	Vir	Lib	Lib	Sc	Sc	Sc	Sag	Sag	Cap	Cap	Aq
May 24	Vir	Lib	Lib	Lib	Sc	Sc	Sag	Sag	Sag	Cap	Cap	Aq
June 1	Vir	Lib	Lib	Sc	Sc	Sc	Sag	Sag	Cap	Cap	Aq	Aq
June 9	Lib	Lib	Lib	Sc	Sc	Sag	Sag	Sag	Cap	Cap	Aq	Pis
June 17	Lib	Lib	Lib	Sc	Sc	Sag	Sag	Cap	Cap	Aq	Aq	Pis
June 25	Lib	Lib	Sc	Sc	Sag	Sag	Sag	Cap	Cap	Aq	Pis	Ar
July 3	Lib	Sc	Sc	Sc	Sag	Sag	Cap	Cap	Aq	Aq	Pis	Ar
July 11	Lib	Sc	Sc	Sag	Sag	Sag	Cap	Cap	Aq	Pis	Ar	Tau
July 18	Sc	Sc	Sc	Sag	Sag	Cap	Cap	Aq	Aq	Pis	Ar	Tau
July 26	Sc	Sc	Sag	Sag	Sag	Cap	Cap	Aq	Pis	Ar	Tau	Tau
Aug 3	Sc	Sc	Sag	Sag	Cap	Cap	Aq	Aq	Pis	Ar	Tau	Gem
Aug 11	Sc	Sag	Sag	Sag	Cap	Cap	Aq	Pis	Ar	Tau	Tau	Gem
Aug 18	Sc	Sag	Sag	Cap	Cap	Aq	Pis	Pis	Ar	Tau	Gem	Gem
Aug 27	Sag	Sag	Sag	Cap	Cap	Aq	Pis	Ar	Tau	Tau	Gem	Gem
Sept 4	Sag	Sag	Cap	Cap	Aq	Pis	Pis	Ar	Tau	Gem	Gem	Can
Sept 12	Sag	Sag	Cap	Aq	Aq	Pis	Ar	Tau	Tau	Gem	Gem	Can
Sept 20	Sag	Cap	Cap	Aq	Pis	Pis	Ar	Tau	Gem	Gem	Can	Can
Sept 28	Cap	Cap	Aq	Aq	Pis	Ar	Tau	Tau	Gem	Gem	Can	Can
Oct 6	Cap	Cap	Aq	Pis	Ar	Ar	Tau	Gem	Gem	Can	Can	Leo
Oct 14	Cap	Aq	Aq	Pis	Ar	Tau	Tau	Gem	Gem	Can	Can	Leo
Oct 22	Cap	Aq	Pis	Ar	Ar	Tau	Gem	Gem	Can	Can	Leo	Leo
Oct 30	Aq	Aq	Pis	Ar	Tau	Tau	Gem	Can	Can	Can	Leo	Leo
Nov 7	Aq	Aq	Pis	Ar	Tau	Tau	Gem	Can	Can	Can	Leo	Leo
Nov 15	Aq	Pis	Ar	Tau	Gem	Gem	Can	Can	Can	Leo	Leo	Vir
Nov 23	Pis	Ar	Ar	Tau	Gem	Gem	Can	Can	Leo	Leo	Leo	Vir
Dec 1	Pis	Ar	Tau	Gem	Gem	Can	Can	Can	Leo	Leo	Vir	Vir
Dec 9	Ar	Tau	Tau	Gem	Gem	Can	Can	Leo	Leo	Leo	Vir	Vir
Dec 18	Ar	Tau	Gem	Gem	Can	Can	Can	Leo	Leo	Vir	Vir	Vir
Dec 28	Tau	Tau	Gem	Gem	Can	Can	Leo	Leo	Vir	Vir	Vir	Lib

135

CHAPTER 9

Stay Healthy and Fit This Millennium Year

Of all the changes in the past few years, those involving our health care may have the most effect on our future well-being. Rather than depending on medical experts, we'll be taking on more and more responsibility for our own health, beginning with adopting a healthier lifestyle.

Astrology can help you sort out your health priorities and put your life on a healthier course. Since before the last millennium, different parts of the body and their potential illnesses have been associated with specific signs of the zodiac. Today's astrologers use these ancient associations not only to locate potential health problems, but also to help clients harmonize their activities with those favored by each sign.

Using the stars as a guide, you can create your own calendar for a healthier millennium, by focusing on the part of the body associated with each sun sign and the general health concerns related to that sign during the dates when each sign is predominant. By the end of the year, you should be healthier from head to toe.

Capricorn (December 22– January 19)

Capricorn, the sign of Father Time, brings up the subject of aging. If sags and wrinkles are keeping you from looking as young as you feel, you may want to investigate plastic surgery during this period. Many foods have anti-aging qualities and might be worth adding to your diet. Teeth are also ruled by this sign, a reminder to have regular cleanings and dental checkups.

Capricorn is also the sign of the workaholic, so be sure not to overdo in your quest for health. Plan for long-term gains and keep a steady, even pace for lasting results. Grim determination can be counterproductive if you're also trying to relieve tension, so remember to include pleasurable activities in your self-care program. Take up a sport for pure enjoyment, instead of pushing yourself to excel.

Here are some other health-producing things to do during Capricorn: Check your office environment for hidden health saboteurs, like poor air quality, poor lighting, and uncomfortable seating. Get an ergonomically designed chair to protect your back, or buy a specially designed back support cushion if your chair is uncomfortable. If you work at a computer, check your keyboard and the height of the computer screen for ergonomic comfort.

Capricorn rules the skeletal structure, which makes this a great time to look at the state of your posture and the condition of your bones and joints. It's never too early to counteract osteoporosis by adding weight-bearing exercise to your routine. If your joints (especially your knees) are showing early signs of arthritis, you may need to add calcium supplements to your diet. Check your posture, which affects your looks and your health. Remember to protect your knees when you work out or play sports, perhaps adding exercises to strengthen this area.

Aquarius (January 20–February 18)

Aquarius, the sign of high-tech gadgets and new ideas, should inspire you with new ways to get fit and healthy. This sign reminds us that we don't have to follow the crowd to keep fit. There are many ways to adapt your exercise routine to your individual needs. If your schedule makes it difficult to get to the gym or take regular exercise classes, look over the vast selection of exercise videos available and take class anytime you want. Or set up a gym at home with portable home exercise equipment.

New Age health treatments are favored by Aquarius, which makes this an ideal month to consider alternative approaches to health and fitness. Since Aquarius rules the circulatory system, you might benefit from a therapeutic massage, a relaxing whirlpool, or one of the new electronic massage machines. If your budget permits, this is an ideal month to visit one of the many wonderful health spas around the country for a spring tune-up.

Calves and ankles are Aquarius territory and should be emphasized in your exercise program. Be sure your ankles are well supported and protect yourself against sprains.

This is also a good time to consider the air quality around you. Aquarians are often vulnerable to airborne allergies and are highly sensitive to air pollution. Do some air quality control on your environment with an air purifier, ionizer, or humidifier. During flu season, read up on ways to strengthen your immune system.

Aquarius is a sign of reaching out to others, a cue to make your health regime more social—doing your exercises with friends could make staying fit more fun.

Pisces (February 19–March 20)

Perhaps it's no accident that we do spring cleaning during Pisces. The last sign of the zodiac, which rules the lymphatic system, is supersensitive to toxins. This is the ideal time to detox your system with a liquid diet or a supervised fast. This may also help you get rid of water retention, a common Pisces problem.

Feet are Pisces territory. Consider how often you take your feet for granted and how miserable life can be when your feet hurt. Since our feet reflect and affect the health of the entire body, devote some time this month to pampering them. Check your walking shoes or buy new ones tailored especially for your kind of exercise. Investigate orthotics, especially if you walk or run a lot. These custom-molded inserts could make a big difference in your comfort and performance.

The soles of our feet connect with all other parts of our body, just as the sign of Pisces embodies all the previous signs. This is the theory behind reflexology, a therapeutic foot massage technique that treats all areas of the body via the nerve endings on the soles of the feet. For the sake of your feet, as well as your entire body, consider treating yourself to a session with a local practitioner of this technique.

Pisces is the ideal time to start walking outdoors again, enjoying the first signs of Spring. Try doing local errands on foot, as much as possible.

Aries (March 21–April 19)

This Mars-ruled sign is a high-energy time of year. It's time to step up the intensity of your workouts, so you'll be in great shape for summer. Aerobics, competitive sports, and activities that burn calories are all favored. Try a new sport that has plenty of action and challenge, like soccer or bike racing. Be sure you have the proper headgear, since Aries rules the head.

Healthwise, if you've been burning the candle at both ends, or repressing anger, this may show up as headaches. The way to work off steam under Aries is to schedule extra time at the gym, take up a racket sport or ping pong—anything that lets you hit an object hard! If there's a martial arts studio nearby, why not investigate this fascinating form of exercise—you too can do Kung Fu! Or get into spring training with your local baseball team!

Taurus (April 20–May 20)

Spring is in full bloom, and what better time to awaken your senses to the beauty of nature? Planting a garden can be a relaxing antidote to a stressful job. Long walks in the woods, listening to the sounds of returning birds, and smelling the spring flowers help you slow down and enjoy the pleasures of the Earth. If you've been longing for a pet, why not adopt one now from your local animal shelter? Walking your new dog could bring you a new circle of animal-loving friends.

This is a month to enjoy all your senses. Add more beautiful music to your library, try some new recipes, take up a musical instrument, or learn the art of massage. This pleasure-loving time can be one of the most sensual in your love life, so plan a weekend getaway to somewhere special with the one you love.

This is also a time to go to local farmers' markets and add more fresh vegetables to your diet. While we're on the subject of food, you may be tempted to overindulge during the Taurus period, so be sure there are plenty of low-calorie treats available. If you are feeling too lethargic, your thyroid might be sluggish. Taurus is associated with the neck and throat area, which includes the thyroid glands and vocal cords.

Since we often hold tension in our neck area, pause several times during the day for a few stretches and head rolls. If you wake up with a stiff neck, you may be using the wrong kind of pillow. Perhaps a smaller, more flexible pillow filled with flax seeds would make a difference.

Gemini (May 21–June 20)

One of the most social times of year, Gemini is related to the nerves, our body's lines of communication, so this would be a great time to combine socializing with exercise—include friends in your exercise routines. Join a friendly exercise class or jogging group. Or learn a Gemini-type sport, such as tennis or golf, which will develop your timing and manual dexterity, and improve your communication with others.

If your nerves are on edge, you may need more fun and laughter in your life. Getting together with friends, going to parties, and doing things in groups brings more perspective into your life.

Since Gemini is also associated with the lungs, this is an ideal time to quit smoking. Investigate natural ways to relieve tension, such as yoga or meditation. Doing things with your hands—playing the piano, typing, doing craftwork—are also helpful.

Those of you who run, race-walk, or jog may want to try hand weights during the Gemini month, or add upper-body exercises to your daily routine.

Cancer (June 21–July 22)

Good health begins at home, and Cancer is the perfect time to do some healthy housekeeping. Evaluate your home for potential toxins in the water or building material. Could you benefit from air and water purifiers, undyed sheets and towels, biodegradable cleaners? How about safer cooking utensils of stainless steel or glass?

This is also a good month for nurturing others and yourself, airing problems and providing the emotional support that should make your home a happier, more harmonious place to live.

Cancer rules digestive difficulties, especially gastric ulcers. Emotionally caused digestive problems—those stomach-knotting insecurities—can crop up under Cancer. Baby yourself with some extra pampering if you're feeling blue.

All boating and water sports are ideal Cancer-time activities. Sometimes just a walk by your local pond or sitting for a few moments by a fountain can do wonders to relieve stress and tension.

If you've been feeling emotionally insecure, these feelings may be sensitized now, especially near the full moon. Being with loved ones, old friends, and family could supply the kind of support you need. Plan some special family activities that bring everyone close together.

The breast area is ruled by Cancer, a reminder to have regular checkups, according to your age and family history of breast-related illness.

Leo (July 23–August 22)

We're now in the heart of summer, the time when you need to consider your relationship to Leo's ruler, the sun. Tans do look great, but in recent years we've all been warned about the permanent damage the sun can do. So don't leave home without a big hat or an umbrella, along with some sunblock formulated for your skin type.

If you've been faithful to your exercise program, you probably look great in your swimsuit. If not, now's the time to contemplate some spot-reducing exercises to zero in on problem areas. This is prime time for outdoor activity—biking, swimming, team sports—that can supplement your routine. Leos like Arnold Schwartzenegger and Madonna are models of the benefits of weight training. Since this is a time to glorify the body beautiful, why not consider what a body-building regime could do for you?

Leo rules the upper back and heart, so consider your cardiovascular fitness and make your diet healthier for your heart. Are you getting enough aerobic exercise? Also, step up exercises that strengthen the Leo-ruled upper back, such as swimming.

If you have planned a vacation for this month, make it a healthy one, a complete change of pace. Spend time playing with children, expressing the child within yourself. The Leo time is great for creative activities and doing whatever you enjoy most.

Virgo (August 23–September 22)

Virgo is associated with the care of the body in general and the maintenance of the abdomen, digestive system, lower liver, and intestines in particular. This is a trouble-shooting time of year, the perfect weeks to check your progress, schedule medical exams and diagnostic tests, and generally evaluate your health. If you need a change of diet, supplements, or special care, consult the appropriate advisers.

It's also a good time to make your life run more efficiently. It's a great comfort to know that you've got a smooth organization backing you up. Go through your files and closets to eliminate clutter; edit your drawers and toss out whatever is no longer relevant to your life.

In this back-to-school time, many of us are taking self-improvement courses. Consider a course to improve your health—nutrition, macrobiotic cooking, or massage, for example.

Libra (September 23–October 22)

Are your personal scales in balance? If you're overdoing in any area of your life, Libra is an excellent time to address the problem. If you have been working too hard or taking life too seriously, what you may need is a dose of culture, art, music, or perhaps some social activity.

If your body is off balance, consider yoga, spinal adjustments, or a detoxification program. Libra rules the kidneys and lower back, which respond to relaxation and tension-relieving exercises. Make time to entertain friends and to be romantic with the one you love. Harmonize your body with chiropractic work; cleanse your kidneys with plenty of liquids.

Since this is the sign of relationships, you may enjoy working out with a partner or with loved ones. Make morning walks or weekend hikes family affairs. Take

a romantic bicycle tour and picnic in the autumn coun-
tryside, putting more beauty in all areas of your life.

Libra is also the sign of grace—and what's more graceful than dance? If ballet is not your thing, why not swing
to a Latin or African beat? Dancing combines art, music,
romance, relaxation, graceful movement, social contact,
and exercise. What more can you ask?

Scorpio (October 23–November 21)

If you have been keeping an exercise program all year,
you should see a real difference—if not a total transformation—now. Scorpio is the time to transform
yourself with a new hair color, get a makeover, change
your style. Eliminate what's been holding you back,
including self-destructive habits. These weeks of Scorpio should enhance your willpower and determination.

The sign rules the regenerative and eliminative organs,
so it's a great time to turn over a new leaf. Sexual activity
comes under Scorpio, so this can be a passionate time
for love. It's also a good time to examine your attitudes
about sex and to put safe sexual practices into your life.

It's no accident that this passionate time is football
season, which reminds us that sports are a very healthy
way to express or diffuse emotions. If you enjoy winter
sports, why not prepare for the ski slopes or ice skating?
Scorpio loves intense, life-or-death competition, so be
sure your muscles are warmed up before going all out.

Sagittarius (November 22–
December 21)

Ruled by a jovial Jupiter, this is holiday time, a time
to kick back, socialize with friends, and enjoy a whirl
of parties and get togethers. High-calorie temptations
abound, so you may want to add an extra workout or
two after hitting the buffet table. Or better yet, head

for the dance floor instead of the hors d'oeuvres. Most people tend to loosen up on resolve around this time of year . . . there's just too much fun to be had.

If you can, combine socializing with athletic activities. Local football games, bike riding, hikes, and long walks with your dog in tow are just as much fun in cooler weather. Let others know that you'd like a health-promoting gift—sports equipment, a gym membership, or an exercise video—for Christmas. Plan your holiday buffet to lessen temptation with plenty of low-calorie choices.

In your workouts, concentrate on Sagittarius-ruled areas with exercises for the hips, legs, and thighs. This is a sports-loving sign, ideal for downhill or cross-country skiing or roller blading and basketball.

You may find the more spiritual kinds of exercise, such as yoga or tai chi, which work on the mind as well as the body, more appealing now. Once learned, these exercises can be done anywhere. Yoga exercises are especially useful for those who travel, especially those designed to release tension in the neck and back. Isometric-type exercises, which work one muscle group against another, can be done in a car or plane seat. If you travel often, investigate equipment that fits easily in your suitcase, such as water-filled weights, home gym devices, or elastic bands.

This sign of expansiveness offers the ideal opportunity to set your goals for next year. Ask yourself what worked best for you this year and where you want to be at the end of 2001. Most important, in holiday-loving Sagittarius-time, go for the health-promoting activities and sports you truly enjoy. These are the best for you in the long run, for they're the ones you'll keep doing with pleasure.

♊ CHAPTER 10

Astrology Adventures on the Internet:

What's New, What's Exciting, and What's Free!

Would you like a free copy of your chart, some sophisticated software to perform all the astrology calculations and give you a beautiful printout, or a screensaver custom designed for your sign? Then boot up your modem and get ready to tour the thousands of astrology websites lighting up cyberspace.

There's a global community of astrologers online with sites that offer everything from chart services to chat rooms to individual readings. Even better, many of the most exciting sites offer *free* software, *free* charts, and *free* articles to download. You can virtually get an education in astrology from your computer screen, sharing your insights with new astrology-minded pals in a chat room or on a mailing list and later meeting them in person at one of the hundreds of conferences around the world.

So if you're curious to see a copy of your chart (or someone else's), a mini-reading, even a personalized zodiac screen saver, or perhaps order a copy of your favorite astrology book, log on!

One caveat, however: Since the Internet is constantly changing, some of these sites may have changed addresses or content, even though this selection was chosen with an eye to longevity. If this happens, there is usually a referral to the new site at the old address.

Free Charts

Go to this Internet address: *http://www.alabe.com.* Astrolabe Software distributes some of the most creative and easy-to-use programs now available. Guests at this site are rewarded with a free chart of the moment you log on. They will also E-mail a copy of your chart, as well as a mini reading.

For an immediate chart printout, surf to this address: *http://www.astro.ch/,* and check into Astrodienst, home of a world atlas that will give you the accurate longitude and latitude worldwide. Once you have entered your birthday and place of birth, your chart will be displayed, ready to be downloaded to your printer. One handy feature of this particular chart is that the planetary placement is written out in an easy-to-read list alongside the chart (an important feature, if you haven't yet learned the astrology glyphs).

Free Software

Go right to this address: *http://www.alabe.com.* There you will find a demo preview of Astrolabe Software, programs that are favored by many professional astrologers. If you're serious about studying astrology, you'll want to check out the latest demo version of "Solar Fire," one of the most user-friendly astrology programs available. Try the program the pros use before you buy—you'll be impressed!

If you would like a totally functional astrology program, go to this address: *http://www.magitech.com/~cruiser1/astrolog.htm.*

Walter Pullen's amazingly complete ASTROLOG program is offered absolutely free at this site. Here is a program that is ultra-sophisticated, can be adapted for all formats—DOS, WINDOWS, MAC, UNIX—and has some very cool features such as a revolving globe and a constellation map. It's a must for those who want to get involved with astrology without paying the big bucks for a professional-caliber program, or for those who want to add ASTROLOG's unique features to their astrology software library. This program has it all!

Another great resource for software is Astro Computing Services. Their website has free demos of several excellent programs. Note especially their Electronic Astrologer, one of the most effective and reasonably priced programs on the market. Go to *http://www. astrocom.com* for software, books, readings, chart services, and software demos.

Free Social Life

Join a newsgroup or mailing list! You'll never feel lonely again, but you will be very busy reading the letters that overflow your mailbox every day, so be prepared! Of the many new groups, there are several devoted to astrology. The most popular is "alt.astrology." Here's your chance to connect with astrologers worldwide, exchange information, and answer some of the skeptics who frequent this newsgroup. Your mailbox will be jammed with letters from astrologers from everywhere on the planet, sharing charts of current events, special techniques, and personal problems. Check the "Web Fest" site below for astrologers on the Festival mailing list, a popular list for professional astrologers and beginners alike.

Free Screen Saver

Matrix New Age Voices offers a way to put your sign in view with a beautifully designed graphic screensaver, downloadable at this site. There are also many other diversions at this site, so spend some enjoyable hours here. Address: *http://thenewage.com/*.

Astrology Course

Schedule a long visit to *http://www.panplanet.com/,* where you will find the Canopus Academy of Astrology, a site loaded with goodies. For the experienced astrologer there are excellent articles from top astrologers. They've done the work for you when it comes to picking the best astrology links on the Web, so be sure to check out those bestowed with the Canopus Award of Excellence.

Astrologer Linda Reid, an accomplished astrology teacher and author, offers a complete online curriculum for all levels of astrology study, plus individual tutoring. To get your feet wet, Linda is offering a beginners' course at this site. A terrific way to get well grounded in astrology.

Visit an Astro-Mall

Surf to: America Online's Astronet at *http://www. astronet.com.* To cater to the thousands of astrology fans who belong to the America Online service, the Astronet area offers interactive fun for everyone. This site is also accessible to outside visitors at the above address. At this writing, there's a special area for teenage astrology fans, access to popular astrology magazines like *American Astrology* and *Planet Earth,* advice to the lovelorn, plus a grab bag of horoscopes, featured guests, a shopping area for books, reports, software, even jewelry.

Find an Astrologer Here

Metalog Directory of Astrology:
http://www.astrologer.com

Looking for an astrologer in your local area? Perhaps you're planning a vacation in Australia or France and would like to meet astrologers or combine your activities with an astrology conference there? Go no further than this well-maintained resource. Here is an extensive worldwide list of astrologers and astrology sites. There is also an agenda of astrology conferences and seminars all over the world.

The A.F.A. Website:
http://www.astrologers.com

This is the interesting website of the prestigious American Federation of Astrologers. The A.F.A. has a very similar address to the Metalog Directory and also has a directory of astrologers, restricted to those who meet their stringent requirements. Check out their correspondence course if you would like to study astrology in depth.

Tools Every Astrologer Needs Are Online:

Internet Atlas:
http://www.astro.ch/atlas/

Find the geographic longitude and latitude and the correct time zone for any city worldwide. You'll need this information to calculate a chart.

The Zodiacal Zephyr:
http://www.zodiacal.com

A great place to start out your tour of the Astrology Internet. It has a wide selection of articles and tools for the astrologer, such as a U.S. and World Atlas, celebrity birth data, information on conferences, software, and tapes. The links at this site will send you off in the right direction.

Astrology World:
http://www.astrology-world.com

Astrologer Deborah Houlding has gathered some of the
finest European astrologers for this terrific website. A
great list of freebies at this site. A must!

Web Fest:
http://hudson.idt.net/~motive/

The imaginative graphics on this beautiful site are a
treat. There's compilation of educational material, as
well as biographies of top astrologers who contribute to
the festival mailing list. Here is the place to look for an
astrologer or an astrology teacher, or for information
about joining the top-notch mailing list.

Astrology Alive:
http://www.astrologyalive.com/

Barbara Schermer has one of the most creative approaches to astrology. She's an innovator in the field and
was one of the first astrologers to go online, so there's
always a cutting edge to this site. Great list of links.

National Council for Geocosmic Research
(NCGR):
http://www.geocosmic.org/

A key stop on any astrological tour of the Net. Here's
where you can find out about local chapters in your area,
or get information on their testing and certification programs. You can order lecture tapes from their nationwide conferences or get complete lists of conference
topics. Good links to resources.

Charts of the Famous

This site has birthdays and charts of famous people to download: *http://www.astropro.com*

You can get the sun and moon sign, plus a biography of the hottest new stars, here: *http://www.celebsite. com*

Best General Search Engine: Yahoo
http://www.yahoo.com

You get the maximum search for your time at Yahoo. This search engine enters your input into other popular search engines.

Matrix Space Interactive:
http://thenewage.com

Browse this New-Age marketplace for free interactive astrology reports, an online astrology encyclopedia, lots of celebrity charts, and information about Matrix's excellent Winstar Plus and other astrology programs. A fun place to spend time.

For Astrology Books

National Clearinghouse for Astrology Books:
http://www.astroamerica.com

A wide selection of books on all aspects of astrology, from basics to advanced, as well as many hard-to-find books.

These addresses also have a good selection of astrology books, some of which are unique to the site.

http://www.panplanet.com
http://thenewage.com
http://www.astrocom.com

Browse the huge astrology list of online bookstore Amazon.com at *http:www.amazon.com/*

Your Astrology Questions Answered

Astrology FAQ (Frequently Asked Questions):
http://www.magitech.com/pub/astrology/info/faq.txt

Questions that are on everyone's mind. Especially useful information when you're countering astrology-bashers.

History and Mythology of Astrology:
http://www.elore.com

Be sure to visit the astrology section of this gorgeous site, dedicated to the history and mythology of many traditions. One of the most beautifully designed sites we've seen.

The Mountain Astrologer:
http//www.mountainastrologer.com/index.html

A favorite magazine of astrology fans, *The Mountain Astrologer,* has an interesting website featuring the latest news from an astrological point of view, plus feature articles from the magazine.

CHAPTER 11

The Sydney Omarr Yellow Pages

Ever wondered where to find astrologers in your area, where to get a basic astrology program for your new computer, or where to take a class with a professional astrologer? Look no further. In this chapter we'll give you the information you need to locate the latest products and services available.

There are very well-organized groups of astrologers all over the country who are dedicated to promoting the image of astrology in the most positive way. The National Council for Geocosmic Research (NCGR) is one nationwide group that is dedicated to bringing astrologers together, promoting fellowship and high-quality education. They have an accredited course system, with a systemized study of all the facets of astrology. Whether you'd like to know more about such specialties as financial astrology or the techniques for timing events, or if you'd prefer a psychological or mythological approach, you'll find the leading experts at NCGR conferences.

Your computer can be a terrific tool for connecting with other astrology fans at all levels of expertise. Even if you are using a "dinosaur" from the 1980s, there are still calculation and interpretation programs available for DOS and MAC formats. They may not have all the bells and whistles or exciting graphics, but they'll get the job done!

If you are a newcomer to astrology, it is a good idea to

learn the glyphs (astrology's special shorthand language) before you purchase a computer program. Use the chapter in this book to help you learn the symbols easily, so you'll be able to read the charts without consulting a book. Several programs, such as Astrolabe's "Solar Fire" for Windows, have pop-up definitions. Just click your mouse on a glyph or an icon on the screen and a window with an instant definition appears.

Astrology software is available at all price levels, from a sophisticated free application like "Astrolog," which you can download from the Internet, to inexpensive programs for under $100, to the more expensive astrology programs such as "Winstar," "Solar Fire," or "Io" (for the Mac), used by serious students and professionals. These are available from specialized dealers and cost approximately $200–$350. Before you make an investment, it's a good idea to download a sample from the company's website or order a demo disk from the company. If you just want to have fun, investigate an inexpensive program such as Matrix Software's "Kaleidoscope," an interactive application with lots of fun graphics. If you're baffled by the variety of software available, most of the companies on our list will be happy to help you find the right application for you needs.

If you live in an out-of-the-way place or are unable to fit classes into your schedule, correspondence courses are available. There are also online courses being offered at astrology websites. Some courses will send you a series of tapes; others use workbooks or computer printouts.

The Yellow Pages:

Nationwide Astrology Organizations and Conferences:

Contact these organizations for information on conferences, workshops, local meetings, conference tapes, or referrals:

National Council for Geocosmic Research

Educational workshops, tapes, conferences, and a directory of professional astrologers are available. For a $35 annual membership fee, you get their excellent educational publications and newsletters plus the opportunity to meet other astrology buffs at local chapter events in cities nationwide. For further information, contact:

Beverly Annen
9307 Thornewood Drive
Baltimore, MD 21234
Phone: 410-882-2856

Or visit their web page: http://www.geocosmic.org

American Federation of Astrologers (A.F.A.)

One of the oldest astrological organizations in the U.S., established 1938, it offers conferences, conventions, and a correspondence course. It will refer you to an accredited A.F.A. astrologer.

P.O. Box 22040
Tempe, AZ 85382
Phone: 602-838-1751
FAX: 602-838-8293

A.F.A.N. (Association for Astrological Networking)

Did you know that astrologers are still being arrested for practicing in some states? AFAN provides support and legal information, working toward improving the public image of astrology. Here are the people who will go to bat for astrology when it is attacked in the media. Everyone who cares about astrology should join!

A.F.A.N.
8306 Wilshire Blvd.
Berkeley Hills, CA 90211

ARC Directory

(Listing of Astrologers Worldwide)
2920 E. Monte Vista
Tucson, AZ 85716
602-321-1114

Pegasus Tapes

(Lectures, Conference tapes)
P.O. Box 419
Santa Ysabel, CA 92070

International Society for Astrological Research

(Lectures, Workshops, Seminars)
P.O. Box 38613
Los Angeles, CA 90038

ISIS Institute

(Newsletter, Conferences, Astrology tapes, Catalog)
P.O. Box 21222
El Sobrante, CA 94820-1222
Phone: 800-924-4747 or 510-222-9436
FAX: 510-222-2202

Computer Software

Astrolabe

Check out the latest version of their powerful "Solar Fire Windows" software, a breeze to use. This company also markets a variety of programs for all levels of expertise, a wide selection of computer astrology readings, and MAC programs. It's a good resource for innovative software as well as applications for older computers.

Box 1750–R
Brewster, MA 02631
800-843-6682

Matrix Software

You'll find a wide variety of software in all price ranges, demo disks at student and advanced level, and lots of interesting readings. Check out "Kaleidoscope," an inexpensive program with beautiful graphics, and "Winstar Plus," their powerful professional software, if you're planning to study astrology seriously.

315 Marion Ave.
Big Rapids, MI 49307
800-PLANETS

Astro Communications Services

Find books, software for MAC and IBM compatibles, individual charts, and telephone readings. Find technical astrology materials here, such as "The American Ephemeris." A good resource for those who do not have computers—they will calculate charts for you.

Dept. AF693, PO Box 34487
San Diego, CA 92163-4487
800-888-9983

Air Software

This is powerful, creative astrology software. For beginners, check out the "Father Time" program, which finds your best days, or "Nostradamus," which answers all your questions. There's also the "Airhead" astrology game, a fun way to test your knowledge.

115 Caya Avenue
West Hartford, CT 06110
800-659-1247

Time Cycles Research

(Beautiful graphic IO Series programs for the MAC)

375 Willets Avenue
Waterford, CT 06385
FAX: 869-442-0625
E-mail: astrology@timecycles.com
Internet: http://www.timecycles.com

Astro-Cartography

(Charts for location changes)

Astro-Numeric Service Box 336-B
Ashland, OR 97520
800-MAPPING

Microcycles

Which software is right for you? The "world's largest astrological software dealer" can help you get up and running. Call for catalogs or demo diskettes:

PO Box 2175
Culver City, CA 90231
800-829-2537

Astrology Magazines

In addition to articles by top astrologers, most have listings of astrology conferences, events, and local happenings.

AMERICAN ASTROLOGY
475 Park Avenue South
New York, NY 10016

DELL HOROSCOPE
P.O. Box 53352
Boulder, CO 89321-3342

PLANET EARTH
The Great Bear
P.O. Box 5164
Eugene, OR 97405

MOUNTAIN ASTROLOGER
P.O. Box 11292
Berkeley, CA 94701

ASPECTS
Aquarius Workshops
P.O. Box 260556
Encino, CA 91426

Astrology Schools:

Though there are many correspondence courses available through private teachers and astrological organizations, up until now there has never been an accredited college of astrology. That is why the following address is so important.

The Kepler College of Astrological Arts and Sciences

By the time this book is published, Kepler College, the first institution of its kind to combine an accredited liberal arts education with extensive astrological studies, should be in operation. A degree-granting college that is also a center of astrology, has long been the dream of the astrological community and will be a giant step forward in providing credibility to the profession.
For more information:

The Kepler College of Astrological Arts and Sciences
P.O. Box 77511
Seattle, WA 98177-0511
Phone: 206-706-0658
or http://www.keplercollege.org

CHAPTER 12

Is Your Life at a Crossroads?
Consider a Personal Reading

Now that the millennium is here, you may wonder if, at this important crossroads, now is the time for you to get a personal reading to plot your future course or help clarify issues in your personal life. Here is some guidance to help you sort through the variety of readings available.

The first thing you'll discover is that there seem to be as many different kinds of readings as there are astrologers. Besides face-to-face readings with a professional astrologer, there are mini-readings at psychic fairs, pay-by-the minute phone readings that can either be tape recorded or a live exchange with an "astrologer," offerings of beautiful computer-generated readings and many pages of "personal" interpretation. If you have access to the Internet, a simple search under "Astrology" will produce a mind-boggling array of websites. Online chat rooms and mailing lists dedicated to astrology are other resources frequented by professional astrologers as well as interested amateurs.

To confuse the matter further, astrologers themselves have specialties. Some are skilled in the technique of horary astrology, which involves answering questions based on the time the question is asked. Some astrologers are psychologically oriented; others are more practical. Some use traditional methods; others use more exotic techniques from India or China.

Though you can learn much about astrology from

books such as this one, nothing compares to a one-on-one consultation with a professional who has analyzed thousands of charts and can pinpoint the potential in yours. With your astrologer, you can address specific immediate problems in your life that may be holding you back. For instance, if you are not getting along with your mate or coworker, you could leave the reading with some new insights and some constructive ways to handle the situation. If you are going through a crisis in your life, an astrologer who is also a trained counselor might help you examine your options . . . and there are many astrologers who now combine their skills with training in psychology.

Before your reading, a reputable astrologer will ask for the date, time (as accurately as possible), and place of birth of the subject of the reading. (A horoscope can be cast about anything that has a specific time and place.) Most astrologers will then enter this information into a computer, which will calculate your chart (perhaps several types of charts related to your situation) in seconds. From the resulting chart or charts, the astrologer will do an interpretation.

If you don't know your exact birth time, you can usually find it filed at the Bureau of Vital Statistics at the city hall or county seat of the state where you were born. If you still have no success in getting your time of birth, some astrologers can estimate an approximate birth time by using past events in your life to determine the chart.

How to Find a Good Astrologer

Your first priority should be to choose a qualified astrologer. Rather than relying on word of mouth or grandiose advertising claims, do this with the same care you would choose any trusted adviser such as a doctor, lawyer, or banker. Unfortunately, anyone can claim to be an astrologer—to date, there is no licensing of astrologers or established professional criteria. However, there are nationwide organizations of serious, committed astrologers that can help you in your search.

Good places to start your investigation are organizations such as the American Federation of Astrologers or the National Council for Geocosmic Research (NCGR), which offers a program of study and certification. If you live near a major city, there is sure to be an active NCGR chapter or astrology club in your area—many are listed in astrology magazines available at your local newsstand. In response to many requests for referrals, the NCGR has compiled a directory of professional astrologers, which includes a glossary of terms and an explanation of specialties within the astrological field. Contact the NCGR headquarters (see the resource list in this book) for information.

As a potentially lucrative freelance business, astrology has always attracted self-styled experts who may not have the knowledge or the counseling experience to give a helpful reading. These astrologers can range from the well-meaning amateur to the charlatan or street-corner gypsy who has for many years given astrology a bad name. Be very wary of astrologers who claim to have occult powers or who make pretentious claims of celebrated clients or miraculous achievements. You can often tell from the initial phone conversation if the astrologer is legitimate. He or she should ask for your birthday time and place and conduct the conversation in a professional manner. Any astrologer who gives a reading based only on your sun sign is highly suspect. Be especially wary of fly-by-night corner gypsies, who claim to be astrologers.

When you arrive at the reading, the astrologer should be prepared. The consultation should be conducted in a private, quiet place. The astrologer should be interested in your problems of the moment. A good reading involves feedback on your part, so if the reading is not relating to your concerns, you should let the astrologer know. Feel free to ask questions and get clarifications of technical terms. The reading should be an interaction between two people, rather than a solo performance. The more you actively participate, rather than expecting the astrologer to carry the reading or come forth with oracular predictions, the more meaningful your experience will be. An astrologer should help you validate your current experience and be frank about possible negative happenings, but suggest a positive course of action.

In their approach to a reading, some astrologers may be more literal, others more intuitive. Those who have had counseling training may take a more psychological approach. Though some astrologers may seem to have an almost psychic ability, extrasensory perception or any other parapsychological talent is not essential. A very accurate picture can be drawn from the data in your horoscope chart.

An astrologer may do several charts for each client, including one for the time of birth and a "progressed chart," showing the evolution from birth to the present time. According to your individual needs, there are many other possibilities, such as a chart for a different location, if you are contemplating a change of place. Relationships between any two people, things, or events can be interpreted with a chart that compares the two horoscopes. Another commonly used device is a composite chart, which uses the midpoint between planets in two individual charts to describe the relationship.

An astrologer will be particularly interested in transits—times when planets will pass over the planets or sensitive points in your chart, which can signal important events in your life.

Many astrologers offer tape-recorded readings, another option to consider. In this case, you'll be mailed a tape of a reading based on your birth chart. Though this reading is more personal than a computer printout and can give you valuable insights, it is not equivalent to a live dialogue with an astrologer, where you can discuss your specific interests and issues of the moment.

About Telephone Readings

Telephone readings come in two varieties. One is a dial-in taped reading, usually by a well-known astrologer.

The other is a live consultation with an "astrologer" on the other end of the line. The taped readings are general daily or weekly forecasts, applied to all members of your sign and charged by the minute. The quality depends on the astrologer. One caution: Be aware that these readings can run up quite a telephone bill, especially if you get into the habit of calling every day. Be sure that you are aware of the per-minute cost of each call beforehand. (It might be wise to keep a timer next to the phone, to limit your calls beforehand.)

Live telephone readings also vary with the expertise of the astrologer. The advantage of a live telephone reading is that your individual chart is used and you can ask about a specific problem. Usually the astrologer on the other end of the line will enter your birth data into a computer and use the chart it generates during the reading. However, before you invest in any reading, be sure that your astrologer is qualified and that you fully understand in advance how much you will be charged.

About Computer Readings

Most of the companies that offer computer programs (such as ACS, Matrix, ASTROLABE) also offer computer-generated horoscope interpretations. These can be quite comprehensive, offering a beautiful printout of the chart plus many pages of information. A big plus is that you'll receive an accurate copy of your chart, which can be used for future reference. The accompanying natal chart interpretation can be a good way to learn about your own chart at your convenience, since most readings interpret the details of the chart in a very understandable way. However, since there is no input from you, the interpretations will be general and may not address your immediate issues.

This is still a good option for a first reading, to get your feet wet, especially since these printouts are much lower in cost than live consultations. You might consider them as either a supplement or preparation for a live reading (study one before you have a live reading to get familiar with your chart and plan specific questions). They also make a terrific gift for someone interested in astrology. If you are considering this type of reading, look into one of the companies on our astrology resource list.

CHAPTER 13

Your Gemini Star Quality

All About Your Gemini Sun Sign

As a Gemini sun sign, you'll find that the qualities associated with this sign resonate through the many roles you play in life. And if there are other Gemini planets in your horoscope, or if your rising sign is Gemini, these conditions will intensify your Gemini-type personality. There'll be no mistaking you for another sun sign! For example, someone with a Gemini sun, Mars, and rising sign (ascendant) is likely to be much more obviously a "Gemini" type than someone whose Gemini sun is combined with a less talkative Scorpio ascendant and an slower-moving Mars in Taurus. However, even if you have a different personality than the typical Gemini, you'll find that many of the traits and preferences described here will still apply to you.

The Gemini Man— Taking It Light and Lively

"What's new?" is the constant question of the Gemini man. You're on a perpetual journey in search of the extraordinary, the startling, the intrigue of life. You're someone who can't bear boredom. Any amount of activity is preferable to being stuck in a rut, so you're forever in motion. Even when you appear to be sitting still, your mind is racing ahead of the pack.

You are a lover of games on every level—and you can

make a game of anything. The most complicated situations are like catnip to your agile mind. Even though you may be very ambitious, you're careful to keep your attitude upbeat rather than overtly aggressive. As one of his staff once described Gemini ex-President George Bush, you are made of "steel with an overlay of tennis."

On the negative side, it may be difficult for you to take anything or anyone too seriously. Weighty matters drag you down. Many Geminis would rather dabble into many different projects, flying from one to the other at the hint of boredom. The Gemini mind is always seeking out new interests, new moves, and new ways to play the game of life. As a mutable air sign, you are able to tap into the undercurrents of life, sensing that the literal, the here and now, is not all there is.

You have the gift of communication with virtually any other type without intruding, always keeping the proper distance and a touch of wit. Frequent social contacts are important to you because you learn best from direct experience. You usually slip away from possessive types who would tie you down or isolate you from others. (The key to keeping you around is to make you feel you'll be missing out on an exciting experience—Gemini can't bear to miss out!)

Many Gemini men rose to power during the 1980s, when their flare for communications helped them become the masters of financial deal making. The list of Gemini billionaires of the decade included real estate mogul Donald Trump (who wrote *The Art of the Deal* before losing much of his fortune), financier Mort Zuckerman, press lord Robert Maxwell, advertising's Maurice Saatchi, and tycoon Armand Hammer. As the decade closed, several of the most dazzling financial wizards became overextended and lost their luster, if not their entire fortunes. Those who will remain in power must get a firm grip on the realities of the millennium and be able to extend their deal-making talents into creative problem solving.

In a Relationship

Since predictable routines and emotional demands can feel confining to a natural freelancer, you may be far more comfortable in the changing whirl of business and social life than in any intense one-on-one relationship. You tend to walk away from difficult situations involving emotions, especially romantic ones. One reason depth of feeling may be difficult for you to understand is that you prefer to operate on a mental rather than an emotional level. You'd rather turn to whatever or whoever is new and different than work through long-standing or deep-rooted problems. As former President George Bush said, "I'm not an emotional kind of guy." Some Geminis avoid emotional responsibilities by refusing to grow up, becoming the Peter Pans of the zodiac and sometimes losing their grip on reality if they have to handle serious matters or crises.

The Gemini man is not averse to beauty when you search for your life partner, but what you really long for is a twin soul, a partner who will be a best friend and companion as well as a lover. On your side of the equation, providing stability, security, or physical amenities are not as high a priority for Gemini as for other signs, even though your bright mind can devise ways to earn a steady, sometimes spectacular, income. Many of your sign often juggle two jobs or careers simultaneously. You're best suited to a free-thinking partner who can adapt to changes and will not object too strenuously to your being constantly on the move. She should also enjoy contact with many projects in various stages of completion. (Barbara Bush fills this bill perfectly!) She'll appreciate your fun-loving view and your amusing, interesting companionship. Though you may not give her emotional reassurance as often as she would like (please work on this!), she'll never be bored.

The Gemini Woman— A Charmed Life

The Gemini woman has an ability to bounce back from difficulties and quick-change her image to suit the next situation. Though you may not have a college education, you've probably done an excellent job of educating yourself by learning from everyone you encounter. You have a remarkable, retentive memory (you are the proverbial "quick study") and are an excellent mimic—you pick up manners, mannerisms, and speech patterns faster than Eliza Doolittle. Your mind races so fast that you often know the answers before the question is asked!

For good examples of Gemini quick studies (fast learners who can match wits with anyone and spin on a dime), look no further than talk show hostess and comedienne Joan Rivers, or soap star Joan Collins, who have adapted their careers to suit every audience. Since you rarely get too attached to anything or anyone, and you are so attuned to what's going on, you can make changes easily and quickly. As Joan Rivers once said, "When someone slams the door in your face, find another door. There are always new doors."

Face it—you'd be miserable in a life of routine. Often you'll do two things at once—hold down two jobs, combine a job with a personal interest, talk on two telephones, have two love affairs concurrently, just to keep life interesting. But you always manage to keep from getting tied down. Isn't it more fun to keep your options open? After all, something or someone more exciting might appear.

"Can we talk?" At some point, you've got to figure out where you're going and get some grounding and focus in your life. Otherwise, you could become like those lost Gemini girls, looking somewhere "Over the Rainbow," as Judy Garland and Marilyn Monroe, both Geminis, portrayed. It is important for you to reconcile those contrary twins within—your feminine emotions with your detached "masculine" intelligence. When you're using your excellent mind correctly and have a clear sense of direction, you can find the right balance of stimulation and security that is your real pot of gold.

In a Relationship

The Gemini woman usually prefers to keep working after marriage, so she can delegate the more mundane chores to someone else. An interesting job also provides the change of scene and social contacts you need to keep from getting bored. Geminis often marry more than once, because it's not easy to find a man who can match your wit and intelligence, allow you the space you need, and at the same time provide solid support. You may find that person later in life, after the men you meet have mellowed and developed more inner security and self-esteem. The type who responds well to your sparkle and joie de vivre is a man who longs to feel young and lively again, one who loves to dance and entertain. Gemini is rarely the sentimental stay-at-home type. You'd much rather have a full social schedule, with some social games, laughter, frivolity, and style—a bit of madness now and then. You love to flirt and need a mate who won't get too jealous. However, if your mate gives you enough personal freedom, you'll provide a life of sparkle and variety.

The Gemini Family

The Gemini Parent

Geminis usually find child rearing satisfying and fulfilling after the child is old enough to communicate verbally. You take a great interest in various stages of development, but you may suffer through the early phases, when the child demands much emotional attention and routine care, taking so much time away from your other activities. Nevertheless, few Geminis let themselves be tied down by parenthood. You'll continue interests outside the home, juggling schedules to suit the needs of the moment. Social activities connected with your children— play groups, parents' groups, school committees—all offer a chance to expand your interests. Far from being an overprotective parent, you'll lean more toward permissiveness and give your children plenty of chances to develop their independence. Ever youthful in outlook, you'll be a great fun-loving pal to your kids. The less rational moods of the earth and water sign children may confound you from time to time, but you'll distract them with delightful games and teach them to laugh off their troubles.

As the child grows older, you may take on the role of teacher, exposing him or her to the world of ideas and mental pursuits. You are a fascinating playmate and a superb storyteller. You know how to make difficult or complicated problems easy to understand when you help with homework. Unlike more possessive parents, Geminis encourage their children to be self-reliant and will help them explore and develop any glimmer of talent or ability.

The Gemini Stepparent

Gemini's sense of humor and lack of possessiveness are tools for forging a good relationship with stepchildren. Your lighthearted, breezy manner can smooth over rough spots in the initial phases, when you'll think of fun things to do together. You'll allow them as much time as they need with your mate, since you have many other activities to pursue. And when emotional problems crop up, you'll use your analytical mind to find an intelligent, workable solution, without getting personally drawn into the situation. Your new family will soon accept you as a nonthreatening companion and friend who is an extra bonus in their lives.

The Gemini Grandparent

You are a sexy senior citizen who is spry and sociable, the life of the party. You love company, especially young people, and are up to the minute on the latest trends. Or you'll regale them for hours with stories of your past adventures (and there will be many). You'll be the most companionable grandparent, never interfering with the house rules, but encouraging the children to be as independent, adventurous, and exciting as you are!

CHAPTER 14

Show Off the Gemini in You

Gemini Self-Expression

Everyone's intrigued by their sun sign personality. But did you know that it also influences the styles that present you at your best, and the colors and sounds that lift your mood? Why not try putting more Gemini style in every area of your life and see if it doesn't make a happier difference!

Gemini at Home

Flexible is the word for the perfect Gemini environment. You need a place that accommodates all your different interests, with plenty of storage space, so you can sweep your projects quickly out of sight when friends drop in. A light, neutral background would allow you to achieve different effects by changing color accents and accessories with your mood. Lots of bookcases, a telephone or three, and furniture you can rearrange in many different ways would provide you with enough variety. You're the sign with a telephone on both sides of the bed and alongside the bathtub. Have a separate room or corner with a desk where you can organize all your lists, Rolodexes, and appointment books, so you won't waste time looking for them. Many Geminis enjoy having houses in more than one place (you're often bicoastal) and keep residences in different cities or a country house, so they can switch environments when bored.

The Gemini Beat

You're a natural disk jockey, who can juggle the beat according to the mood of the moment. Your music tastes are usually eclectic, with a wide variety of sounds, but you also pay attention to the words as well as the melody, so the witty lyrics of Cole Porter and the poetry of Bob Dylan appeal. So does abstract classical music—nothing too heavy or loud that might distract from conversation or bring on the blues. Create your own mix of sounds on tapes, so you can change moods frequently, perhaps combining Paul McCartney with Paula Abdul, some rap music, a bit of country and western, opera, Cole Porter, Judy Garland, and some continental tunes from Charles Aznavour.

Great Vacation Adventures for Gemini

Stay away from desert islands, unless you need some peace and quiet to write your novel. Stick to places where there's a lively social scene, some interesting exotic scenery, and local characters to provide good conversation. You might improve your language skills by visiting a foreign country—you'll have no trouble communicating in sign language, if necessary. Consider a language school in the South of France or Switzerland, where you'll mix with fellow students of many nationalities.

Lightness is the key to Gemini travel. Don't weigh yourself down with luggage. Dare to travel with an empty suitcase, and get some interesting clothes and supplies at your destination—imagine how fast you'll speed through the airport!

Keep a separate tiny address book for each city, so the right numbers are always handy. Invest in beautifully designed travel cases and briefcases, since you're on the go so much. Spend some time looking for the perfect luggage, portable notebook computers (with a modem), and cellular telephones.

Your Gemini Colors

Soft gray, pale yellow, and airy Wallis Windsor blue are Gemini colors. Sound bland? That's because these are great background colors, the ones you can live with over a period of time. They'll adapt to different seasons and climates, and they won't compete with your personality or distract from your total image. You can change the look of these colors at will, accenting them with bright touches or blending with other pastels. And they can tolerate a frequent change of accessories, according to your look of the moment.

Gemini Fashion Tips

You have fun with fashion and never take your fashion image too seriously. Some great fashion icons, like the Duchess of Windsor, were born under your sign and you couldn't find better inspiration than this legendary fashion devotée. We remember Wallis Simpson for her witty way with accessories, like those fabulous jewels she wore with casual aplomb (some engraved with secret messages from the Duke). Yet she never varied her signature swept-back hairdo or her elegantly simple style of dressing.

Gemini always likes to do something interesting with your clothes, to get them talking about you! Like Cyndi Lauper, you can be downright outrageous! Play up your expressive hands with a perfect manicure and beautiful rings. A hairstyle that you can wear several different ways could satisfy your need for variety. Joan Rivers transforms her classic style into a tumble of curls with a few hot rollers.

Gemini Fashion Leaders

Since you have such a changeable personality, you'll probably experiment with every kind of look before you settle on the style that becomes you best. Usually you're up to the minute, however, with a touch of the newest trend coming down the runway. The fashion duo Dolce and Grabbana, the with-it looks of Anna Sui, or the newest androgynous menswear styles would be fun for you to try on for size.

Gemini Edibles

No matter what you order, you'll always want a bit of what everyone else is eating! Buffet tables are ideal ways for Geminis to sample a little bit of everything. Fortunately, your sign rarely has to worry about weight. However, to keep down calorie intake, try ordering a meal of different appetizers. Then you'll have a little bit of a lot of things, which is your favorite way to dine!

CHAPTER 15

Unleash Your Gemini Potential—Find the Work You Love!

The Gemini Route to Success

Gemini in Charge

Gemini is fun to work for—sociable, witty, and clever. Your office will be a beehive of activity, with telephone lines busy and clients and coworkers coming and going. You operate best as a dealmaker, an entrepreneur rather than a designer or producer. You often change your mind, so you should hire assistants who are adaptable enough to keep up with you, yet who are organized enough to provide direction and structure. If a project gets bogged down, you will change course rapidly, rather than stick it through. Sometimes you have so many projects going on at once that others are dizzy, yet you are known for innovative ideas and cool analysis of problems. You are especially gifted in making a deal, coordinating many of the diverse aspects of a project. What is lacking in job security you make up for in opportunities for others to experiment, to develop flexibility and a sense of gamesmanship.

Gemini in the Workplace

The Gemini worker shines in a job full of variety and quick changes. The key: You must be stimulated mentally. Financial security alone rarely motivates you. You can learn a job quickly but you leave it just as quickly once it becomes routine. You work beautifully on a team, where your light sense of humor, friendliness, and ability to express yourself clearly are appreciated. Your position should be dealing with the public in a sales or communications position. You are also skilled at office politics. It's all part of the game to you, and you rarely get emotionally involved. Let someone else do the record keeping, financial management, or accounting. You can handle a position where you report to several different people or juggle several different assignments, though you may do less well if the job requires intense concentration, patience, and perseverance.

Your Gemini Career Strategy

Gemini has many winning cards to play in the career game. Your quick mind works best in a career where there is enough mental stimulation to keep you from getting bored. High-pressure situations that would be stressful to others are stimulating to you. Many things happening simultaneously—phones ringing off the hook, daily client meetings, constant changes—are all exciting to you. Your ability to communicate with a variety of people works well in sales, journalism, public relations, agent or broker work, personnel or consulting—literally any job that requires verbal or writing skills. You who learn languages easily could be a language teacher or interpreter. Manual dexterity is another Gemini gift that can find craft, musical, or medical expression, especially surgery or chiropractic.

Avoid a job that is too isolated, routine, detail oriented, or confining. Stay away from companies that are hidebound, with rigid rules, looking instead for a place that gives you strong backup as well as free rein. Gemini often works well in a freelance position, provided they have a solid support system.

To get ahead fast, pick a job with variety and mental stimulation. Play up your best attributes.

- Verbal and written communication skills
- Ability to handle pressure
- Charm and sociability
- Manual dexterity
- Ability to learn quickly
- Analytical ability

Gemini Success Stories

Study the careers of these colorful Geminis, some of them legends in their own time. Most are featured in biographies, business magazine profiles, or reference books. You might get some valuable tips on what to do—and what not to do—to make the most of your sign's money-making potential:

Donald Trump
Robert Maxwell
Mortimer Zuckerman
Sam Wanamaker
Katharine Graham (*Washington Post*)
Charles and Maurice Saatchi (advertising)
Laurence Rockefeller
Baron Guy de Rothschild

CHAPTER 16

Gemini Celebrities—From Hollywood to the Halls of Power

Here's a list of the current crop of celebrities born under your Gemini sun sign. Though it's fun to see who shares your birthday, this list can also be a useful tool to practice what you've learned so far about astrology. Use it to compare similarities and differences between the stars who embody Gemini traits and those who don't. Look up the other planets in the horoscope of your favorites to see how their influence might color the sun sign emphasis.

Naomi Campbell (5/22/70)
Douglas Fairbanks (5/23/1883)
Roseanne Cash (5/24/50)
Bob Dylan (5/24/41)
Patti LaBelle (5/24/44)
Priscilla Presley (5/23/45)
Miles Davis (5/23/26)
Dixie Carter (5/25/39)
Connie Selleca (5/25/55)
Ian McKellen (5/25/39)
Anne Heche (5/25/63)
Helena Bonham Carter (5/26/66)
John Wayne (5/26/07)
Peggy Lee (5/26/20)
Stevie Nicks (5/26/48)
Philip Michael Thomas (5/26/49)
Louis Gossett, Jr. (5/27/36)

Tony Hillerman (5/27/25)
Siouxie Sioux (5/27/57)
Vincent Price (5/27/11)
Gladys Knight (5/28/44)
Sondra Locke (5/28/47)
Annette Bening (5/29/58)
Anthony Geary (5/29/47)
Kevin Conway (5/29/42)
Bob Hope (5/29/03)
Rupert Everett (5/29/59)
John F. Kennedy (5/29/17)
Benny Goodman (5/30/09)
Prince Ranier (5/31/23)
Joe Namath (5/31/50)
Clint Eastwood (5/31/30)
Brooke Shields (5/31/65)
Lea Thompson (5/31/61)
Sharon Gless (5/31/43)
Peter Yarrow (5/31/38)
Tom Berenger (5/31/50)
Morgan Freeman (6/1/37)
Andy Griffith (6/1/26)
Jonathan Pryce (6/1/47)
Ron Wood (6/1/47)
Edward Woodward (6/1/30)
Pat Boone (6/1/34)
Rene Auberjonois (6/1/40)
Marilyn Monroe (6/1/26)
Hedda Hopper (6/2/1890)
Sally Kellerman (6/2/37)
Stacey Keach (6/2/41)
Marvin Hamlisch (6/2/44)
Curtis Mayfield (6/3/42)
Tony Curtis (6/3/25)
Deniece Williams (6/3/51)
Michelle Phillips (6/4/44)
Dr. Ruth Westheimer (6/4/28)
Parker Stevenson (6/4/52)
Bruce Dern (6/4/36)
Marky Mark (6/5/71)
Bill Moyers (6/5/34)

Sandra Bernhard (6/6/55)
Jessica Tandy (6/7/09)
Tom Jones (6/7/40)
James Ivory (6/7/28)
Liam Neeson (6/7/52)
Prince (6/7/58)
Kathy Baker (6/8/50)
Barbara Bush (6/8/25)
Joan Rivers (6/8/33)
Michael J. Fox (6/9/61)
Johnny Depp (6/9/63)
Elizabeth Hurley (6/10/65)
Tara Lipinski (6/10/82)
Grace Mirabella (6/10/30)
Lionel Jeffries (6/10/26)
Prince Philip (6/10/21)
Gene Wilder (6/11/35)
Chad Everett (6/11/37)
Adrienne Barbeau (6/11/45)
George Bush (6/12/24)
Timothy Busfield (6/12/57)
Tim Allen (6/13/53)
Ally Sheedy (6/13/62)
Christo (6/13/35)
Basil Rathbone (6/13/1892)
Donald Trump (6/14/46)
Yasmine Bleeth (6/14/68)
Boy George (6/14/61)
Steffi Graf (6/14/69)
Waylon Jennings (6/15/37)
Mario Cuomo (6/15/32)
Courteney Cox (6/15/64)
Helen Hunt (6/15/63)
Yasmine Bleeth (6/16/68)
Corin Redgrave (6/16/39)
Dean Martin (6/17/17)
Joe Piscopo (6/17/51)
Roger Ebert (6/18/42)
Isabella Rossellini (6/18/52)
E. G. Marshall (6/18/10)
Paul McCartney (6/18/41)

Paula Abdul (6/19/63)
Kathleen Turner (6/19/54)
Danny Aiello (6/20/33)
John Goodman (6/20/52)

CHAPTER 17

Astrological Outlook for Gemini in 2000

March, May, and December will be memorable for you this year, along with the Mercury keynote that denotes change, travel, variety, and words, both verbal and written. During March, the pressure is on, but you will be up to it. The time element will be very important. Your career gets a boost, since important people take an interest in your welfare. A Capricorn helps you deal with interest rates, tax and license requirements, and legal matters.

During May, you might feel reborn. Enlightenment replaces an aura of fear and ignorance of what is going on in your life. Secrets spring out of the closet. Though you'll need to be discreet, it will not always be possible. The focus this month will be on institutions, hospitals, museums, and houses of worship. A Taurus lets you in on a secret that you already were aware of—money is involved. Valuables that had been kept under lock and key will be loose. During May, an array of planets will be in your twelfth house—you come to grips with yourself and perhaps have a fleeting memory of what you might have been or were in a previous incarnation.

During December, the focus will be on public acceptance of your efforts, your creations, and you as an individual. The spotlight also falls on legal affairs, the possibility of a partnership or marriage, or both. The emphasis will be on where you live, your lifestyle and finances in connection with forming a life-long association, perhaps marriage.

During August and September, and up to mid-October,

Saturn will be in your sign, Gemini. Once again the pressure is on and financial promises are not guaranteed, as financial aid that seemed assured might not come through or a project becomes more expensive than you originally anticipated.

If you're single, this could be a year of marriage. An addition to your family is also a distinct possibility during September or December.

During the year 2000, people who play important roles in your life will be Virgo, Sagittarius, and another Gemini, with these letters, in their names: E, N, W.

These numbers can be considered lucky throughout the year—5, 1, 4.

Use the information contained in your Daily Guides as your diary in advance, along with these monthly forecasts. Both Daily Guides and Monthly Forecasts equal a one–two punch to help you conquer obstacles and make the most of current trends. Start now to digest your forecasts for the year 2000.

CHAPTER 18

Eighteen Months of Day-by-Day Predictions—July 1999 to December 2000

All times are calculated for EST and EDT.

JULY 1999

Thursday, July 1 (Moon in Aquarius) The puzzle pieces fall into place. Preparations for the upcoming holiday proceed, and Sagittarius and another Gemini figure prominently. These persons could have the following letters in their names: C, L, U. The financial picture brightens as your set of values and standards is taken seriously.

Friday, July 2 (Moon in Aquarius) The Aquarian moon relates to the adventure of discovery, exploration, publishing, and the possibility of meeting someone who might be your soulmate. Taurus, Leo, and Scorpio are drawn to you, and could have these letters in their names: D, M, V. The answer to your question: A mechanical defect cannot be ignored, including those in your automobile and home.

Saturday, July 3 (Moon in Aquarius to Pisces 12:24 a.m.) Get ready for change, travel, and variety; by tomorrow, your career gets a boost. You no longer will be hampered by a whimpering relative. Success is indicated via words, both verbal and written. A flirtation lends spice, and it could become more serious than you originally anticipated. Lucky lottery: 5, 50, 51, 10, 12, 17.

Sunday, July 4 (Moon in Pisces) Today's Pisces

186

moon relates to dealings and confrontations with people in authority. Review the U.S. Constitution and Jefferson's Declaration of Independence. Rather than be embarrassed, be proud—you'll receive numerous compliments and this could be one of your most memorable holidays.

Monday, July 5 (Moon in Pisces to Aries 7:21 a.m.) Recovery! Much energy is extended on the Fourth, while today you regain your strength and vitality, feeling flattered by compliments showered on you. The Neptune keynote blends with your Mercury, creating a combination of mystery, intrigue and intelligence. Pisces figures prominently.

Tuesday, July 6 (Moon in Aries) What a Tuesday! The lunar position highlights friends, hopes, wishes, and an ability to be Svengali while the rest of the world is your Trilby. Accept the challenge of a time schedule, responsibility, and the need to bring order out of chaos. Capricorn will play an astounding role.

Wednesday, July 7 (Moon in Aries to Taurus 11:22 a.m.) Lucky lottery: 9, 19, 1, 10, 40, 50. Stress universal appeal, learning about the mores and diets of people in other lands. Review your own potential, refusing to settle for second best. A love relationship heats up, and a spark that brought you together with a special person reignites. Aries is in the picture.

Thursday, July 8 (Moon in Taurus) Dining in an out-of-the-way place could be featured. Highlight mystery and intrigue, and perhaps enjoy the performance of a skilled magician. Make a fresh start, highlighting independence and realizing your aura of sex appeal. Leo and Aquarius figure in today's dynamic scenario; look for these letters in their names—A, S, J.

Friday, July 9 (Moon in Taurus to Gemini 1:00 p.m.) The moon keynote emphasizes dealings with the public as you promote special products that appeal to women. Highlight cooperative efforts, personality, special appearances, and decisions relating to marriage. A Cancer invites you to dine, so you'll be in for a treat of seafood, perhaps lobster.

Saturday, July 10 (Moon in Gemini) A live Saturday night! Your cycle is high and your popularity increases. The moon position emphasizes timing and sex appeal. The emphasis is on entertainment, fashion, the way you wear clothes, and your body image. What you chased becomes available, as you're told, "You are the right person, the one we have been seeking!" Your lucky number is 3.

Sunday, July 11 (Moon in Gemini to Cancer 1:27 p.m.) The moon in your sign relates to the high cycle, so stand tall, express your opinions, and refuse to be a wallflower. A Taurus tells a secret about a hospital or a relative. A Leo returns from a short trip, talking about news and gossip. A Scorpio concentrates on health and employment.

Monday, July 12 (Moon in Cancer) It's a money day! The cash flow resumes as the moon is in its own sign, Cancer, which relates to that section of your horoscope associated with income and the value of your possessions. Solid friendships form, and you no longer wish you had more friends, although you now might yearn for your precious privacy. Another Gemini is involved.

Tuesday, July 13 (Moon in Cancer to Leo 2:26 p.m.) The new moon in Cancer tells of fresh financial opportunities on a Tuesday you'll long remember. A lost object is located; you'll be saying, "This is more like it!" Taurus, Libra, and Scorpio will be drawn to you, and are likely to have these letters in their names: F, O, X.

Wednesday, July 14 (Moon Leo) Define your terms, get promises in writing, and realize the truth of Samuel Goldwyn's statement: "A verbal promise is not worth the paper it's written on!" You'll perceive places and relationships in their true light. Don't rush, for time is on your side. Perfect techniques, streamline methods, and get rid of clutter.

Thursday, July 15 (Moon in Leo to Virgo 5:39 p.m.)   Focus on responsibility and the pressure of a deadline. The Leo moon emphasizes siblings, close neighbors, and ideas that require time to become viable. Capricorn, Cancer, and Leo play outstanding roles, and they could have these letters in their names—H, Q, Z. The fortunate number is 8.

Friday, July 16 (Moon in Virgo)   During this weekend, you'll hear from people in distant cities or foreign lands. A reunion is indicated with someone who once played an important role in your life. Emotional wounds heal, and you'll bask in the glory of the past. But don't retrograde. Aries plays a role.

Saturday, July 17 (Moon in Virgo)   Make a new start, exercising independence of thought and action. Avoid lifting heavy objects. Don't wear your heart on your sleeve, for people sense your sensitivity and some may take advantage. A bright light shines at home base, so you won't have to go far afield for luck. It's right where you live!

Sunday, July 18 (Moon in Virgo to Libra 12:19 a.m.)   A Sunday family reunion! The moon is in the area of your chart associated with security, protection, and plans for buying or selling. Attention revolves around directions, motivation, and proposals that include partnership and marriage. Special: Don't give up something of value for nothing. Cancer and Capricorn play perplexing roles.

Monday, July 19 (Moon in Libra)   Pressures are relieved now, as the Jupiter keynote, Libra moon, relates to the affairs of the heart. The focus is on sensuality, attractiveness, and accelerated social activity. Listen, Gemini: This could be one of your perfect days. Sagittarius and another Gemini play entertaining, dramatic roles.

Tuesday, July 20 (Moon in Libra to Scorpio 10:30 a.m.)   Be willing to revise, review, and rewrite, to tear down in order to rebuild. The lunar position highlights creativity, style, challenge, children, and a relationship that is more serious than you wish at this time. Music, dancing, and dining out are featured. Taurus and Scorpio are involved.

Wednesday, July 21 (Moon in Scorpio)   Analyze your prospects, both personal and professional. Check your handwriting, digging deep into the mantic arts and sciences, including astrology and number divination. Give full rein to your intellectual curiosity, as you ask questions, explore, and learn. Virgo, Sagittarius, and another Gemini play fascinating roles, and have these letters in their names—E, N, W.

Thursday, July 22 (Moon in Scorpio to Sagittarius, 10:48 p.m.)   Attention revolves around art objects, luxury items, and gifts. The Scorpio moon is associated with work methods, basic issues, household pets, and employment. A coworker, in display of passion, temper, says sorrowful things and will later apologize. Taurus and Libra become true friends.

Friday, July 23 (Moon in Sagittarius)   Hold tight! Within 24 hours, you get what you want, including added recognition and a profitable legal agreement. The theme should be, "Don't give up the ship!" Be patient as you wait and win. Be aware of the element of deception, and protect yourself in emotional clinches. Pisces and Virgo figure prominently.

Saturday, July 24 (Moon in Sagittarius)   It's a serious Saturday! What people took for a display of humor they now take seriously, so be guarded in your remarks. Someone who extracts a promise of love is not joking, and might extract more in the future than you can afford. Capricorn and Cancer dominate this scenario, and have these letters in their names—H, Q, Z.

Sunday, July 25 (Moon in Sagittarius to Capricorn 11:08 a.m.)   A job well done! You'll hear those words and as a result, reach an agreement. You'll be offered a chance to elevate your prestige and to earn more money. Marriage figures prominently, along with a partnership proposal. Show off your ability to overcome distance and language obstacles. Libra is involved.

Monday, July 26 (Moon in Capricorn)   Imprint your style, refusing to be discouraged by naysayers. Some people, in a display of jealousy, will condemn your independence, inventiveness, and lifestyle. Realize this is a passing phase, and the very people who condemn will later become your valuable allies. Leo and Aquarius are represented.

Tuesday, July 27 (Moon in Capricorn to Aquarius 9:54 p.m.)   Get down to business! Get your budget straight and show you are capable of meeting a deadline. Deal gingerly with a Capricorn who is reluctant to try new things. By contrast, Cancer is enthusiastic, offering to help with funding. This cycle highlights promotion, production, direction, motivation, and your marital status.

Wednesday, July 28 (Moon in Aquarius)   The full moon, lunar eclipse, highlights travel, philosophy, metaphysics, and publishing. The emphasis is on your ninth house. Spiritual values surge forward, highlighting sentiment in connection with a romance. The spotlight is also on foreign lands, bilingual people, and introduction to ethnic cuisine. Sagittarius is involved.

Thursday, July 29 (Moon in Aquarius)   Some people attempt to twist the facts, so be careful to strive for the true picture, refusing to be intimidated by those who claim to know those in power. State clearly, "I don't care who you know, I know who I am and that is what is important!" Taurus, Leo and Scorpio play memorable roles, and have these letters in their names—D, M, V.

Friday, July 30 (Moon in Aquarius to Pisces 5:27 a.m.)   Within 24 hours, the moon will relate to your career, promotion, and ability to take charge of your own fate.

You asked for an opportunity to rewrite the script of your life—write it the way you would like it to be and so it will be. Virgo, Sagittarius, and another Gemini play outstanding roles, and have these letters in their names—E, N, W.

Saturday, July 31 (Moon in Pisces)   Family members express appreciation for your past efforts and favors. Focus on music, entertainment, and gifts. Beautify your surroundings to be prepared to welcome important guests. This is one Saturday night you won't soon forget! Lucky lottery: 6, 50, 15, 9, 22, 33.

AUGUST 1999

Sunday, August 1 (Moon in Pisces to Aries 12:47 p.m.)   On this Sunday, you wrestle with problems concerning where you are and where you are going. The Pluto keynote highlights upsets, sudden changes, and basic issues of health, employment, and household pets. Taurus, Leo, and Scorpio play memorable roles, and could have these letters in their names: D, M, V.

Monday, August 2 (Moon in Aries)   You'll be saying, "This is the kind of Monday I would always welcome!" The Aries moon represents your ability to win friends among the powerful, and to succeed in matters of speculation and romance. The Mercury keynote coincides with your ability to get your message across and to win with words. Your lucky number is 5.

Tuesday, August 3 (Moon in Aries to Taurus 5:09 p.m.)   Lucky numbers: 6, 9, 15. Attention revolves around gifts that help beautify your surroundings, including your home. Focus on music, style, panache, and a romantic interlude that gets your creative juices flowing. Taurus, Libra, and Scorpio play leading roles, and could have these letters in their names—F, O, X.

Wednesday, August 4 (Moon in Taurus)   Lucky lottery: 7, 12, 50, 19, 10, 1. The lunar position highlights secrets and the need to communicate with someone temporarily confined to home or hospital. A project that appears to be falling apart can be restored by networking. Pisces figures prominently.

Thursday, August 5 (Moon in Taurus to Gemini 7:57 p.m.)   For racing luck, try these selections at all tracks: Post position special—number 8 p.p. in the ninth race. Pick six: 8, 5, 4, 2, 1, 1. Watch for these letters in the names of potential winning horses or jockeys: H, Q, Z. Hot daily doubles: 8 and 5, 2 and 1, 3 and 7. Older horses and favorites will be in the money.

Friday, August 6 (Moon in Gemini)   Round out a project, finishing what was started three months ago. The moon in your sign coincides with the high cycle, so take the initiative, imprint your style, and make a new start in a different direction. You'll be drawn to the language and history not only of your own country but of foreign lands. You could be dining with someone who is bilingual, very likely an Aries.

Saturday, August 7 (Moon in Gemini to Cancer 9:53 p.m.)   What a Saturday! The sun keynote, moon in Gemini, might cause some people to claim, "You are all over the place!" The astrological and numerical cycles point to independence, vitality, and sex appeal. Leo and Aquarius are drawn to you and will make no secret of it. Lucky lottery: 1, 19, 27, 48, 46, 12.

Sunday, August 8 (Moon in Cancer)   Attention revolves around people who confess to you, as another Gemini talks about a business partnership or marriage—or both. A puzzle is solved concerning finances, home building, and the need to reach the public with the promotion of a product appealing to women. A Cancer plays a role.

Monday, August 9 (Moon in Cancer to Leo 11:56 p.m.)   Your cycle is high for reaping rewards for creative endeavors. It's an unusual Monday, with the focus on your style, wardrobe, and entertainment involving activities associated with politics or charity. A reminder: Keep resolutions about exercise, diet, and nutrition. A Sagittarian could dominate this exciting scenario.

Tuesday, August 10 (Moon in Leo) You will be asking, "Is this déjà vu?" The scenario highlights familiar places and faces. The moon in Cancer represents an emphasis on locating lost articles, earning more money, and learning the value of personal possessions. You move closer to your ultimate goal, even though you may not be aware of it.

Wednesday, August 11 (Moon in Leo) The new moon, with a solar eclipse in Leo, activates a tendency to scatter your forces and to get involved in a wild-goose chase. The Mercury keynote emphasizes an opportunity to advance via your skills as a writer. Refuse to be limited, for today there are no limitations! Virgo plays an outstanding role. Your lucky number is 5.

Thursday, August 12 (Moon in Leo to Virgo 3:22 a.m.) Attention revolves around home decorating and gifts of affection and love. Love could be in bloom and you might not even be conscious of it. The Leo moon represents romance, creativity, panache, and success in matters of speculation. Taurus and Libra will play colorful roles.

Friday, August 13 (Moon in Virgo) This Friday the 13th is not unlucky, for you'll have time on your hands. An opportunity exists to perfect methods, to streamline procedures, and to get rid of clutter. Special: A psychic impression or a prophetic dream deserves more-than-usual attention. Don't equate delay with defeat!

Saturday, August 14 (Moon in Virgo to Libra 9:24 a.m.) A powerful Saturday! The Saturn keynote highlights durability and survival under trying conditions. The Virgo moon equates to your home and the completion of long-standing negotiations. Property value will be called to your attention, perhaps in a dramatic way. Capricorn figures prominently. Your lucky number is 8.

Sunday, August 15 (Moon in Libra) Elements of timing and luck ride with you. Correspondence relates to people in transit and to those making their homes in foreign lands. As your horizons expand, you overcome distance and language barriers. A love relationship heats up and your soulmate could be involved. Aries and Libra play outstanding roles.

Monday, August 16 (Moon in Libra to Scorpio 6:40 p.m.) Lucky numbers: 1, 16, 7. Past promises surge to the forefront. Be sure others realize you have not forgotten, but are timing your moves. The spotlight is on initiative, independence, originality, and a fresh start in a different direction. New love on the horizon, and the current affair of the heart regains its spark. Leo is in a dramatic role.

Tuesday, August 17 (Moon in Scorpio) For racing luck, try these selections at all tracks: Post position special—number 6 p.p. in the fifth race. Pick six: 2, 3, 4, 1, 6, 5. Watch for these letters in the names of potential winning horses or jockeys: B, K, T. Hot daily doubles: 2 and 3, 2 and 2, 6 and 4. Hometown jockeys will have racing luck.

Wednesday, August 18 (Moon in Scorpio) Lucky lottery: 3, 33, 10, 12, 22, 15. It's an excellent day for dining out, preparing a program of social activity for a group that features art, literature, and book reviews. You'll be complimented on your appearance. An addition to your wardrobe improves your image, and a new hairstyle also enhances your sex appeal. Sagittarius is involved.

Thursday, August 19 (Moon in Scorpio to Sagittarius 6:32 a.m.) You emerge triumphant as a problem is solved that involved timing or bureaucratic red tape. By tomorrow, you'll win allies. The spotlight will be on partnership and marriage. Tonight, you could be emotionally involved with a Scorpio who waxes eloquent with such statements as, "Life is cold without you!"

Friday, August 20 (Moon in Sagittarius)   You'll welcome more freedom, including the freedom to speak, write, and publish. On a personal level, a flirtation lends spice and might be the precursor to a trip that no one is supposed to know about—be discreet! Virgo, Sagittarius, and another Gemini play fascinating roles, and could have these letters in their names: E, N, W.

Saturday, August 21 (Moon in Sagittarius to Capricorn 6:59 p.m.)   Beautiful surroundings! Saturday features music, style, panache, and wining and dining with the elite. A gift received represents a token of deep affection. Special: Recall resolutions about diet and nutrition, for moderation must be the key word. A domestic adjustment involves your lifestyle or marital status.

Sunday, August 22 (Moon in Capricorn)   What was previously acceptable will no longer suffice. Funding can be made available if you experiment, explore, and make inquiries. Someone close to you, perhaps a Sagittarius, will show how to follow the money. Pisces and Virgo also play important roles, and could have these letters in their names: G, P, Y.

Monday, August 23 (Moon in Capricorn)   The Capricorn moon relates to the assets of other people, as you are trusted to make the most of what is available. Attending an auction could be part of this unusual scenario. A riddle is solved, as Cancer and Capricorn people appear at almost the last minute. Get your priorities in order, and be aware of a time element or deadline.

Tuesday, August 24 (Moon in Capricorn to Aquarius 5:49 a.m.)   Finish what you start, realizing that, within 24 hours, a long-distance communication will verify your views. Tonight you'll hear sincere words of love that will boost your morale. You'll be musing, "What goes around does come around!" Aries and Libra are in the picture, and have these letters in their names: I and R.

Wednesday, August 25 (Moon in Aquarius)   Lucky lottery: 1, 11, 22, 33, 41, 44. Answer to question: Go for it! It's an excellent day to make a fresh start and to participate in a pioneering project. Love vibrations auger sensuality and sex appeal, and Leo and Aquarius, who figure prominently in this department, and are likely to have these letters in their names: A, S, J.

Thursday, August 26 (Moon in Aquarius to Pisces 1:50 p.m.)   The full moon in Aquarius relates to philosophy, the higher mind, journeys, publishing, and getting your message across via a vigorous program. The moon keynote blends with your Mercury significator, so your writings and teachings will earn praise. A Cancer plays an important role.

Friday, August 27 (Moon in Pisces)   For racing luck, try these selections at all tracks: Post position special—number 5 p.p. in the seventh race. Pick six: 1, 3, 7, 2, 1, 5. Watch for these letters in the names of potential winning horses or jockeys: C, L, U. Hot daily doubles: 1 and 3, 7 and 7, 8 and 5. Foreign horses score upsets; Sagittarian jockeys win.

Saturday, August 28 (Moon in Pisces to Aries 7:09 p.m.)   The Pluto keynote with the moon in your tenth sector adds up to a rare opportunity for promotion, production, and dealings with controversial people. Special: Check references and bring your source material up to date. Knowledge of graphology would be helpful; you'll come across strange handwriting.

Sunday, August 29 (Moon in Aries)   Storytelling is featured, as quotations from the Bible are interpreted. Studies of theology and comparative religions prove fruitful. Take notes, write ideas, and welcome a clash of opinions. Emphasize tolerance without backing down from your principles. Virgo and Sagittarius are represented.

Monday, August 30 (Moon in Aries to Taurus 10:41 p.m.) Attention revolves around your ability to beautify your home and to blend the color red into other schemes. The Venus keynote highlights gifts, music, art objects, luxury items, and the tendency to indulge your sweet tooth. Taurus, Libra, and Scorpio play leading roles, and could have these letters in their names: F, O, X.

Tuesday, August 31 (Moon in Taurus) Within 24 hours, a secret is revealed in connection with your income potential, a lost article, or your ability to deal with someone who is attractive, sentimental, and temperamental. Tonight, see a relationship as it exists, not merely as you wish it were. Have your antennae up for a possible deception—someone wants something for nothing and you are the prime target.

SEPTEMBER 1999

Wednesday, September 1 (Moon in Taurus) You learn what requires your immediate attention and you can do something about it. Proofread your material; you'll discover an error that, when attended to, will save money and prevent embarrassment. Virgo, Sagittarius, another Gemini in picture, with these letters in their names: E, N, W.

Thursday, September 2 (Moon in Taurus to Gemini 1:25 a.m.) The Venus keynote is highlighted, so no matter how far you may wander, you'll return home. The emphasis is on the way your voice sounds, entertainment, and gifts that help beautify your surroundings. Special: Keep your resolutions concerning exercise, diet, and nutrition. Libra plays a role.

Friday, September 3 (Moon in Gemini) Be sure terms are made crystal clear. Find out what is expected from you and what you might expect in return. The moon is in your sign, so your cycle is high. Take the initiative now that circumstances are turning in your favor. Pisces and Virgo are featured, and are likely to have these letters in their names—G, P, Y.

Saturday, September 4 (Moon in Gemini to Cancer 4:10 a.m.)   The results of previous efforts surface, which could mean money in the bank. Wear shades of pink and purple, attend a social gathering, and speak your mind. You'll win allies and love. Capricorn and Cancer figure in this dynamic scenario, and could have these letters in their names: H, Q, Z. Your lucky number is 8.

Sunday, September 5 (Moon in Cancer)   Lucky numbers: 12, 9, 31. The moon position emphasizes your ability to retrieve what had been lost, missing, or stolen. On this Sunday, people want to hear you and see you, and some want to test your veracity. Speak the truth and you have nothing to fear! Aries and Libra play dramatic roles.

Monday, September 6 (Moon in Cancer to Leo 7:29 a.m.)   The answer to your question: Affirmative. New love is positive, so make a fresh start in a new direction. An exciting world awaits. Leo and Aquarius dominate this revelatory scenario, and they will have these letters in their names—A, S, J. Money appears from a surprise source.

Tuesday, September 7 (Moon in Leo)   Romance mingles with legal commitments, partnership, and marital status. An element of deception exists, so keep your guard up and insist on a clear, written definition of terms. You'll have a backstage view, but don't tell everything you see or know, since discretion is the better part of valor. A Cancer is in the picture.

Wednesday, September 8 (Moon in Leo to Virgo 11:57 a.m.)   Finding how the other half lives will be the motive for action. Social work figures prominently. Use entertainment to inspire others to study, work, and regain self-esteem. Your sense of humor will be transformed into profundity. Lucky lottery: 3, 33, 12, 22, 44, 45.

Thursday, September 9 (Moon in Virgo)   The new moon in Virgo represents home, security, family, and purchase of furniture. Money outlay is necessary; it adds up to a good investment. The cycle continues high, putting you in the right place at a crucial moment. People take you seriously today, so avoid making commitments unless you're prepared to honor them.

Friday, September 10 (Moon in Virgo to Libra 6:16 p.m.)   Focus on writing, disseminating information, and being in contact with someone who shares your hobby and interests. What begins as a flirtation could lead to a physical attraction—and after that, who knows! What you seek is close at hand, possibly in your home. Virgo, Sagittarius, and another Gemini play exciting roles, and have these initials in their names: E, N, W.

Saturday, September 11 (Moon in Libra)   Return home! The Libra moon relates to children, challenge, change, and exciting experiences. A travel invitation awaits, and a gift received adds to your wardrobe and represents a token of something more than affection. Highlight diplomacy. Money owed will be paid, but not if you force issues. Lucky lottery: 6, 7, 14, 13, 12, 22.

Sunday, September 12 (Moon in Libra)   Wait up! Someone who thinks much of you asks you to wait. This person, very likely a Pisces, deserves your attention. Focus on the stirring of creative juices. By listening and waiting, you will be ahead of the game. Pisces and Virgo play roles, and could have these letters in their names: G, P, Y.

Monday, September 13 (Moon in Libra to Scorpio 3:08 a.m.)   Results! Let others know you mean business, insisting on creative control and refusing to let others water down your principles or talents. A love relationship smolders. Capricorn and Cancer figure in this fascinating scenario and are likely to have these letters in their names: H, Q, Z.

Tuesday, September 14 (Moon in Scorpio) Finish what you start, accenting a sharpening of tools. Basic issues dominate, including ways to earn a living. Keep your health resolutions, including those involving exercise, diet, and nutrition. Highlight universal appeal by studying the language, food, and customs of foreign lands. Aries plays a role.

Wednesday, September 15 (Moon in Scorpio to Sagittarius 2:35 p.m.) It's the day you've been waiting for— a breakthrough! Light shines in areas previously dark. People appreciate your worth and will say so. Stress independence, originality, and self-esteem. A member of the opposite sex displays passionate feelings. Leo is represented. Your lucky number is 1.

Thursday, September 16 (Moon in Sagittarius) What you missed two weeks ago will again become available. Focus on property value, a love relationship, and taking charge of the direction of your life. Partnership and marriage dominate. A Cancer does care and will prove it by extending a dinner invitation. Capricorn also plays a role.

Friday, September 17 (Moon in Sagittarius to Capricorn 3:14 a.m.) Highlight diversity, versatility, and intellectual curiosity. The moon in your seventh house equates to the public reaction to your efforts. The spotlight also falls on legal affairs, written agreements, and marriage. Someone outside your family attempts to horn in on benefits. Have none of it! Another Gemini is involved.

Saturday, September 18 (Moon in Capricorn) A fascinating Saturday! The Capricorn moon highlights public appearances and tests of your popularity. Fight for your legal rights, realizing a relationship has consequences. You'll be asked pointed questions about marriage. Taurus, Leo, and Scorpio play outstanding roles, and have these letters in their names: D, M, V.

Sunday, September 19 (Moon in Capricorn)   There's a release from a burden! Today's scenario highlights greater freedom of thought and action, as a member of the opposite sex, possibly a writer or journalist, plays an important role. The lunar position emphasizes mystery, intrigue, the occult, and information about a possible inheritance. Virgo plays a top role.

Monday, September 20 (Moon in Capricorn to Aquarius 2:38 p.m.)   Harmony is restored! Confusion no longer exists in connection with where you live, your lifestyle, or your marital status. A boat that rocked perilously is once again headed for smooth sailing. Someone who said, "I'll never see you again!" could be at your doorstep within three days. Libra is in the picture.

Tuesday, September 21 (Moon in Aquarius)   For racing luck, try these selections at all tracks: Post position special—number 1 p.p. in the sixth race. Pick six: 1, 5, 3, 2, 4, 1. Put your antenna up for these letters in the names of potential winning horses or jockeys: G, P, Y. Hot daily doubles: 1 and 5, 7, 3 and 8. A slippery track causes upsets and is a danger to jockeys.

Wednesday, September 22 (Moon in Aquarius to Pisces 10:51 p.m.)   Lucky lottery: 8, 11, 12, 22, 33. 4. The Aquarian moon relates to philosophy, theology, and the mantic arts and sciences, including astrology. The Saturn keynote equates to elements of time, deadline, responsibility, and an intensified relationship. Capricorn and Cancer play fascinating roles.

Thursday, September 23 (Moon in Pisces)   A relationship begins or ends—what goes around, comes around. The Pisces moon relates to your ability to control your own fate and destiny. The Mars keynote highlights action in connection with future prospects, travel, or a search for your soulmate. Aries and Libra play outstanding roles.

Friday, September 24 (Moon in Pisces)   Make a fresh start, letting those close to you realize that you appreciate everything they do, but from now on you're going to live your own life. Imprint your style, stressing originality, independence, and innovation. Special: Avoid lifting heavy objects! Leo and Aquarius dominate this scenario, and have these letters in their names: A, S, J.

Saturday, September 25 (Moon in Pisces to Aries 3:34 a.m.)   What a Saturday night! The full moon in your eleventh house equates to spectacular doings. Your popularity surges as people are drawn to you. A bold member of the opposite sex confesses, "I want you so much I can hardly keep your hands off you!" Lucky lottery: 2, 12, 20, 13, 30, 40.

Sunday, September 26 (Moon in Aries)   Good fortune smiles in connection with finance and romance. New clothing improves your body image, while concern about your weight represents a loss of energy that might be better used in a creative project. The Aries moon shows you get what you want by taking the initiative. You'll surprise yourself as the cash flow resumes and you could be holding a Cornucopia of Plenty.

Monday, September 27 (Moon in Aries to Taurus 5:51 a.m.)   Be willing to revise, review, and rewrite, and to rebuild on a more solid structure. The moon in Taurus relates to hospitals, museums, motion pictures, and secret meetings. The Pluto keynote warns that discretion is necessary. Dining in an out-of-the-way place might seem safe, but don't let your guard down. Taurus plays a dynamic role.

Tuesday, September 28 (Moon in Taurus)   Welcome a change of scene, for a short trip could be just what the doctor ordered! The Taurus moon represents romance, a clandestine arrangement, and a gift representing a token of love. There's a genuine bargain in connection with an art object that could be obtained at auction. A Sagittarian plays a role.

Wednesday, September 29 (Moon in Taurus to Gemini 7:21 a.m.)   The cycle shoots upwards. The moon in your sign represents a time when everything you do turns out right. Focus on personality, initiative, charm, humor, and profundity. Designate where the action will be by accepting an opportunity to speak, to interview, and to be interviewed. Lucky lottery: 6, 50, 15, 24, 1, 13.

Thursday, September 30 (Moon in Gemini)   What appeared to be a loss will boomerang in your favor. People of opposing views concede that you are the leader, at least for today. Wear shades of pink and purple, imprinting your style and refusing to follow others. Psychic impressions prove valid, so heed your instincts and follow your heart. A Pisces figures prominently.

OCTOBER 1999

Friday, October 1 (Moon in Gemini to Cancer 9:31 a.m.)   The first day of October relates to an overall cycle—romance, art, music, ability to beautify your surroundings. Attention revolves around the home, family relationships, being diplomatic without being gullible. Taurus and Libra play roles, are likely to have these letters in their names: F, O, X.

Saturday, October 2 (Moon in Cancer)   Lucky lottery: 7, 12, 4, 40, 22, 9. A secret liaison dominates and you'll consider this a lively Saturday night! You'll hear whispers of sweet nothings, but maintain your emotional equilibrium and your sense of humor. A Pisces talks about career, business, and how you can improve personal conditions.

Sunday, October 3 (Moon in Cancer to Leo 1:13 p.m.)   Find out where you stand in connection with property, home, or a possible inheritance. The Saturn keynote emphasizes timing, responsibility, durable goods, and dealings with people who make the world go around. No slouches! You receive meaningful compliments from those you respect. Your lucky number is 8.

Monday, October 4 (Moon in Leo) What you've been waiting for will arrive. A relative is involved, and travel information is exciting. Study conditions in other lands and get familiar with distance, language, and cuisines. Let go of an unsavory situation by being with the one you love, not one you merely tolerate. Aries is represented.

Tuesday, October 5 (Moon in Leo to Virgo 6:40 p.m.) Highlight showmanship and publicity. Advertise your wares, paying special attention to color coordination. Develop a product that appeals to children. Imprint your style, stressing originality and an unusual format or thesis. Special: Avoid lifting heavy objects! Leo and Aquarius are involved, with these letters in their names: A, S, J.

Wednesday, October 6 (Moon in Virgo) Lucky lottery: 2, 12, 16, 7, 4, 11. Focus on partnership, home, property values, and a decision relating to marriage. A Cancer says, "I want to be involved with you, business or otherwise!" You'll be sought after and wined and dined. Capricorn will also figure in this provocative scenario.

Thursday, October 7 (Moon in Virgo) On this Thursday, social invitations abound. Enjoy but don't scatter your forces, for some people are not serious and merely want attention. Be up to date on fashion and current events. New clothes improve your body image. Stay close to home base if possible, for a surprise is being planned. Don't make it necessary to send a search party.

Friday, October 8 (Moon in Virgo to Libra 1:52 a.m.) For racing luck, try these selections at all tracks: Post position special—number 4 p.p. in the eighth race. Pick six: 4, 4, 8, 1, 7, 1. Look for these letters in the names of potential winning horses or jockeys: D, M,

V. Hot daily doubles: 4 and 4, 8 and 7, 1 and 1. Favorites win and a veteran jockey will be honored.

Saturday, October 9 (Moon in Libra)   The new moon in Libra on this Saturday night spells creativity, style, romance, and expressions of passion. If you are merely playing games, it might be best to move on. People take you seriously in the love department. You'll be saying, "This is one Saturday night I won't soon forget!" Your lucky number is 5.

Sunday, October 10 (Moon in Libra to Scorpio 10:01 a.m.)   It's a harmonious Sunday! The Libra moon highlights children, teaching, and spiritual awareness. The Venus keynote emphasizes food, luxury, and the joy of being with loved ones. Attention revolves around your home and a different kind of music. Libra and Aries help make this a memorable time.

Monday, October 11 (Moon in Scorpio)   Meditate, transforming a tendency to brood into positive concepts, thoughts, ideas, and predictions. You'll be on the go, even if you don't move an inch geographically. Your morale is elevated by a Pisces who declares, "You will never really be alone because I'm always going to be with you!"

Tuesday, October 12 (Moon in Scorpio to Sagittarius 10:18 p.m.)   For racing luck, try these selections at all tracks: Post position special—number 8 p.p. in the ninth race. Pick six: 8, 5, 4, 1, 3, 2. Watch for these letters in the names of potential winning horses or jockeys: H, Q, Z. Hot daily doubles: 8 and 5, 8 and 8, 1 and 7. Favorites come in the money; Capricorn jockeys have racing luck.

Wednesday, October 13 (Moon in Sagittarius)   In matters of speculation, stick with the number 9. The moon relates to love, money, and health. You'll be asked intimate questions by someone who has no right to ask, so maintain your equilibrium and your dignity. Dine on foreign cuisine, giving attention to different customs and languages.

Thursday, October 14 (Moon in Sagittarius) A surprise dinner invitation! A romantic Leo proposes a trip out of town. An Aquarian also has travel on his mind, but at a far distance. Express gratitude, turning on your Gemini charm, and transforming humor into profundity. Make a fresh start, exercising independence of thought and action. Your lucky number is 1.

Friday, October 15 (Moon in Sagittarius to Capricorn 10:04 a.m.) The moon relates to that section of your horoscope that involves partnership, public response to your efforts, and marital status. The moon keynote blends with your Mercury, so you can now articulate your feelings without being embarrassed. A Cancer plays an outstanding role.

Saturday, October 16 (Moon in Capricorn) What appears a disaster will almost as if by magic be transformed into something pleasurable. The emphasis is on publishing, advertising, entertainment, and accelerated social activity. Questions about marriage will be answered, with a blend of amusement, seriousness, and degree of consternation. Lucky lottery: 3, 36, 4, 12, 23, 33.

Sunday, October 17 (Moon in Capricorn to Aquarius 11:17 p.m.) Everything comes out even! Concern over bank figures and accounting procedures will be erased. Taurus, Leo, and Scorpio play outstanding roles, and will have these letters in their names: D, M, V. A Taurus reveals a secret, which has to do with a clandestine relationship.

Monday, October 18 (Moon in Aquarius) Monday is off to fast start! The Mercury keynote relates to mental activity that includes reading, writing, teaching, and absorbing knowledge. You are restless, but this can be transformed into creative energy. A flirtation lends spice, but don't let it get out of hand! Virgo will figure prominently.

Tuesday, October 19 (Moon in Aquarius) Lucky
numbers: 6, 3, 9. The Aquarian moon relates to philosophy, theology, and an ability to get your message across.
Spiritual values are enhanced, and publishing and advertising opportunities should not be ignored. A relative
talks you into a short trip, but unless you're careful, this
could turn out to be a wild-goose chase.

*Wednesday, October 20 (Moon in Aquarius to Pisces
8:33 a.m.)* Take it easy! Take time to catch your
emotional breath. It's an excellent day for meditation,
reviewing relationships, and seeing people and places as
they are, and not merely as you wish they were. A Pisces
does have your best interests at heart and will prove it.
Lucky lottery: 5, 50, 51, 12, 6, 18.

Thursday, October 21 (Moon in Pisces) Power play!
Today's scenario features the need to take charge of
your own fate. You'll be dealing with the element of
time as you meet and beat a deadline. The spotlight is
on promotion, production, and an ability to bring order
out of chaos. Capricorn and Cancer play roles, with
these letters in their names: H, Q, Z.

*Friday, October 22 (Moon in Pisces to Aries 1:42
p.m.)* The emphasis is on completion as you receive
additional information about a possible long journey
overseas. Highlight universal appeal, being sensitive to
the ways other people feel about romance, love, and
marriage. Aries and Libra figure in this scenario, and
are likely to have these letters in their names: I and R.

Saturday, October 23 (Moon in Aries) Bright lights
this Saturday night! The sun keynote plus Aries moon,
sends you off and running! Focus on popularity and a
new start in a different direction. A love relationship
heats up. Highlight showmanship, color coordination,
and original ways of expressing your feelings. Leo is represented. Your lucky number is 1.

*Sunday, October 24 (Moon in Aries to Taurus 3:25
p.m.)* The full moon in Taurus stimulates areas of

your life associated with secret missions, hospitals, and charitable organizations. A visit to a museum helps coordinate your feelings and opinions. Get in touch with someone temporarily confined to home or hospital. Proposals are received, either partnership or marriage.

Monday, October 25 (Moon in Taurus)   Today is not lacking in excitement! The Jupiter keynote promotes joy, social activity, and awareness of spiritual values. A discussion with Sagittarius proves fruitful. Give full play to your curiosity about comparative religions. Another Gemini fulfills an emotional need.

Tuesday, October 26 (Moon in Taurus to Gemini 3:33 p.m.)   Play your cards close to your chest, for someone wants to trick you. Have none of it! Speak frankly, saying, in effect, "I feel you are desirable and I like you, but I won't stand for trickery." Within 24 hours, your cycle moves up in a dramatic way. Events will occur to bring you closer to your goal, as circumstances will move in your favor.

Wednesday, October 27 (Moon in Gemini)   Lucky lottery: 5, 51, 3, 30, 12, 22. It's an excellent day for reading, writing, teaching, and finding a creative outlet for your special talent. A short trip involves a relative. Research verifies your views and you know once and for all that you are on the right track. Virgo, Sagittarius, and another Gemini dominate this fascinating scenario.

Thursday, October 28 (Moon in Gemini to Cancer 4:09 p.m.)   Racing luck—selections apply to all tracks: Post position special—number 2 p.p. in the fourth race. Pick six: 2, 2, 6, 2, 5, 5. Watch for these letters in the names of potential winning horses or jockeys: F, O, X. Hot daily doubles: 2 and 2, 6 and 5, 6 and 6. Local boys make good, including jockeys and horses.

Friday, October 29 (Moon in Cancer)   Define terms, finding out what is expected of you, and what you can expect in return for your efforts, creative, financial, emotional. Get your promises in writing. Above all, avoid self-deception. The passing parade makes you feel that this must be déjà vu! Today's scenario highlights familiar faces and places.

Saturday, October 30 (Moon in Cancer to Leo 6:47 p.m.) Lucky lottery: 8, 12, 4, 40, 17, 26. Deal gingerly with someone accustomed to having his own way. Let it be known, however, that you refuse to be coerced or pressured into making snap decisions. The moon in its own sign, Cancer, relates to your income and ability to locate lost articles. Capricorn is involved.

Sunday, October 31—Daylight Saving Time Ends (Moon in Leo) Take special care around fire and dangerous weapons. Headstrong action relates to romance and to a desire to get away from it all. Halloween brings forth memories of the great Houdini, for magicians around the world celebrate this as National Magic Day in his honor. Aries and Libra take center stage.

NOVEMBER 1999

Monday, November 1 (Moon in Leo to Virgo 11:07 p.m.) Family affairs dominate, and you will be consulted about investments and savings. Be diplomatic, but don't equate delay with defeat. Your psychic impressions prove reliable. Pisces and Virgo figure in this scenario, and they could have these letters in their names: G, P, Y.

Tuesday, November 2 (Moon in Virgo) What was missed yesterday becomes available today. Focus on responsibilities and deadlines. A relationship is intense and controversial. The lunar position emphasizes a relative who offers advice about a home or building. Capricorn and Cancer are in this picture, and they will have these letters in their names: H, Q, Z.

Wednesday, November 3 (Moon in Virgo) Lucky lottery: 9, 6, 15, 26, 37, 4. Extra recognition is due. Today's cycle highlights romance, sensitivity, creativity, and the higher mind. The moon position emphasizes family reunions and your ability to overcome a temporary financial dry spell. Aries and Libra play featured roles, and they will have these letters in their names: I and R.

Thursday, November 4 (Moon in Virgo to Libra 6:57 a.m.)   The sun keynote blends with your Mercury significator to make this a day of enlightenment. Make a fresh start and be open to the possibility of new love. Avoid lifting heavy objects. Don't break too many hearts! There's an aura of sentimentality, along with the excitement of discovery and sex appeal. Leo will play a dramatic role.

Friday, November 5 (Moon in Libra)   Almost without warning, visitors arrive bringing news of marriage. The Libra moon relates to that part of your horoscope associated with creativity, style, adventure, and sex appeal. The sale or purchase of property is also featured. Cancer and Capricorn are in the picture, with these letters in their names: B, K, T.

Saturday, November 6 (Moon in Libra to Scorpio 4:46 p.m.)   It's an excellent Saturday night for socializing! The Jupiter keynote blends with your Mercury, and the Libra moon lends an aura of excitement. You'll be saying that this is one Saturday you'll long remember. A young person seeks permission to participate in an outlandish activity. Your lucky number is 3.

Sunday, November 7 (Moon in Scorpio)   What seemed long ago and far away will be practically at your doorstep. Work methods are highlighted and tools are brought to razor-sharpness as you refuse to be satisfied with mediocre work. Taurus, Leo, and Scorpio figure in this scenario, and they will have these letters in their names—D, M, V.

Monday, November 8 (Moon in Scorpio)   The new moon in Scorpio coincides with a change of schedule in connection with work. More money is available to develop your product or talent. Use words, verbal and written, for the more you express ideas, the better. A flirtation lends spice, but keep it under control or you will pay dearly.

Tuesday, November 9 (Moon in Scorpio to Sagittarius 4:15 a.m.)   Finish a project. Within 24 hours, you'll be offered a contract. Attention will revolve around a public appearance, partnership, or marriage. Tonight, music plays and the aura of romance fills the air. Taurus, Libra, and Scorpio dominate this scenario, and they will have these letters in their names: F, O, X.

Wednesday, November 10 (Moon in Sagittarius)   Define terms, finding out exactly what is expected of you and what you can expect in return for your energy and your financial and creative contributions. The Sagittarius moon brings you in contact with people whose ideas clash with your own. The lunar position is also associated with partnership, public relations, and marriage.

Thursday, November 11 (Moon in Sagittarius to Capricorn 5:00 p.m.)   No fooling! People take you seriously, and though previously you could get away with ironic humor, today people are sensitive and many are dull. So be deliberate in all statements and in policy matters. The element of time plays a major role, so meet a deadline and bring order out of a chaotic situation.

Friday, November 12 (Moon in Capricorn)   Light really does shine at the end of the tunnel. People seek reassurances from you that the world is not falling apart. The emphasis is on humanitarianism, distance and language, and a very warm romance. Finish rather than begin, keeping in touch with someone in a foreign land.

Saturday, November 13 (Moon in Capricorn)   Answer to a question: Yes, in connection with your career, ambition, and the possibility or a promotion. On this Saturday, you exude optimism, along with an aura of creativity and sex appeal. You'll make a fresh start and the world will look different. A Leo sparks style and panache, helping you realize your own worth. Your lucky number is 1.

Sunday, November 14 (Moon in Capricorn to Aquarius 5:46 a.m.) On this Sunday, attention revolves around family, home, security, and a decision relating to accounting procedures and license requirements for a projected deal involving venture capital. Cancer and Capricorn are in the limelight, and they could have these letters in their names: B, K, T. There's a management shakeup!

Monday, November 15 (Moon in Aquarius) The Aquarian moon relates to travel and philosophy. Attention revolves around comparative religions. You'll be musing, "This certainly is a most unusual Monday!" A long-distance call verifies opinions providing encouragement for possible investment in an import–export activity. Sagittarius is involved.

Tuesday, November 16 (Moon in Aquarius to Pisces 4:21 p.m.) A dedicated Scorpio makes a declaration of loyalty. Proofread material and check references. The lunar aspect emphasizes sentimentality, romance, and your ability to bring together people whose views clash. A Taurus reveals a secret relating to financial well-being. Scorpio is also in the picture.

Wednesday, November 17 (Moon in Pisces) Lucky lottery: 5, 50, 10, 12, 7, 13. Put your thoughts on paper, communicating with someone who formerly excited you physically, mentally, and emotionally. An old flame could burn again! The Pisces moon relates to your business and career, and to associations with those in executive capacities. Virgo plays a role.

Thursday, November 18 (Moon in Pisces to Aries 10:57 p.m.) Attention revolves around trips, music, art objects, and the pleasure principle. Someone who previously passed you by will attempt to make amends. Be diplomatic and don't force issues, so that you'll get what you deserve. That will be enough to please and delight. Libra figures in this scenario.

Friday, November 19 (Moon in Aries)   Remember the aphorism, "Einstein declares God does not play dice with the Universe!" Apply this to your own universe. Avoid unnecessary risks, seeing people, places, and relationships as they are not, not merely as you wish they were. Don't play dice with your own happiness and security!

Saturday, November 20 (Moon in Aries to Taurus 1:26 a.m.)   There's fun, pleasure, and romance for you on this Saturday night! The Aries moon relates to your eleventh house, that section of your horoscope associated with friends, hopes, wishes, and good fortune in finance and romance. Your past efforts pay dividends, especially with a relationship that went asunder—it could be back on track. Your lucky number is 8.

Sunday, November 21 (Moon in Taurus)   Spiritual values surface. People are drawn to you for answers to questions like, "Why am I here and where do I go from here?" You are "Svengali" and the world is your "Trilby." That is an awesome responsibility! Aries and Libra play meaningful roles, and could have these letters in their names: I and R.

Monday, November 22 (Moon in Taurus)   The Taurus moon relates to mystery, intrigue, and money and ways to earn it. The sun keynote blends with your Mercury, emphasizing fitness, vitality, and independence of thought and action. You'll make the most of secret knowledge. Leo and Aquarius play exciting roles.

Tuesday, November 23 (Moon in Taurus to Gemini 1:14 a.m.)   The full moon is in your sign and you'll be asking in a humorous way, "Is this déjà vu all over again?" Today's scenario highlights what seemed to have already occurred as you meet familiar places and faces. Property ownership is questioned, so have legal proof available. Cancer and Capricorn make their presence known.

Wednesday, November 24 (Moon in Gemini) For racing luck, try these selections at all tracks: Post position special—number 7 p.p. in the seventh race. Pick six: 3, 3, 6, 4, 7, 5. Watch for these letters in the names of potential winning horses or jockeys: C, L, U. Hot daily doubles: 3 and 3, 7 and 7, 4 and 5. Upsets occur, and apprentice jockeys shine.

Thursday, November 25 (Moon in Gemini to Cancer 12:29 a.m.) The cycle is high for this Thanksgiving! Distance and language obstacles are overcome, and a Scorpio makes an appearance despite the previous statement, "I probably won't be able to be there!" Your humor, goodwill, wit, and wisdom will be much appreciated. You will hear these words, "If it were not for you, this Thanksgiving would fall apart at the seams!"

Friday, November 26 (Moon in Cancer) Be analytical and take nothing for granted. Someone of the opposite sex lends spice. You'll be drawn in two directions. Another Gemini helps you make up your mind. Get promises in writing, putting forth a proposal or format that you long have had in mind but didn't have the time to complete.

Saturday, November 27 (Moon in Cancer to Leo 1:19 a.m.) Tender, loving care—that will be the general feeling for you on this Saturday. A family member who last week walked out in a huff will be back, offering the hand of friendship and expressions of love. The spotlight is also on music, gifts, fine arts, and your ability to dance to your own tune. Lucky lottery: 6, 50, 1, 7, 8, 11.

Sunday, November 28 (Moon in Leo) Sharpen your tools, define your terms, and deal with a Leo whose forces are scattered. The two of you—Gemini and Leo—will make a winning team. Highlight investigative reporting. Transform humor into profundity, seeing people, situations, places, relationships in a realistic light. Pisces plays a fantastic role.

Monday, November 29 (Moon in Leo to Virgo 5:11 a.m.) The Saturn keynote means attention must be paid to time limitations and to a relationship. Saturn represents time, responsibility, discipline, and durable goods, so play the game for keeps. Capricorn and Cancer figure in this scenario, with these letters in their names— H, Q, Z.

Tuesday, November 30 (Moon in Virgo) What a way to finish November! The Mars keynote, Virgo moon, relates to clearing away emotional debris, especially in connection with employment. Round out a project, reaching beyond the immediate to the excitement of discovery and the thrill of romance. Aries and Libra dominate this scenario, and have these letters in their names: I and R.

DECEMBER 1999

Wednesay, December 1 (Moon in Virgo to Libra 12:29 p.m.) You'll review the past with satisfaction. Within 24 hours there's serious consideration about partnership, legal documents, and marriage. Capricorn and Cancer figure in this fascinating scenario, and will have these letters in their names: H, Q, Z. Your lucky number is 8.

Thursday, December 2 (Moon in Libra) Focus on distance, language, and your ability to communicate with someone in a foreign land. The Libra moon represents the section of your horoscope associated with a public response to efforts, legal rights, and your marital status. You'll exhibit universal appeal as people are drawn to you with questions and problems, often of a most intimate nature.

Friday, December 3 (Moon in Libra to Scorpio 10:35 p.m.) You've been waiting for a chance to express new ideas and to take greater charge of your own destiny. This could be it! The Libra moon highlights creativity, style, variety, challenge, children, and an aura of sensuality. Leo and Aquarius figure in this dramatic scenario, and have these letters in their names: A, S, J.

Saturday, December 4 (Moon in Scorpio)   On this Saturday, you'll realize the effect you have on others. You have the power to change plans and to put aside annoyances that deter progress. A secret meeting takes place, which involves Taurus and enables you to know once and for all where you stand and why you are here. Lucky lottery: 2, 13, 11, 22, 33, 16.

Sunday, December 5 (Moon in Scorpio)   A tinge of the occult! As you dig deep for information about spiritual values and theology, you perhaps learn more than you care to know. A hiding place is involved, along with revisionist history. Sagittarius and another Gemini figure in this fascinating scenario, and could have these letters in their names: C, L, U.

Monday, December 6 (Moon in Scorpio to Sagittarius 12:27 p.m.)   For racing luck, try these selections at all tracks: Post position special—number 4 p.p. in the eighth race. Pick six: 2, 4, 8, 4, 6, 6. Watch for these letters in the names of potential winning horses or jockeys: D, M, V. Hot daily doubles: 2 and 4, 4 and 8, 6 and 5. A veteran jockey could take a spill; favorites generally will be in the money.

Tuesday, December 7 (Moon in Sagittarius)   The new moon falls in that section of your horoscope associated with people whose ideas oppose your own, legal agreements, and marriage, Special: If you don't know what to do, do nothing! The Mercury keynote relates to communication, dissemination of information, and a clash of ideas that leads to flirtation and physical attraction.

Wednesday, December 8 (Moon in Sagittarius to Capricorn 11:14 p.m.)   Virgo and Sagittarius have lately been playing important roles in your life. Today and tonight, Taurus, Libra, and Scorpio will figure prominently. You'll know them because of these letters in their names: F, O, X. Decorating, remodeling, and music figure prominently, along with serious consideration of where you live and your lifestyle.

Thursday, December 9 (Moon in Capricorn)   Within 24 hours, you'll gain information about the financial status of people close to you, including your partner or mate. Tonight, play the waiting game, exercising your powers of perception. Find out what is expected of you and what to expect in return. Pisces and Virgo play roles.

Friday, December 10 (Moon in Capricorn)   On this Friday, you'll hear people say, "Let's get down to business!" The Saturn keynote means others take you seriously and your words have impact, so be careful of what you say and to whom you say it. Capricorn and Cancer figure in this scenario, and are likely to have these letters in their names: H, Q, Z.

Saturday, December 11 (Moon in Capricorn to Aquarius 11:59 a.m.)   You'll remember this Saturday! The Mars keynote means action, aggressiveness, and an invitation to romance. Aries plays an important role, relating to that section of your chart associated with hopes, wishes, desires, and sex appeal. The Capricorn moon dictates that you dig deep for information and that you reject the superficial. Your lucky number is 9.

Sunday, December 12 (Moon in Aquarius)   Look beyond the immediate, stressing innovation, inventiveness, and originality as you dare to be different. Whatever you do, maintain your creative control, refusing to permit too much rewriting on the part of others. Don't permit your own style to be buried. Leo plays a romantic role.

Monday, December 13 (Moon in Aquarius to Pisces 11:18 p.m.)   The Aquarian moon relates to philosophy, theology, and biographies of mystics such as Madame Blavatsky. The moon keynote relates to a special appeal to the public, especially women. Attention will revolve around your home, family, tradition, and an exciting dining experience. Your marital status also figures prominently.

Tuesday, December 14 (Moon in Pisces)   Highlight diversity and versatility, and be open to fun-and-frolic. Your Gemini sense of humor and of the ridiculous will surge forward. People with unsavory schemes, including how to get rich without working, will run for their lives when encountering you. Sagittarius and another Gemini play top roles.

Wednesday, December 15 (Moon in Pisces)   Be willing to revise, review, and rewrite, and to rebuild on a more solid structure. The Pisces moon relates to your career, prestige, and standing in the community, and to your ability to take charge of your own destiny. Check your credit card accounts, and be sure your bank book figures are correct. Special: Your telephone bill could be incorrect.

Thursday, December 16 (Moon in Pisces to Aries 7:30 a.m.)   For racing luck, try these selections at all tracks: Post position special—number 3 p.p. in the second race. Pick six: 5, 3, 8, 7, 3, 3. Keep your antenna up for these letters in the names of potential winning horses or jockeys: E, N, W. Hot daily doubles: 5 and 3, 3 and 2, 1 and 7. Speed horses refuse to give up the lead and upsets occur.

Friday, December 17 (Moon in Aries)   The Aries moon means you are going to win friends and influence people. Attention revolves around music, home, family, and the acquisition of an art object or a luxury item. Your voice sounds different, and your marital status figures prominently. Your lucky number is 6.

Saturday, December 18 (Moon in Aries to Taurus 11:45 a.m.)   What a Saturday! You'll be regarded as mystical, glamorous, intriguing, and challenging. Don't tell all—protect your precious privacy. Let others do the "confessing." Pisces and Virgo play outstanding roles, and are likely to have these letters in their names: G, P. Y. Lucky lottery: 7, 51, 12, 8, 22, 13.

Sunday, December 19 (Moon in Taurus)   You'll be reminded about how many shopping days remain before Christmas. You'll also be made aware of your budget, how much to spend on whom, and the need to solidify your holiday plans. The Taurus moon means that you should keep secrets. Don't tell all concerning your budget, and don't ruin a surprise others plan for you by saying, "I know what is going to happen!"

Monday, December 20 (Moon in Taurus to Gemini 12:39 p.m.)   Highlight universality, the higher mind, recognition of beauty in art, and music, and sentimentality in romance. Finish what you start, reaching beyond the immediate. Your skill at predicting the future will be noticed and people will approach you for readings. Aries and Libra play paramount roles and have these letters in their names: I and R.

Tuesday, December 21 (Moon in Gemini)   The moon in your sign, plus the sun keynote, assures that the world will appear new to you, so display originality, daring, and a pioneering spirit. A different kind of love is on the horizon, and, in a current affair of the heart, the spark that brought you together in the first place will soon reignite. You will be a Gemini in love.

Wednesday, December 22 (Moon in Gemini to Cancer 11:52 a.m.)   Lucky lottery: 22, 5, 7, 17, 12, 30. Focus on direction and on motivation in connection with your home and marriage. Emotional responses are heightened as a Cancer invites you to dine and seeks to entice you romantically and in business. A Capricorn will also play a fascinating role.

Thursday, December 23 (Moon in Cancer)   Keep your plans flexible, for someone who supposedly purchased tickets for a play or concert confides, "I am so sorry, but I did not have the time and, when I thought of it, it was too late!" This will provide the opportunity for a heart-to-heart talk with someone who seemingly feels that forgetfulness is a virtue.

Friday, December 24 (Moon in Cancer to Leo 11:32 a.m.) It's Christmas Eve, bringing dissention about money, gifts, and invitations. Even so, your day will be pleasant, and in some areas spiritual. You'll receive a gift that obviously is impractical and will be considered a closet gift. It will never be used, but don't make a federal case of it. Instead, use your sense of humor to express your feelings.

Saturday, December 25 (Moon in Leo) Merry Christmas! Relatives are involved and excitement prevails. People relate anecdotes and you'll be told how attractive you are, which will boost your ego. As a matter of fact, you will exude an aura of sensuality, perceptiveness, and sex appeal. Virgo, Sagittarius, and another Gemini figure in this Christmas tableau.

Sunday, December 26 (Moon in Leo to Virgo 1:34 p.m.) One holiday is finished, so now you can get ready for New Year's Eve. Check your invitation list. Be together with your family, if possible. Today highlights sense of music and drama, and your ability to win your way via diplomacy. Changes occur at home in connection with decorating, remodeling, and your marital status. Libra will figure in this dynamic scenario.

Monday, December 27 (Moon in Virgo) This may not be a blue Monday. The Virgo moon relates to changes at your home base and an exciting dialogue with a family member, usually reticent when it comes to talking. Regard this as an excellent way to prepare for the year 2000. Communication will be of major importance. Pisces and Virgo figure in this fascinating scenario.

Tuesday, December 28 (Moon in Virgo to Libra 7:14 p.m.) On this Tuesday, you come to terms spiritually and financially, and you decide why you are here and where you are going. The shadow of the twenty-first cen-

221

tury is felt, and you'll be aware of a time limitation. You'll also feel deadline pressure. A relationship that is controversial and intense is also on your mind.

Wednesday, December 29 (Moon in Libra)   Lucky lottery: 29, 6, 5, 50, 20, 1. Finish what you start. Find out where you will be on New Year's Eve and with whom, and then review your resolutions. Excitement! You become aware that you are approaching the new century and that the upcoming year will be one of change, travel, and romance.

Thursday, December 30 (Moon in Libra)   Make a fresh start, turning on the charm to exude a magnetic appeal. Some people confide their love and physical attraction, saying, "I can hardly keep my hands off you!" Leo and Aquarius play outstanding roles, and they could have these letters in their names: A, S, J. Your lucky number is 1.

Friday, December 31 (Moon in Libra to Scorpio 4:36 a.m.)   New Year's Eve! The moon shows clearly that music will be involved in your New Year's Eve celebration. When the clock strikes midnight, you'll be kissed by more people than in previous years. The moon keynote emphasizes romance and resolutions about lifelong friendships. Questions about marriage loom large.

Happy New Year!

JANUARY 2000

Saturday, January 1 (Moon in Scorpio)   The Neptune keynote blends with the moon in Scorpio to emphasize your financial condition in connection with decorating, remodeling, or a possible change of residence. On this first day of the year 2000, you will know where you stand with money and love.

222

Sunday, January 2 (Moon in Scorpio to Sagittarius 4:33 p.m.) The Scorpio moon translates into mystery, intrigue, tax and license requirements, and the financial status of someone close to you, perhaps your partner or mate. The Saturn keynote represents pressure, a deadline, or an emotional involvement that, escalator-like, is up and down, from cold to hot and at times too hot not to cool down.

Monday, January 3 (Moon in Sagittarius) Finish what you start, attending to legal details. Review contracts to maintain creative control. Attention revolves around your partnership and your marital status. Aries and Libra play meaningful roles, and will have these letters, initials in their names—I and R. Language study is both essential and rewarding.

Tuesday, January 4 (Moon in Sagittarius) The answer to your question: Affirmative. Make a fresh start, highlighting independence, originality, and a willingness to give and receive love. The Sagittarian moon emphasizes cooperative efforts, your public image, and marriage. Leo and Aquarius play roles, and they could have these letters in their names—A, S, J.

Wednesday, January 5 (Moon in Sagittarius to Capricorn 5:24 a.m.) Lucky lottery: 2, 12, 20, 10, 8, 18. The Capricorn moon places the spotlight on other people's money, and the need to learn more about accounting and financial procedures that involve the knowledge of percentages. Cancer and Capricorn are in the picture, and have these letters in their names—B, K, T.

Thursday, January 6 (Moon in Capricorn) The new moon emphasizes a reunion with an older person who once played an important role in your life. The financial picture is involved. A major discussion will involve banks, the stock market, and investments. Sagittarius and another Gemini figure in this scenario, and they could have these initials in their names—C, L, U.

Friday, January 7 (Moon in Capricorn to Aquarius 5:53 p.m.)   Practical matters dominate, including shelter, basic security, and long-term negotiations that could be concluded in your favor. Taurus, Leo, and Scorpio are in the picture, and are likely to have these letters in their names—D, M, V. A hiding place is discovered—exciting!

Saturday, January 8 (Moon in Aquarius)   For racing luck, these selections apply to all tracks: Post position special—number 3 p.p. in the second race. Pick six: 5, 3, 2, 1, 8, 2. Look for these letters in the names of potential winning horses or jockeys: E, N, W. Hot daily doubles: 5 and 3, 3 and 2, 5 and 5. Sagittarian jockeys ride and win with long shots.

Sunday, January 9 (Moon in Aquarius)   Attention revolves around your lifestyle, where you live, a family gathering, and a serious discussion about future prospects and theology. The Aquarian moon tells of travel talk, as well as interest in language, distance, and communication. Music is involved. You'll be intrigued by architecture, design, and color coordination.

Monday, January 10 (Moon in Aquarius to Pisces 4:59 a.m.)   Time is on your side, so perfect your techniques, streamline your procedures, and be willing to play the waiting game. See people, places, and situations in a realistic light, refusing to fall victim to self-deception. Trust your psychic impressions—follow a hunch and your heart. Pisces and Virgo are in this picture, and may have these initials in their names—G, P, Y.

Tuesday, January 11 (Moon in Pisces)   In the midst of confusion, you arrive at the truth—you discern the need for timing and added responsibility, and you take the lead in making this knowledge crystal clear to others. As a result, the focus will be on production, promotion, and a valid opportunity to increase your income. Your lucky number is 8.

Wednesday, January 12 (Moon in Pisces to Aries 1:48 p.m.) Within 24 hours, many of your desires, hopes, and aspirations could be fulfilled. Tonight, make clear your intentions, permitting a special person to save face. Plans suddenly are solid; you no longer are a prisoner of inertia or preconceived notions. Lucky lottery: 9, 19, 29, 40, 50, 51.

Thursday, January 13 (Moon in Aries) The Aries moon relates to the eleventh sector of your horoscope, so focus on your ability to win friends and influence people and to have luck in money and love. It has been observed that some people with this aspect do not appreciate it or make the most of it. This will not be in your case—you will be a big winner!

Friday, January 14 (Moon in Aries to Taurus 7:38 p.m.) Focus on direction, motivation, and your ability to know a good thing when you see it. There's much speculation regarding your home, security, family, and marital status. You'll muse, "Finally I see my way clear—I do know why I am here!" A Cancer will play an interesting role.

Saturday, January 15 (Moon in Taurus) Luck rides with you! These numbers could be fortunate—3, 2, 20. The Taurus moon represents glamour, intrigue, mystery, and discovering your hidden wealth. Sagittarius and another Gemini play roles, and are likely to have these initials in their names—C, L, U. A Saturday to remember!

Sunday, January 16 (Moon in Taurus to Gemini 10:25 p.m.) Revise, review, rewrite, remodel—and accept the challenge of being new and different. The Taurus moon represents delicious secrets. You'll dine in an out-of-the-way place. Taurus, Leo, and Scorpio figure in this scenario, and will have these letters in their names—D, M, V.

Monday, January 17 (Moon in Gemini) It's your cycle high, so designate where the action will be, imprint your style, read and write, and disseminate information. A flirtation is featured that could amount to fun and frolic, but could also be more serious than you originally anticipated. Take nothing for granted; don't permit anyone to take you for granted!

Tuesday, January 18 (Moon in Gemini to Cancer 11:01 p.m.)   The spotlight revolves around your home, your ability to beautify your surroundings, and the acquisition of an art object or a luxury item—or both. A family member reveals the good news regarding your income. Music is involved, so dance to your own tune. Your voice is different, pleasing, and compelling. Libra is in this picture.

Wednesday, January 19 (Moon in Cancer)   Lucky lottery: 7, 12, 17, 2, 4, 6. The lunar position highlights basic structure and design, along with your ability to increase your earnings. There's fine dining tonight. A family member suggests, "Let us be more of a family from tonight on!" Pisces and Virgo are in the picture, and have these letters in their names—G, P, Y.

Thursday, January 20 (Moon in Cancer to Leo 10:59 p.m.)   Lucky numbers: 8, 12, 2. The focus is on responsibility and meeting a deadline. An intense relationship survives, despite emotional fireworks. You'll be dealing with people who know plenty about money and how to earn it. Listen and learn, but avoid being obsequious. Capricorn is involved.

Friday, January 21 (Moon in Leo)   The full moon, lunar eclipse, falls in Leo, so take special care in traffic and be careful of what you say—a snide remark intended to be humorous will be taken seriously. Relatives are especially sensitive, so steer clear of disputes involving religion and politics. Aries plays a dynamic role.

Saturday, January 22 (Moon in Leo)   You prove that you can beat the game. Focus on speculation, physical attractiveness, and sex appeal, leading to a romance that is exciting beyond your dreams. No doubt, it'll be a Saturday night you won't soon forget! Imprint your style, refusing to follow others. Take a risk involving future prospects requiring a pioneering spirit. Your fortunate number is 1.

Sunday, January 23 (Moon in Leo to Virgo 12:08 a.m.) On this Sunday, be with people who are important to you. Agreements can be reached concerning the sale or purchase of property, a business partnership, or marriage. The emphasis is on direction, motivation, and learning how far you can go in trusting someone who has captured your heart. A Cancer is involved.

Monday, January 24 (Moon in Virgo) What a Monday! The telephone rings, bringing an invitation to attend a special meeting or social affair tonight. You'll be musing, "No other Monday has ever started in this lively way!" A Sagittarius and another Gemini play featured roles, and they could have these letters in their names— C, L, U.

Tuesday, January 25 (Moon in Virgo to Libra 4:10 a.m.) The Libra moon relates to children, challenge, change, variety, and the creative process. You'll express an interest in theater and drama, and consider the possibility of acting lessons. Check your references. Be selective, choosing quality over quantity. Taurus, Leo, and Scorpio are in this picture, and they may have these letters in their names—D, M, V.

Wednesday, January 26 (Moon in Libra) Everything appears to add up to excitement, adventure, exploration, and creativity. You won't be standing still—even if you don't move an inch geographically! Your mind and your creative processes are revved up, and you'll exude an aura of sensuality, fitness, and sex appeal. You will have luck with these numbers: 3, 2, 5.

Thursday, January 27 (Moon in Libra to Scorpio 12:02 p.m.) There are needed repairs that can wait for tomorrow—save tonight for creative expression in romance. Focus on domestic issues, art, music, literature and a possible encounter with a Libran who fascinates you—and will be fascinated by you in return. Aries also plays a role.

Friday, January 28 (Moon in Scorpio)   Focus on the need for additional time. Someone who hesitates to give the answers to direct questions should be suspect—play your cards close to your chest. Be cautious in traffic, more so than usual. Also take care in places near water, especially swimming pools.

Saturday, January 29 (Moon in Scorpio to Sagittarius 11:18 p.m.)   An apparent casual acquaintance wants more then mere friendship—be aware of it and protect yourself in close quarters. Capricorn and Cancer figure in today's scenario, and they will have these letters in their names: H, Q, Z. An engine problem in your automobile can be corrected if you are selective in choosing a mechanic.

Sunday, January 30 (Moon in Sagittarius)   The spotlight falls on distance, language, travel, communication, and participation in a humanitarian project. Mail previously unopened reveals the story of people in dire straits. Open your heart, realizing that The Golden Rule is more than a mere saying. Aries and Libra are in this picture, and have these initials in names—I and R.

Monday, January 31 (Moon in Sagittarius)   Make a fresh start in a different direction—let your spiritual values surface. The Sagittarian moon relates to contacts with people associated with legal affairs. Focus on publicity, public relations, and tests of integrity. This lunar position highlights cooperative efforts and marriage.

FEBRUARY 2000

Tuesday, February 1 (Moon in Sagittarius to Capricorn 12:10 p.m.)   On this first day of February, Saturn dominates. The moon is in your eighth house, which means that you should be cautious without being timid. Be open minded without being gullible. Deal with the element of time, for a deadline must be met. A Cancer will play an outstanding role.

Wednesday, February 2 (Moon in Capricorn) Free yourself from the tentacles of someone who would like to exploit you. Your financial picture is puzzling. Dig deep for information; get the facts about tax and license requirements. A love relationship improves following or during a journey. Aries and Libra figure in this dynamic scenario.

Thursday, February 3 (Moon in Capricorn) Let go of the status quo, shaking off any tendency to be lethargic. Focus on mystery, intrigue, and a fresh start in a new direction. A lost article is located once you stop looking. The message tonight becomes crystal clear. A young person is involved. Leo and Aquarius round out this fascinating scenario.

Friday, February 4 (Moon in Capricorn to Aquarius 12:31 a.m.) Back on familiar ground, memories of travel persist. Attendance at a conference devoted to publishing or education will prove fruitful and could result in meeting your soulmate. Cancer and Capricorn are in the picture, and have these letters in their names—B, K, T.

Saturday, February 5 (Moon in Aquarius) Lucky lottery: 11, 7, 17, 22, 33, 18. The new moon and solar eclipse in Aquarius tells of disturbances in connection with future prospects, as well as problems in traffic, both air and ground. Forces are scattered, so don't attempt to do everything at once and do not try to please everyone.

Sunday, February 6 (Moon in Aquarius to Pisces 11:02 a.m.) Within a matter of hours, the lunar position will promote your hopes, wishes, and desires as well as the ability to win friends and influence people. You are on a roll—this could be the start of something big. Taurus, Leo, and Scorpio will figure in today's dramatic scenario.

Monday, February 7 (Moon in Pisces)   Words, both verbal and written, will play important roles. The moon position verifies that this is your day to win big. You'll have luck in matters of speculation, and people will be entranced by your ability to pick long-shot winners. Your fortunate number is 5.

Tuesday, February 8 (Moon in Pisces to Aries 7:18 p.m.)   Attention revolves around expenses in connection with decorating, remodeling, beautifying your surroundings, and carrying on a courtship. You'll be musing, "I never would have predicted this kind of Tuesday!" A domestic adjustment involves where you live and your marital status.

Wednesday, February 9 (Moon in Aries)   Lucky lottery: 7, 1, 10, 19, 12, 18. Define your terms and find out what is expected of you and what you can anticipate in return. Look before leaping. See people, places, and relationships as they are and not merely as you wish they might be. A mysterious Pisces will play a fascinating role.

Thursday, February 10 (Moon in Aries)   The emphasis is on power, responsibility, challenge, and a relationship that heats up. The Aries moon represents your eleventh house, which means that you can expect action in connection with romance, pioneering efforts, and your ability to erase past errors. Someone important to your career will declare, "You most certainly have proven yourself a valuable asset!"

Friday, February 11 (Moon in Aries to Taurus 1:21 a.m.)   Look beyond the immediate, unlocking a door that previously was shut tight. Missing mementos will be found; photographs that you thought lost for good will reappear almost as if by magic. Finish what you start, paying special attention to language, where people live, and how they respond to money and love.

230

Saturday, February 12 (Moon in Taurus)   Your cycle is such that areas of life previously dark will receive more light. Do not fear the unknown! A relative recently returned from a trip has much to say, and is fascinating though slightly arrogant, and must be catered to if peace is to reign. Leo is in this picture. Your lucky number is 1.

Sunday, February 13 (Moon in Taurus to Gemini 5:23 a.m.)   The moon in your sign represents a time when you are at the right place in an almost magical manner. Events transpire to bring you closer to your goal of fulfillment. Even as you read these lines, circumstances move in your favor. Make personal appearances, letting people know there are two ways of doing things—"The wrong way and my way!"

Monday, February 14 (Moon in Gemini)   Elements of timing and luck continue to ride with you, so highlight your diversity and versatility. Make inquiries and demand answers, not evasions. Sagittarius and another Gemini play meaningful roles, and will have these letters in their names—C, L, U. Look for many Valentine cards—you'll get them!

Tuesday, February 15 (Moon in Gemini to Cancer 7:46 a.m.)   For racing luck, these selections apply at all tracks: Post position special—number 4 p.p. in the fourth race. Pick six: 1, 2, 8, 4, 3, 5. Look for these letters in the names of potential winning horses or jockeys: D, M, V. Hot daily doubles: 1 and 2, 4 and 4, 8 and 3. Scorpio jockeys have racing luck.

Wednesday, February 16 (Moon in Cancer)   Lucky lottery: 5, 15, 16, 2, 12, 20. Today's scenario highlights mobility and variety. A flirtation lends spice and could also provide inspiration. The financial picture relates to efforts made four months ago. A dinner invitation is extended. Improve relations with a Cancer by accepting.

Thursday, February 17 (Moon in Cancer to Leo 9:12 a.m.)   Attention revolves around your personal environment and money spent to beautify your surroundings.

You receive a gift representing a token of esteem. The cycle is such that you make the right moves at a crucial moment. People ask, "How did you do it?" Your honest response: "I don't know, it just happened!"

Friday, February 18 (Moon in Leo)   Lie low; play the waiting game. Be especially careful in traffic—some drivers apparently are intent on blocking your way or causing accidents. Pisces and Virgo play significant roles and could have these letters in their names—G, P, Y.

Saturday, February 19 (Moon in Leo to Virgo 10:54 a.m.)   On this Saturday, with the full moon and Saturn keynote, you accomplish what previously seemed impossible. Trips, visits, relatives, and party time seem to coalesce. The quest for success suddenly appears within reach, as the right people will no longer be out when you call. Your fortunate number is 8.

Sunday, February 20 (Moon in Virgo)   The Mars keynote and Virgo moon tell of the completion of negotiations, property value, and a reunion with a family member who is dynamic, inventive, and at times bombastic. Realize that this too shall pass. Put the finishing touches on a project. Make plans for a display. Aries plays a top role.

Monday, February 21 (Moon in Virgo to Libra 2:21 p.m.)   The key is to be perceptive and to use your powers of analysis. Be aware of body language and subtle innuendoes. Express yourself, be who you are. Don't imitate or plagiarize. Leo and Aquarius figure in this fascinating scenario, and are likely to have these letters in their names—A, S, J.

Tuesday, February 22 (Moon in Libra)   For racing luck, these selections apply at all tracks: Post position special—number 6 p.p. in the fifth race. Pick six: 2, 2, 1, 4, 6, 8. Look for these letters in the names of potential winning horses or jockeys: B, K, T. Hot daily doubles: 2 and 2, 4 and 2, 2 and 7. Cancer jockeys ride favorites and win.

Wednesday, February 23 (Moon in Libra to Scorpio 8:58 p.m.) The Libra moon promotes a variety of experiences and romantic episodes. Dinner and dance music would fit the bill. An air of frivolity exists, so be serious without having a long face. A smile and light banter will get you everywhere! Sagittarius and another Gemini will play featured roles. Your lucky number is 3.

Thursday, February 24 (Moon in Scorpio) If you are patient, you win. If you lose your cool, you lose. Today's scenario highlights details, as well as the necessity for proofreading and reading between the lines. A Taurus helps you overcome fear, doubt, and apprehension. Work gets done as a result of cooperation from someone previously distant.

Friday, February 25 (Moon in Scorpio) The Scorpio moon relates to basic issues, care of pets, and dealing with someone who is passionate toward you but who in actuality leaves you cold. Be diplomatic, without watering down your principles or feelings. It's an excellent day for reading and writing, disseminating information, and reporting on current events.

Saturday, February 26 (Moon in Scorpio to Sagittarius 7:10 a.m.) Within 24 hours, your attention will revolve around legal matters, credibility and reliability, and proposals that include partnership and marriage. Tonight, the emphasis is on lifestyle, gifts, and music, the need to control your sweet tooth. Taurus, Libra, and Scorpio are in this picture, and they may have these initials in their names—F, O, X.

Sunday, February 27 (Moon in Sagittarius) Appropriately, spiritual values surface. You'll explain your religious feelings in a way that enlightens rather than offends. People comment, "When you discuss theology, you inspire, so you should have a pulpit of your own!" The Sagittarian moon coincides with serious consideration of your future prospects in connection with partnership or marriage.

Monday, February 28 (Moon in Sagittarius to Capricorn 7:45 p.m.) Results! Previous efforts pay dividends, so focus on production, promotion, and the successful exploitation of your product, or talent. Wear dark colors. Proceed in your campaign to obtain funding for a unique project. A Cancer and a Capricorn play instrumental roles, and they may have these letters in their names—H, Q, Z.

Tuesday, February 29 (Moon in Capricorn) On this "leap day," you locate missing objects. You learn once and for all where you stand in the romance department. No matter what the answer, the truth will set you free! Look beyond the immediate. Communicate with someone in a distant city or foreign land.

MARCH 2000

Wednesday, March 1 (Moon in Capricorn) On this Wednesday, the first day of March, the moon is in Capricorn, Mars keynote, indications that point to universality and the need to break free from the prison of inertia. Your contacts and friendships broaden on a day of action, not mere contemplation.

Thursday, March 2 (Moon in Capricorn to Aquarius 8:14 a.m.) Make a fresh start in a new direction. Enlightenment replaces puzzlement, especially in areas of tax and license requirements. You also learn more about the financial status of someone who would be your partner or mate. Be sure to say, "Let me examine the books!"

Friday, March 3 (Moon in Aquarius) Focus on direction and motivation. The Aquarian moon relates to communication, travel, idealism, theology. An unorthodox visitor causes talk, but makes up for it with amusing anecdotes. Do not rush to judgment! Cancer and Capricorn play leading roles, and have these letters in their names—B, K, T.

Saturday, March 4 (Moon in Aquarius to Pisces 6:31 p.m.) Social activities accelerate and your popularity increases. Your curiosity is spurred by a charming Sagittarius. Be up-to-date on fashion and current events, for your opinions will be sought. You could be interviewed by the media. Gemini will also play a provocative role. Your lucky number is 3.

Sunday, March 5 (Moon in Pisces) You might be musing, "This is not like any Sunday I expected!" Details unravel in connection with a mystery. A decision is reached in connection with decorating, remodeling, or the process of rebuilding. Taurus, Leo, and Scorpio figure in this scenario, and have these letters in their names—D, M, V.

Monday, March 6 (Moon in Pisces) The new moon in Pisces represents career motivation and conferences with an older person, possibly your teacher, employer, or father. The written word plays a major role. Virgo, Sagittarius, and another Gemini figure in this dynamic scenario, and may have these letters in their names—E, N, W.

Tuesday, March 7 (Moon in Pisces to Aries 1:55 a.m.) The Aries moon relates to your eleventh sector, that area of your horoscope that concerns friends, the fulfillment of desires, and good fortune in finance and romance. Attention revolves around your domestic environment and the acquisition of an art object or luxury item.

Wednesday, March 8 (Moon in Aries) Focus on your ability to perceive the truth in a relationship. Terms are defined, so find out what is expected from you and what you might anticipate in return. An element of deception is present, so protect yourself at close quarters. Pisces and Virgo play outstanding roles, and have these initials in their names—G, P, Y.

Thursday, March 9 (Moon in Aries to Taurus 7:02 a.m.) For racing luck, these selections apply at all tracks: Post position special—number 8 p.p. in the ninth race. Pick six: 8, 5, 1, 7, 4, 4. Look for these letters in the names of potential winning horses or jockeys: H, Q, Z. Hot daily doubles: 8 and 5, 4 and 4, 1 and 7. Veteran jockeys ride favorites into the Winner's Circle.

Friday, March 10 (Moon in Taurus) Focus on completing a project, gaining prestige, and investigating the possibility of promoting a product or talent in a foreign land. The emphasis is on showmanship, communication, and expressions of love. Aries and Libra play fascinating roles, and are likely to have these letters in their names—I and R.

Saturday, March 11 (Moon in Taurus to Gemini 10:46 a.m.) Lucky lottery: 11, 2, 20, 22, 3, 5. The answer to question: Extricate yourself from an untenable situation, making a fresh start in a new direction. Make personal appearances, wearing blends of yellow and gold. Make room for adventure and romance. A Leo will play outstanding role.

Sunday, March 12 (Moon in Gemini) Close scrutiny is required in connection with a division of property. Circumstances move in your favor. You'll be at the right place at a crucial moment—almost effortlessly. The moon in your sign emphasizes personality and sex appeal. A Cancer and another Gemini will dominate this exciting scenario.

Monday, March 13 (Moon in Gemini to Cancer 1:52 p.m.) There's something to celebrate tonight! Domestic relationships stabilize. The Jupiter keynote symbolizes transformation of a controversy into a joyous harmony. Sagittarius and another Gemini are in featured roles, and they have these letters in their names: C, L, U. You'll have luck with the number 3.

Tuesday, March 14 (Moon in Cancer) Proofreading is necessary—it will also be to your advantage to read between the lines. The moon in Cancer represents income potential, the ability to locate lost articles, and an opportunity to encounter a member of the opposite sex destined to play a major role in your life.

Wednesday, March 15 (Moon in Cancer to Leo 4:44 p.m.)   Lucky lottery: 15, 22, 3, 4, 40, 13. Financial gain is indicated through the use of words, both verbal and written. Be an investigative reporter. Find out why things happened, rejecting superficial explanations. A short trip is necessary in connection with a relative who seeks help in locating a legal document.

Thursday, March 16 (Moon in Leo)   Attention revolves around what is precious to you. Take care when handling crystal, dishes, and art objects. Focus on where you live, your marital status, and obtaining your money's worth. Taurus and Libra figure in this scenario, and may have these letters in their names—F, O, X.

Friday, March 17 (Moon in Leo to Virgo 7:49 p.m.)   On this St. Patrick's Day, you find yourself with relatives, some of whom might not know the meaning of moderation. Refuse to drive with heavy drinkers. Find out where you are going and why, refusing to become involved in a wild-goose chase. Pisces plays a dynamic role.

Saturday, March 18 (Moon in Virgo)   Lucky lottery: 18, 6, 5, 50, 32, 36. The Virgo moon relates to your home and property, and to one completion of long-term negotiations. The spotlight falls on added responsibility, more authority, and the chance to hit the financial jackpot. Be aware of a deadline—meet it and beat it under budget.

Sunday, March 19 (Moon in Virgo to Libra 10:57 p.m.)   On this Sunday, reach beyond the immediate, permitting spiritual values to surface. A long-standing block to progress will be removed, freeing you to create, to travel, and to love. During a journey to attend a conference, you could encounter someone destined to play an important role in your life.

Monday, March 20 (Moon in Libra)   The full moon relates to more freedom of thought and action. Within 24 hours, the puzzle pieces fall into place—you will imprint your own personality and style. Focus on children, challenge, change, and a variety of sensations. Leo and Aquarius are involved.

Tuesday, March 21 (Moon in Libra)   The Libra moon relates to that area of your horoscope associated with creativity, passion, and physical attraction. The moon keynote emphasizes style, panache, romance, and learning once and for all that you are attractive and desirable. A young person expresses undying gratitude.

Wednesday, March 22 (Moon in Libra to Scorpio 6:17 a.m.)   For racing luck, these selections apply at all tracks: Post position special—number 7 p.p. in the first race. Pick six: 1, 7, 3, 4, 1, 5. Look for these letters in the names of potential winning horses or jockeys: C, L, U. Hot daily doubles: 1 and 7, 3 and 3, 5 and 4. Gemini and Sagittarius jockeys will be in the Winner's Circle.

Thursday, March 23 (Moon in Scorpio)   Get ready to revise, rewrite, and rebuild to get your basic issues settled, especially those involving a Scorpio. Questions revolve around money, payments, and a possible inheritance. Someone who once professed love will now act as if you are a stranger. Stay cool.

Friday, March 24 (Moon in Scorpio to Sagittarius 3:43 p.m.)   Focus on communication, reading and writing, and disseminating information. Keep resolutions concerning exercise, diet, and nutrition—your fitness report will turn out to be excellent. A flirtation could exceed the proscribed limits. Know when to say, "Enough is enough!"

Saturday, March 25 (Moon in Sagittarius)   Attention revolves around your ability to entertain people who did you favors in recent past. Stick close to home base if possible. No matter how far you might wander, you'll need to return to familiar ground. Missing keys are involved; another Gemini lends support.

Sunday, March 26 (Moon in Sagittarius)   Look beyond the immediate, realizing that what you have been seeking will be at your doorstep. A lost love returns. The Sagittarian moon represents confirmation of your views and your marital status. Pisces and Virgo figure in this scenario, and have these initials in their names—G, P, Y.

Monday, March 27 (Moon in Sagittarius to Capricorn 3:52 a.m.)   Get your priorities in order. Find out exactly who is to pay for what. Deal with someone familiar with budgets and tax and license requirements. Sweep aside opposition by showing all the facts and figures. Capricorn and Cancer figure in this scenario, and have these initials in their names—H, Q, Z.

Tuesday, March 28 (Moon in Capricorn)   For racing luck, these selections apply to all tracks: Post position special—number 8 p.p. in the first race. Pick six: 8, 1, 7, 2, 4, 8. Look for these letters in the names of potential winning horses or jockeys: H, Q, Z. Hot daily doubles: 8 and 1, 3 and 6, 4 and 5. Aries jockeys ride speed horses and will be in the money.

Wednesday, March 29 (Moon in Capricorn to Aquarius 4:35 p.m.)   Lucky lottery: 29, 1, 18, 17, 27, 38. Within 24 hours, your views are verified and you'll win allies among the high and mighty. Focus on distance, language, and the ability to comprehend abstract, complex subjects. What you dreamed last night contains prophetic symbols.

Thursday, March 30 (Moon in Aquarius)   A Cancer becomes your staunch ally, despite personal differences. The Aquarian moon relates to philosophy, theology, travel, exploration, and discovery. The moon keynote represents a reunion with your family, as well as a decision regarding the sale or purchase of property. A question concerns marriage.

Friday, March 31 (Moon in Aquarius)   This Friday represents an opportunity for showing appreciation for a gift received, relating to art. Focus on diversity, versatility, humor, and intelligence in deciding questions about one value of property. A Sagittarius and another Gemini will play vital roles, and may have these letters in their names—C, L, U.

APRIL 2000

Saturday, April 1 (Moon in Aquarius to Pisces 3:13 a.m.)   A fun-loving Leo takes April Fool's Day seriously—don't believe everything you hear! The Pisces moon represents your career, ambition, production, and promotion. The answer to your question: Yes, a fresh start is in order. Show what you can do! Lucky lottery: 28, 10, 50, 13, 12, 22.

Sunday, April 2—Daylight Saving Time (Moon in Pisces)   A family relationship is under strain. The focus continues on direction, motivation, business plans, and opportunities. Sunday dining with your family proves pleasant and beneficial. After a Cancer makes a declaration of loyalty, others follow suit. A Capricorn observes, "A good meal and good wine solves all problems. Ain't that the truth?"

Monday, April 3 (Moon in Pisces to Aries 11:33 a.m.)   The moon gets ready to enter the area of your horoscope relating to fulfillment and good fortune in finance and romance. Tonight, make it clear that you don't intend to be part of a nefarious scheme or an unsavory relationship. A Sagittarius and another Gemini play leading roles.

Tuesday, April 4 (Moon in Aries)   The new moon in your eleventh sector means that you now can win friends

240

and influence people in ways that were previously difficult to imagine. Taurus, Leo, and Scorpio figure in this
dynamic scenario, and are likely to have these letters in
their names—D, M, V.

*Wednesday, April 5 (Moon in Aries to Taurus 3:30
p.m.)*   On this Wednesday you could have luck with
these numbers—5, 3, 2. The emphasis is also on learning
by teaching, and using words to your advantage, both
verbal and written. A flirtation lends spice, and it could
lead to something much more serious. Virgo plays a role.

Thursday, April 6 (Moon in Taurus)   Attention revolves around beauty, art, music, and a domestic adjustment that proves pleasant and beneficial. A Taurus
confides a secret and lends an aura of glamour. A Libra
says, "When I am with you, I have a feeling of exaltation!" You'll luck with the number 6.

*Friday, April 7 (Moon in Taurus to Gemini 3:59
p.m.)*   On this Friday, overcome a tendency to brood,
transforming your dark mood into positive meditation.
An intuitive flash is rare and beautiful. You will experience it and know why you are here, where you are going,
and what to do about it. Pisces is in this picture.

Saturday, April 8 (Moon in Gemini)   Lucky lottery:
8, 51, 35, 6, 16, 22. Get your priorities lined up. Accept
the challenge of overtime work. A relationship is exciting and controversial, and it will prove durable. Capricorn and Cancer figure in this dramatic scenario and
could have these letters in their names—H, Q, Z.

*Sunday, April 9 (Moon in Gemini to Cancer 8:16
p.m.)*   Speculation revolves around a possible overseas journey. The moon in your sign relates to your intuitive intellect and initiative, responding to your high
cycle by being at the right place at a crucial moment.
Aries and Libra offer suggestions and assure you they
will be loyal. They could have these letters in their
names: I and R.

Monday, April 10 (Moon in Cancer)   An investment opportunity should not be overlooked. A Leo claims to have inside information—try it, at least this one time! Special: Avoid lifting heavy objects. Make room for a new, different kind of love, refusing to limit your imagination or your inspiration.

Tuesday, April 11 (Moon in Cancer to Leo 9:16 p.m.)   For racing luck, these selections apply at all tracks: Post position special—number 6 p.p. in the fifth race. Pick six: 2, 2, 1, 5, 6, 7. Watch for these letters in the names of potential winning horses or jockeys: B, K, T. Hot daily doubles: 2 and 2, 6 and 5, 3 and 8. Cancer-born jockeys come from behind to win photo finishes.

Wednesday, April 12 (Moon in Leo)   The elements of timing and luck ride with you. In matters of speculation, stick with the number 3. A Leo provides a legitimate shortcut. Highlight humor, diversity, versatility, and the thrill of exploration and discovery. Sagittarius and another Gemini figure in this scenario.

Thursday, April 13 (Moon in Leo)   You're on solid ground, so be confident, refusing to give up something of value for a mere temporary thrill. Many persons regard you tonight as a bulwark against ignorance and prejudice. Although you do not seek that role, accept it with dignity. Scorpio dominates this scenario.

Friday, April 14 (Moon in Leo to Virgo 3:19 a.m.)   The Virgo moon relates to your property values. A family member is engaged in a long-term negotiation and your role is to serve as a morale booster. Mercury is the ruling planet for both you and Virgo, bringing unspoken understanding and sympathy. A clash of ideas proves stimulating. Don't feel you must agree on everything.

Saturday, April 15 (Moon in Virgo)   Be diplomatic, avoiding forcing the issues and seeking a reunion with a family member has felt neglected. Special: Remember recent resolutions about exercise, diet, and nutrition.

Your sweet tooth fights back, but don't let it win! Music is involved, so listen and enjoy. Your lucky number is 6.

Sunday, April 16 (Moon in Virgo to Libra 8:36 a.m.) On this Sunday, your spiritual values surface. The moon is in the last degree of Virgo. The dominant digit is 7. Synchronized, this adds up to critical analyses of a recent recurring dream involving water and a possible confession of infidelity. Pisces plays the top role.

Monday, April 17 (Moon in Libra) What a Monday! Just when one mountain has been climbed, another challenge appears. The emphasis is on elements of timing and surprise—pressure is exerted by someone who seems intent on getting their money's worth. A relationship is strong and controversial, but ultimately durable.

Tuesday, April 18 (Moon in Libra to Scorpio 3:36 p.m.) For racing luck, these selections apply at all tracks: Post position special—number 8 p.p. in the ninth race. Pick six: 3, 6, 7, 1, 8, 2. Be alert for these letters in the names of potential winning horses or jockeys: I and R. Hot daily doubles: 3 and 6, 4 and 7, 8 and 1. Aries jockeys ride speed horses and will be in the money.

Wednesday, April 19 (Moon in Scorpio) Make a fresh start in a new direction. A coworker declares, "I would not be here if it were not for you!" The sixth-house emphasis highlights fitness and your ability to get the job done. Imprint your style, accenting originality and independence of thought and action. Your lucky number is 1.

Thursday, April 20 (Moon in Scorpio) On this Thursday, attention revolves around cooperative efforts, and discussions that include partnership and the possibility of going into business or changing your marital status. There's a sumptuous dinner tonight—it might be swordfish accompanied by new potatoes. Capricorn plays a role.

243

Friday, April 21 (Moon in Scorpio to Sagittarius 12:59 a.m.) Dig deep for information. Attend a social gathering during which you might meet your future mate—or maybe even your soulmate. A legal dilemma requires close scrutiny. The law is on your side, but take nothing for granted. A Sagittarian expresses true feelings.

Saturday, April 22 (Moon in Sagittarius) For racing luck, these selections apply at all tracks: Post position special—number 4 p.p. in the fourth race. Pick six: 1, 4, 2, 4, 1, 8. Watch for these letters in the names of potential winning horses or jockeys: D, M, V. Hot daily doubles: 1 and 4, 4 and 4, 5 and 8. Taurus and Scorpio jockeys could ride and win with long shots.

Sunday, April 23 (Moon in Sagittarius to Capricorn 12:48 p.m.) This could be your last chance to express your views about marriage—sparks of attraction fly and a clash of ideas is exciting and dynamic. Don't let a good thing get away! Within 24 hours, this scenario undergoes an abrupt change—things become less romantic, more practical, and possibly even profitable. Sagittarius is involved.

Monday, April 24 (Moon in Capricorn) The Capricorn moon relates to your interest in the occult, handling other people's money, and forming an opinion on the afterlife. This entire scenario is one of discovery and exploration as you dig deep for information and stand tall for the truth. Libra will play a dramatic role.

Tuesday, April 25 (Moon in Capricorn) Define your terms, finding out exactly what is expected of you and what you might anticipate in return. Something has been kept hidden, so speak up, find out what it is, then decide what to do about it. Questions revolve around investments, inheritance, and financial procedures.

Wednesday, April 26 (Moon in Capricorn to Aquarius 1:43 a.m.) The Aquarian moon relates to travel, publishing, and questions about theology, theosophy, and the mantic arts and sciences. Your priorities fall into place. Refuse to be awed by someone who plays the role of big shot. Capricorn and Cancer figure in major shakeups. You will have luck with the number 8.

Thursday, April 27 (Moon in Aquarius)   Stress universality. Look forward to a reunion with someone who has played an important role in your life. Focus on the adventure of discovering how the other half lives, including the other half of the world. Don't be limited by those who lack vision, faith, and inspiration.

Friday, April 28 (Moon in Aquarius to Pisces 1:06 p.m.)   Long-range prospects come into sharp, clear focus. Obtain the necessary signatures and legal documents. An immigration law could figure prominently. A fiery Leo relates stories, some of which fall into the category of tall tales. Be amused rather than confused. Your lucky number is 1.

Saturday, April 29 (Moon in Pisces)   On this Saturday, business mixes with pleasure. Focus on proposals, either career and marriage. You'll be feted as people vie to be in your company. There's an excellent dining experience tonight, featuring charcoal-broiled lamb chops. A Cancer is involved.

Sunday, April 30 (Moon in Pisces to Aries 8:55 p.m.)   On this last Sunday of April, you'll be provided with information relating to a promotion, production, or career advancement. You will be saying a nostalgic good-bye to April—Sagittarius and another Gemini form a team that is exciting, productive, and creative. You will have luck with the number 3.

MAY 2000

Monday, May 1 (Moon in Aries)   Prepare for the great conjunction and lunar aspects to take place on the 3rd and 4th—today, strengthen your personal beliefs and convictions. Deal gingerly with Cancer and Capricorn who are likely to have these letters in their names—B, K, T.

Tuesday, May 2 (Moon in Aries)   The stock markets act as if suddenly gone mad. Pay personal attention to your investments, protecting your possessions and being aware of the need for future security. There is world turmoil in a matter of days—self-reliance will be of special importance. Sagittarius and another Gemini play leading roles.

Wednesday, May 3 (Moon in Aries to Taurus 12:54 a.m.)   An important conjunction gets under way, as much that happens will be kept secret in the beginning. It will be once again as if the government was keeping news of UFOs confidential. However, this has to do with world markets, not flying saucers or invasions from Mars. Scorpio plays a featured role.

Thursday, May 4 (Moon in Taurus)   Keep your plans flexible. The lunar position highlights what occurs behind your back. Deviousness is involved. Don't be paranoid, but at the same time, don't be too willing to trust others. There will be shakeups all around you. Be willing to help others, but also protect your own assets and possessions. Virgo is represented.

Friday, May 5 (Moon in Taurus to Gemini 2:24 a.m.)   Attention revolves around your home, family, security, and threats that come from who knows where. The spotlight falls on cause, delineation, and synchyronicity—come to terms with who you are, why you are here, and what your prospects are for the future. Taurus, Libra, and Scorpio are in the picture, and have these letters in their names—F, O, X.

Saturday, May 6 (Moon in Gemini)   The moon in your sign highlights your initiative, personality, sensuality, creativity, and sex appeal. Your timing is on target, as people look to you for leadership. Attention revolves around your family, home, safety measures, love, and marriage. Pisces, and Virgo play outstanding roles and have these letters in their names—G, P, Y.

Sunday, May 7 (Moon in Gemini to Cancer 3:14 a.m.)   On this Sunday there is a blend of spirituality and practicality. Ideas are exchanged and evaluated. It turns out that playing the waiting game is your best policy now. Someone previously arrogant will come to earth and help you set priorities.

Monday, May 8 (Moon in Cancer)   Family requirements take precedence where your budget is concerned. Focus on finances involved with travel, education, and getting your message across to a wider audience. Aries and Libra play leading roles, and will have these letters in their names—I and R.

Tuesday, May 9 (Moon in Cancer to Leo 5:02 a.m.)   For racing luck, these selections apply to all tracks: Post positions special—number 7 p.p. in the third race. Pick six: 1, 7, 7, 2, 5, 3. Look for these letters in the names of potential winning horses or jockeys: A, S, J. Hot daily doubles: 1 and 7, 1 and 1, 5 and 5. Leo jockeys participate in daily-double wins.

Wednesday, May 10 (Moon in Leo)   Lucky lottery: 18, 10, 2, 12, 5, 50. Focus on how you look to the public and how you regard reactions to your efforts and products. The lunar position emphasizes an array of ideas that require time to reach fulfillment. A Cancer is involved.

Thursday, May 11 (Moon in Leo to Virgo 8:42 a.m.)   Your intuitive intellect is honed to razor sharpness. Almost effortlessly, you'll know what to do and when to do it. Within 24 hours, a decision is reached about basic values, property rights, and a fair division. Sagittarius and another Gemini figure in this scenario, with these letters in their names—C, L, U.

Friday, May 12 (Moon in Virgo)   Forces that were scattered will be settled to your advantage. The Virgo moon relates to security, family, and long-term negotiations. You will be dealing with people who have a sharp critical sense—all may not be pleasant, but untimely it will be honest. Taurus and Scorpio are involved.

Saturday, May 13 (Moon in Virgo to Libra 2:28 p.m.)   It's an excellent day for special studies, advertising, writing, and publishing. Give full rein to your intellectual curiosity, making inquiries, asking questions, and finding out where you stand in a love relationship. No need for more guesswork in this department! Your lucky number is 5.

Sunday, May 14 (Moon in Libra)   Focus on your family, harmony in relation to music, and decisions that previously aroused controversy. Be kind without being weak, be open minded, without being gullible. A domestic adjustment is featured that applies to where you live, your income potential, or your marital status.

Monday, May 15 (Moon in Libra to Scorpio 10:18 p.m.)   Go slow, play the waiting game, and maintain an aura of mystery, intrigue, and glamour. The moon in your fifth house denotes personal magnetism, the spark of creativity, and an aura of sensuality and sex appeal. The spotlight is on children, challenge, change, and a variety of sensations. Pisces is involved.

Tuesday, May 16 (Moon in Scorpio)   You'll be musing, "I did not expect to relax on this Tuesday, but I never figured it would be this active and vital!" The Scorpio moon relates to your house of work and repairs, and on the need to cooperate with people who share your interests. Capricorn plays a dynamic role.

Wednesday, May 17 (Moon in Scorpio)   Lucky lottery: 9, 33, 8, 12, 18, 22. Highlight universality. Be a Renaissance person. Expand an area of interests. Acknowledge to yourself that without love, your life is not complete. What was started long ago and was dormant will be revived due to your dedication and inspiration.

Thursday, May 18 (Moon in Scorpio to Sagittarius 8:10 a.m.)   The lunar phase emphasizes closeness in connection with your work and your relationships. Do not attempt to separate yourself from what goes on in the world around you. People depend on you, relying on your decisions and actions. Leo and Aquarius figure in this scenario, and are likely to have these letters in their names—A, S, J.

Friday, May 19 (Moon in Sagittarius)   For racing luck, these selections apply at all tracks: Post position special—number 2 p.p. in the second race. Pick six: 2, 2, 4, 7, 1, 1. Look for these letters in the names of potential winning horses or jockeys: B, K, T. Hot daily doubles: 2 and 2, 7 and 7, 1 and 5. Cancer-born jockeys ride heavily weighted horses to the Winner's Circle.

Saturday, May 20 (Moon in Sagittarius to Capricorn 8:02 p.m.)   Very social! The Sagittarian moon relates to public appearances, acknowledgements of successful efforts, applause, legal agreements, and your marital status. You'll be invited to travel and to present your opinions regarding entertainment and sports. Lucky lottery: 25, 7, 3, 30, 12, 9.

Sunday, May 21 (Moon in Capricorn)   Restrictions and delays ultimately prove favorable. Become knowledgeable about tax and license requirements and investments, as well as the financial status of someone who would like to be close to you. Taurus, Leo, and Scorpio play memorable roles, and they will have these initials in their names—D, M, V.

Monday, May 22 (Moon in Capricorn)   Get ready for a change of itinerary, keeping your plans flexible. You will be chosen to write a program and to present possibilities to potential investors. Today's scenario includes engagement parties and dealing with slick customers. Sagittarius plays a top role.

Tuesday, May 23 (Moon in Capricorn to Aquarius 9:01 a.m.)   Within 24 hours, when the moon moves into

Aquarius, travel will be emphasized, along with speculative ventures and romance. Tonight, you learn whether or not it will be necessary to move furniture. Focus on entertainment at home, discussions relating to property values, and your income potential.

Wednesday, May 24 (Moon in Aquarius)   Lucky lottery: 24, 12, 19, 10, 1. 7. The tendency today will be toward romance—act and respond first and think about it later. However, it will be to your advantage to make room for logic—don't give up something of value for a mere whispered promise. Virgo is represented.

Thursday, May 25 (Moon in Aquarius to Pisces 9:08 p.m.)   On this Thursday, you feel compelled to express to another person questions about love, romance, marriage, and money. Following your initial doubts, fear and embarrassment, you will be assured that you did the right thing and no longer are holding in pent-up feelings. Capricorn is involved.

Friday, May 26 (Moon in Pisces)   Spiritual values surface. You could gain national attention or at the very least promote your product or talent in a way that enables you to knock on the doors of fame and fortune. Get rid of superfluous material; let go of an obligation that you were foolish to assume in the first place.

Saturday, May 27 (Moon in Pisces)   Make a fresh start, resolving that no longer will you be held captive by a guilty conscience. You have earned the right to be free and easy, independent, original, dynamic, and adventurous. Leo and Aquarius will play dramatic roles, and have these letters in their names—A, S, J. Your lucky number is 1.

Sunday, May 28 (Moon in Pisces to Aries 6:08 a.m.)   The spotlight is on decisions involving partnership, public relations, and marriage. The Aries moon relates to your eleventh house, which includes friends, hopes, wishes, and good fortune in matters of finance and romance. You will appeal to the public in general and women specifically—a dinner invitation may be extended by a Cancer.

Monday, May 29 (Moon in Aries)   Exalted feeling, Monday or no Monday! The moon position, Jupiter keynote, guarantees joie de vivre. Special: Remember your resolutions concerning moderation, exercise, diet, and nutrition. Everything goes your way, but don't get in the way of your own luck by abusing it. Sagittarius is involved.

Tuesday, May 30 (Moon in Aries to Taurus 11:03 a.m.)   The moon is leaving Aries—by tomorrow, secrets will be disclosed and confidential material will be in your hands. Tonight, untie the Gordian Knot thread by thread. You will discover that your assets are more valuable than you originally anticipated. A Scorpio will play a dynamic role.

Wednesday, May 31 (Moon in Taurus)   A gift received is under wraps. Interpretation: Someone who presents something of sentimental value may not have been morally free to have done so. The key word is secret; the need for discretion is obvious. Virgo, Sagittarius, and another Gemini figure are in this scenario, with these letters in their names—E, N, W.

JUNE 2000

Thursday, June 1 (Moon in Taurus to Gemini 12:35 p.m.)   Throughout June, your vitality makes a comeback as your personality surfaces. People are fascinated by you and say so. Focus today on publicity, direction, motivation, and a decision relating to partnership or marriage. Sagittarius and another Gemini play instrumental roles.

Friday, June 2 (Moon in Gemini)   What was out of order will be fixed. This cycle is such that events transpire to bring you close to your ultimate goal. The an-

swer to your question: Take the initiative; make a fresh
start; love plays a featured role. The puzzle pieces fall
into place concerning investments, the financial status of
a loved one, and the news of an inheritance.

**Saturday, June 3 (Moon in Gemini to Cancer 12:31
p.m.)**   Lucky lottery: 5, 50, 3, 13, 12, 22. On this Saturday, people vie for your company—you'll hear these
words, "You are so much fun to be with!" You'll also
be complimented on your way with words. At least one
person will comment, "Now you are more like the Gemini I know!"

Sunday, June 4 (Moon in Cancer)   The emphasis is
on where you live, your lifestyle, and your cash flow. A
family member concedes, "You are right; we will do
things your way!" Focus on dealings with a Libran who
once played a major role in your life. Taurus and Scorpio will also figure prominently, with these letters in
their names—F, O, X.

**Monday, June 5 (Moon in Cancer to Leo 12:47
p.m.)**   Monday gets off to a slow start but picks up
steam. The moon in its own sign, Cancer, relates to finding lost articles, your income potential, and being at the
right place in connection with a loved one. Look behind
the scenes for the answers. Transform a tendency to
brood into positive meditation.

Tuesday, June 6 (Moon in Leo)   For racing luck,
these selections apply to all tracks: Post position special—number 8 p.p. in the ninth race. Pick six: 2, 7, 1,
3, 4, 3. Look for these letters in the names of potential
winning horses or jockeys: H, Q, Z. Hot daily doubles:
2 and 7, 4 and 4, 8 and 5. Capricorn and Cancer jockeys
will be in the money.

**Wednesday, June 7 (Moon in Leo to Virgo 2:58
p.m.)**   Lucky lottery: 9, 5, 13, 23, 11, 51. A temporary
separation from a loved one sharpens your anticipation
for a reunion. The scenario highlights travel, language,
and your ability to reach beyond the immediate. Aries

and Libra figure in this scenario, and will have these initials in their names—I and R.

Thursday, June 8 (Moon in Virgo)   Answer: Affirmative. Let go of the status quo, refusing to be the prisoner of inertia. A Virgo will be at your side when and if a crisis occurs. Make personal appearances, wearing bright colors and showing what you can do. Special: Avoid lifting heavy objects.

Friday, June 9 (Moon in Virgo to Libra 8 p.m.) Once again you are concerned with your own selections and opinions. The key is to stop wondering what other people think. Concentrate instead on your own thoughts and actions. A Cancer family member provides information, but some of it is actually misinformation. The question of your marital status looms large.

Saturday, June 10 (Moon in Libra)   You'll have luck with these numbers: 6, 7, 9. Highlight your diversity, experimentation, and intellectual curiosity. Be up to date on current events and fashion. You can charm people in the media. Some will ask, "What is the secret of your popularity?" A Sagittarian is involved.

Sunday, June 11 (Moon in Libra)   On this Sunday, with the moon in Libra, attention revolves around affairs of heart, speculation, a love relationship, and children. Attend to details; get work done early. Tonight is the time to relax with people who appreciate you. Taurus, Leo, and Scorpio are represented.

Monday, June 12 (Moon in Libra to Scorpio 3:56 a.m.)   An enthusiastic Scorpio encourages, "Let's get started on a project and show the world!" The written word is of major importance, so record your ideas and dreams. A flirtation lends spice, but know when to say, "Enough is enough!" Virgo and another Gemini play interesting roles, and have these letters in their names— E, N, W.

Tuesday, June 13 (Moon in Scorpio)   Focus on harmony, music, style, and contact with someone who displays bravado. Remember, "It takes two to tango!" Do not become involved in the emotional problems of others—unless you're careful, you will find yourself taking the blame for something you had nothing to do with.

Wednesday, June 14 (Moon in Scorpio to Sagittarius 2:19 p.m.)   Lucky lottery: 7, 14, 33, 3, 17, 9. Within 24 hours, you will have a clear answer to queries about partnership, legal agreement, and marriage. You are close to the cutting edge of society. You are in the game—decide tonight to play it! Pisces is involved.

Thursday, June 15 (Moon in Sagittarius)   The Sagittarian moon relates to how you appear to the world and what participation in world affairs might mean to you. Focus on your strength of will, responsibility, and your willingness to meet and beat a deadline. The moon position emphasizes working together with someone whose ideas might be opposite your own.

Friday, June 16 (Moon in Sagittarius)   The full moon emphasizes creativity, style, and the conviction that love conquers all. Special: Let go of a burden you had no right to carry in the first place! Be free to explore, travel, engage in creative activities, and love. Aries plays an astonishing role.

Saturday, June 17 (Moon in Sagittarius to Capricorn 2:27 a.m.)   Lucky lottery: 1, 10, 12, 8, 4, 33. The Capricorn moon relates to the occult, which means discovering what had been hidden, your ability to deal with someone who hides wealth. Emphasize independence, courage, originality, and a willingness to make a fresh start in a new direction.

Sunday, June 18 (Moon in Capricorn)   Getting together with a family member who recently was recalcitrant will prove to be the highlight. You'll receive valid information about stocks and bonds, property value, and the character of a person you are enamored with. A Cancer is involved.

Monday, June 19 (Moon in Capricorn to Aquarius 3:26 p.m.)   No Blue Monday for you! Within 24 hours, you might be involved with a travel agent. Tonight, there's fun and frolic. You'll turn on your Gemini charm. Don't scatter your forces, but at the same time, be willing to test and to explore areas previously unknown.

Tuesday, June 20 (Moon in Aquarius)   The Aquarian moon highlights travel, exploration, higher education, spirituality, and learning through the process of teaching others. Stick to the unorthodox. Don't be afraid to face the music played by a bully. This means don't be intimidated! Scorpio plays a dominant role.

Wednesday, June 21 (Moon in Aquarius)   Focus on reading and writing, experimentation, advertising, publishing, and getting your message across. Deal with a quixotic person known for changing his mind at the last minute. Pretend this does not bother you, even if it does. Virgo is involved. Lucky lottery: 50, 12, 18, 22, 13, 46.

Thursday, June 22 (Moon in Aquarius to Pisces 3:52 a.m.)   It will feel like you're coming home. The lunar position emphasizes the joy of return, giving you a reason to celebrate your good fortune in finance and romance. Today's scenario emphasizes the acquisitions of an art object or a luxury item. Someone in your home displays musical talent.

Friday, June 23 (Moon in Pisces)   Be sure the terms are clearly defined; find out what it is you are to do, and what you might anticipate in return. Protect yourself at close quarters. An aura of deception could exist. This could be too much of a good thing—a relationship runs hot and cold. Pisces is represented.

Saturday, June 24 (Moon in Pisces to Aries 1:56 p.m.)   Lucky lottery: 24, 2, 6, 8, 12, 13. What was nebulous will be solid, and you'll wonder, "What did I do that was so right? I wish I knew so that I can repeat it!" Ride with the tide. Don't get in the way of your own luck. Capricorn and Cancer are in the picture, with these letters in their names—H, Q, Z.

Sunday, June 25 (Moon in Aries)   A relationship that was finished will be revived. The Phoenix rises from its own ashes. The Aries moon coincides with your hopes, wishes, and desires. The spark that brought you together with that special person will be reignited. Don't let false pride keep you from saying, "I want to be with you no matter who is right or wrong!"

Monday, June 26 (Moon in Aries to Taurus 8:20 p.m.)   A fresh start! It will seem as if you were reborn. Wear bright colors; speak up; make special appearances; be receptive to the adventure of romance. No matter what your chronological age, you'll be dynamic, lively, and creative, with an amazing display of panache. Your lucky number is 1.

Tuesday, June 27 (Moon in Taurus)   You'll be asking, "Is this déjà vu?" Today's scenario highlights familiar places and faces. Married or single, male or female, your love life prospers. Comfort and security replaces sensationalism. There's an exquisite dining experience tonight, when a Cancer displays culinary skills.

Wednesday, June 28 (Moon in Taurus to Gemini 11:01 p.m.)   Lucky numbers: 12, 22, 18. The Taurus moon relates to secrets, institutions, and the need to communicate with someone temporarily confined to home or hospital. By so doing, the networking process gets under way. Sagittarius and another Gemini play meaningful roles, and may have these letters in their names—C, L, U.

Thursday, June 29 (Moon in Gemini)   The moon in Gemini relates to your high cycle. You have excellent timing and an ability to designate where the action will be. During this cycle, you exude an aura of sensuality and sex appeal. You also will transform humor into profundity. Taurus, Leo, and Scorpio play featured roles.

Friday, June 30 (Moon in Gemini to Cancer 11:11 p.m.) What you started early in the month can be completed on this last day. Circumstances move in your favor, but be selective and discriminating. Choose only the best, despite those who might chortle, "Who in the world do you think you are!" Answer: "I am the best there is and you better know it!"

JULY 2000

Saturday, July 1 (Moon in Cancer) The new moon, solar eclipse, is in the sign of the nation's birthday, Cancer. This serves as reminder of holiday preparations. The Fourth is practically upon you, so focus on costs, preparations and plans, and concerns relating to your income potential and expenses. Scorpio is involved.

Sunday, July 2 (Moon in Cancer to Leo 10:39 p.m.) On this Sunday, you'll experience the euphoria of freedom in connection with thought and action. Reading Thomas Jefferson's Declaration of Independence proves informative and inspiring. People with you today will be disabused of the idea that being patriotic is square. Sagittarius is involved.

Monday, July 3 (Moon in Leo) Attention revolves around your children, challenge, change, intellectual curiosity, and decorations in conjunction with the holiday festivities tomorrow. Taurus, Libra, and Scorpio play outstanding roles, and will have these letters in their names—F, O, X. Your lucky number is 6.

Tuesday, July 4 (Moon in Leo to Virgo 11:20 p.m.) A reunion with a fiery-tempered Leo that occurred yesterday will hold for the holidays. This will be one Fourth of July that you'll not soon forget! A celebration that begins in one home will move to another due to the insistence of a relative. Pisces plays the top role.

Wednesday, July 5 (Moon in Virgo)   On this Wednesday, the keynote is power, authority, and the awareness of a deadline. The moon position highlights your property value, basic issues, and the necessity for repair work. Capricorn and Cancer figure prominently, and they could have these letters in their names—H, Q, Z. Lucky lottery: 22, 33, 8, 18, 9, 50.

Thursday, July 6 (Moon in Virgo)   The keynote is universal appeal, so highlight understanding, and sympathy, being willing to fight if the cause is right. On a personal level, a breakup might happen. But if it does, it is temporary. Love is on the horizon, new or old. Aries plays a significant role, helping to make a major wish come true.

Friday, July 7 (Moon in Virgo to Libra 2:48 a.m.)   The answer to your question: Affirmative. A new love is on the horizon. Highlight independence, letting go of the status quo. The answer is in the sky for you to take a pioneering course. This means do not be afraid to be different—imprint your style, avoid heavy lifting, speak up, wear bright colors, and be ready for a romantic episode.

Saturday, July 8 (Moon in Libra)   For racing luck, these selections apply at all tracks: Post position special—number 6 p.p. in the fifth race. Pick six: 2, 2, 4, 6, 6, 1. Look for these letters in the names of potential winning horses or jockeys: B, K, T. Hot daily doubles: 2 and 2, 1 and 4, 5 and 6. Veteran Cancer-born jockeys ride the favorites and win.

Sunday, July 9 (Moon in Libra to Scorpio 9:49 a.m.)   Blend humor and entertainment with education and greater knowledge of spiritual values. Your unique ability to transform fun into profundity surfaces. People—perhaps too many at once—want to be with you. Sagittarius and another Gemini play leading roles, and they could have these initials in their names—C, L, U.

Monday, July 10 (Moon in Scorpio)   The facts of life become evident, as this day features reality and the puzzle pieces that finally fall into place. Taurus, Leo, and Scorpio play prominent roles, and could have these letters in their names—D, M, V. It's necessary for you to read between the lines!

Tuesday, July 11 (Moon in Scorpio to Sagittarius 8:06 p.m.)   Focus on reading and writing, disseminating information, and using your instinctive knowledge of psychology and astrology. Investigative reports figure prominently, so learn the truth and face the music. Virgo, Sagittarius, and another Gemini are in this scenario.

Wednesday, July 12 (Moon in Sagittarius)   Lucky numbers: 12, 6, 9. Attention revolves around your lifestyle, decorating, remodeling, color coordination, and a decision relating to where you live and your marital status. Special: Remember recent resolutions about exercise, diet, and nutrition. Your fitness report might prove instrumental in achieving your goal.

Thursday, July 13 (Moon in Sagittarius)   On this Thursday, with the Neptune keynote and the moon in Sagittarius, you'll perform what appears to be a miracle, though the miracle is actually a blend of fact and fantasy. The Neptune influence encourages a display of extrasensory perception and psychic phenomena.

Friday, July 14 (Moon in Sagittarius to Capricorn 8:28 a.m.)   For racing luck, these selections apply at all tracks: Post position special—number 9 p.p. in the eighth race. Pick six: 4, 8, 2, 7, 5, 5. Look for these letters in the names of potential winning horses or jockeys: H, Q, Z. Hot daily doubles: 4 and 8, 8 and 8, 2 and 7. Capricorn jockeys win photos finishes.

Saturday, July 15 (Moon in Capricorn)   The answer to your question: Reach beyond the immediate and you will not be deterred by distance or language barriers. A love relationship flourishes during a journey. If you are single, you could meet your soulmate. The Capricorn moon relates to money belonging to others, as well as more knowledge of tax and license requirements.

Sunday, July 16 (Moon in Capricorn to Aquarius 9:27 p.m.)   On this Sunday, you feel refreshed and renewed, and you have knowledge that you can conquer the world if you are ready to give it up. The full moon and lunar eclipse fall in Capricorn, emphasizing a possible inheritance, percentages in connection with a loan, and expressions of physical attraction.

Monday, July 17 (Moon in Aquarius)   An exciting discovery is on the agenda tonight! This could involve a family member who has been hiding wealth. The Aquarian moon relates to information and education in connection with foreign lands, as well as romance involving travel, possibly to attend or participate in an educational conference.

Tuesday, July 18 (Moon in Aquarius)   Do things your way, but make your way unorthodox. Emphasize your intellectual curiosity. Investigate and publish. An unusual connection exists with a university. Focus on diversity, versatility, doing work that brings pleasure, fun, and accelerated social activity. Sagittarius is involved.

Wednesday, July 19 (Moon in Aquarius to Pisces 9:45 a.m.)   Be willing to revise, review, rewrite, and ultimately to tear down in order to rebuild. Within 24 hours, a tempting offer is received. It's not easy to decide, because it means more responsibility and less time at home. A Pisces plays an interesting role and is on the fence about whether or not you should accept.

Thursday, July 20 (Moon in Pisces)   The emphasis continues on appointments, basic resources, and your ability to write your way into and almost out of anything. A flirtation figures prominently—keep it under control. Don't give up something of value for nothing. A short trip out of town is okay.

Friday, July 21 (Moon in Pisces to Aries 8:10 p.m.) Someone in a position of authority expresses a liking for you and your work, but the flattery also contains hidden meaning. Don't go too far! Attention revolves around your home, family, financial security, and the acquisition of an art object or a luxury item. Libra is in this picture.

Saturday, July 22 (Moon in Aries) Play the waiting game! Your first offer is not good, but by the third time around, you will be sitting pretty. The Aries moon relates to your eleventh house, which means that you'll win friends and influence people among the higher-ups. You'll display remarkable skill in picking winners and overcoming odds. Your lucky number is 7.

Sunday, July 23 (Moon in Aries) What appeared to be a bust will boomerang in your favor. Your past record will be considered. Your credits far outnumber debits. A relationship is controversial and colorful, but you must decide whether or not it is worth the trouble. Cancer, and Capricorn play outstanding roles.

Monday, July 24 (Moon in Aries to Taurus 3:45 a.m.) What seemed to never end will be completed. By sticking with it, you gain admiration and recognition. Learn more about the language. Give serious consideration to an offer that would take you on a journey overseas. Aries and Libra are in the picture, and have these letters in their names—I and R.

Tuesday, July 25 (Moon in Taurus) Light shines on areas previously obscured and darkened. Your money situation will be out in the open, so remember the aphorism, "Don't cast the first stone!" Shenanigans have taken place—but this is a new day and it would not hurt to forget and forgive. Leo plays a dramatic role.

261

Wednesday, July 26 (Moon in Taurus to Gemini 8:03 a.m.) Lucky lottery: 26, 2, 12, 11, 22, 18. The moon is moving into your sign. Your cycle is high, so designate where the action will be. What was hidden is revealed and works to your favor. Refuse to be frightened into premature action. A Cancer figures in this scenario.

Thursday, July 27 (Moon in Gemini) Pressure is relieved. This is your day of vindication! The moon in your sign highlights your personality, and your ability to win your way and to be at the right place at a crucial moment. You'll exude an aura of sensuality and sex appeal. Sagittarius and another Gemini play exciting roles. Your lucky number is 3.

Friday, July 28 (Moon in Gemini to Cancer 9:31 a.m.) Check your handwriting samples: Play the role of detective, examining clues and following your intuition and your heart. Money is at stake. You'll hold the right cards. A Leo declares, "You are not getting paid enough for your product or talent, so double your price!" Scorpio is in this picture.

Saturday, July 29 (Moon in Cancer) Lucky lottery: 5, 22, 4, 40, 1, 10. Pay attention to the study of the mantic arts and sciences, including number divination and astrology. What begins as a fascinating hobby could be transformed into a paying proposition. A Virgo plays an instrumental role.

Sunday, July 30 (Moon in Cancer to Leo 9:24 a.m.) The emphasis is on beautifying your surroundings, being confident in connection with your home, security, family, and income potential. The moon in its own sign, Cancer, coincides with locating a lost article and obtaining needed material at a legitimate bargain prices. Libra is involved.

Monday, July 31 (Moon in Leo) On this last day of July, a blue moon and solar eclipse occurs in Leo, meaning trips, visits, relatives, and a tendency to try to please everyone and to be everywhere. Avoid self-deception; see people, places, and relationships in a more realistic light. Take time to perfect your skills.

AUGUST 2000

Tuesday, August 1 (Moon in Leo to Virgo 9:28 a.m.) On this Tuesday, the first day of August, the spotlight falls on numerous activities, from walking, reading, and writing, to learning through the process of teaching others. A visit from a relative comes as a surprise, not entirely pleasant. Virgo, Sagittarius, and another Gemini figure in this dynamic scenario.

Wednesday, August 2 (Moon in Virgo) Lucky lottery: 6, 12, 16, 24, 30, 20. Attention revolves around your lifestyle, where you live, your income potential, and your marital status. A Libra confides true feelings. You'll feel good as a result! Taurus, Libra, and Scorpio play leading roles, and have these letters in their names—F, O, X.

Thursday, August 3 (Moon in Virgo to Libra 11:32 a.m.) Focus on durable goods, household products, and repair work. Remind the person who borrowed from you that the time for repayment is overdue. Define terms, finding out what you can expect for contributions—mental, emotional, financial. Pisces will play an outstanding role.

Friday, August 4 (Moon in Libra) It's the precursor to a lively weekend! The lunar position highlights creativity, style, variety, fitness, and sex appeal. Get your priorities lined up. Be knowledgeable about timing and a deadline. A relationship gets serious, involving someone fascinated by the occult.

Saturday, August 5 (Moon in Libra to Scorpio 5:05 p.m.) A project begun some time ago could be completed by tonight. An Aries becomes your staunch ally, helping you win friends and influence people. Be prepared to make an intelligent concession about distance or language. You will have luck with the number 9.

Sunday, August 6 (Moon in Scorpio)   Power play! Work your personal magic, turning on the charm to make a fresh start and welcome the opportunity for adventure and romance. Don't follow others. Express your own style: Highlight your personality, initiative, and originality. Leo and Aquarius are involved, and have these letters in their names—A, S, J.

Monday, August 7 (Moon in Scorpio)   A decision involves whether to dig deep or to be superficial and keep things pleasant. Answer: Another person is involved, likely born under Cancer. Money will be paid if you persist and if you have courage enough to get at the truth no matter how deep you have to dig.

Tuesday, August 8 (Moon in Scorpio to Sagittarius 2:31 a.m.)   For racing luck, these selections apply to all tracks: Post position special—number 5 p.p. in the seventh race. Pick six: 3, 3, 1, 4, 2, 8. Watch for these letters in the names of potential winning horses, or jockeys— C, L, U. Hot daily doubles: 3 and 3, 8 and 1, 5 and 4. Gemini and Sagittarius jockeys bring home long shots.

Wednesday, August 9 (Moon in Sagittarius)   A roadblock will be removed; you'll benefit as a result. The Sagittarian moon relates to legal documents, public relations, cooperative efforts, and your marital status. Those who disagree with you will at the same time concede that you possess imagination and talent. You will have luck with the number 4.

Thursday, August 10 (Moon in Sagittarius to Capricorn 2:45 p.m.)   The emphasis is on deciding whether you are in lust or in love. The Mercury keynote highlights communication, the exchange of ideas, and relating your ambitions to a member of the opposite sex who does seem to have your best interests at heart. Virgo and Sagittarius play roles.

Friday, August 11 (Moon in Capricorn)   What was taken away is due to be returned—if you are patient and diplomatic. Someone deliberately hid an object that you need to complete a project. Maintain your emotional equilibrium, but make it clear that enough is enough. Taurus plays a significant role.

Saturday, August 12 (Moon in Capricorn)   On this Saturday, spend time meditating. A dilemma dissolves if you permit it to. You cannot solve every mystery, nor can you please everyone—know it, and respond accordingly. Play the waiting game. If you don't know what to do, do nothing! Pisces plays a role.

Sunday, August 13 (Moon in Capricorn to Aquarius 3:44 a.m.)   On this Sunday, you'll be surprised by an Aquarian who declares, "I find it a privilege to share this Sunday and its spiritual implications with you!" The spotlight is on timing, recognition of priorities, realization that a deadline must be met—within 24 hours.

Monday, August 14 (Moon in Aquarius)   You'll be asking, "Is this déjà vu?" It seemed you recently had the same experience that looms large today. Familiar places and faces are highlighted—you will know what to do and when to do it. Be finished with an obligation that belongs to another—no more false altruism!

Tuesday, August 15 (Moon in Aquarius to Pisces 3:42 p.m.)   The full-moon position relates to a decision involving a travel agent. The emphasis is on the unorthodox, and on a trip that could prove rewarding and informative. During the trip you could meet your soulmate. Spiritual values should not be overlooked. Leo plays a dramatic role.

Wednesday, August 16 (Moon in Pisces)   Lucky lottery: 12, 18, 22, 32, 14, 17. The Pisces moon relates to your career, community activity, leadership, and the fulfillment of a secret ambition. On a more mundane level, check the plumbing—rust in your water requires attention pronto. A Cancer is in the picture.

Thursday, August 17 (Moon in Pisces)   For racing luck, these selections apply to all tracks: Post position special—number 3 p.p. in the third race. Pick six: 7, 1, 3, 6, 6, 8. Watch for these letters in the names of potential winning horses or jockeys—C, L, U. Hot daily doubles: 7 and 1, 2 and 3, 3 and 3. Long shots win the third race with Sagittarian jockeys.

Friday, August 18 (Moon in Pisces to Aries 1:45 a.m.)   The lunar position coincides with good fortune in finance and romance. The Aries moon in your eleventh sector is as good as it can get—you win friends and influence people; you have luck in matters of speculation. Some insist, "You must be psychic!"

Saturday, August 19 (Moon in Aries)   On this Saturday, extend the hand of friendship to an Aries who is intent on helping you to succeed. Caution: Don't look a gift horse in the mouth; do not ask too many questions! The emphasis is on charm, flirting, writing, and reveling in a clash of ideas. Your lucky number is 5.

Sunday, August 20 (Moon in Aries to Taurus 9:32 a.m.) Within 24 hours, you'll be dealing with institutions, hospitals, theaters, and concepts of home improvement. You'll get secret backing from a Taurus who states, "I know that everything I do for you will be repaid handsomely!" Music is in this picture.

Monday, August 21 (Moon in Taurus)   Play the waiting game—visit someone temporarily confined to home or hospital. Focus on patience, meditation, and understanding of a problem faced by someone you admire. Maintain an aura of intrigue; don't tell all. Do not confide or confess. Play your cards close to the chest.

Tuesday, August 22 (Moon in Taurus to Gemini 2:56 p.m.)   Money is on the line! Your secret plan will be received enthusiastically—a green light flashes for progress. Cancer and Capricorn figure in this dynamic scenario, and are likely to have these letters in their names: H, Q, Z. Line up your priorities!

Wednesday, August 23 (Moon in Gemini)   Lucky lottery: 39, 9, 3, 30, 50, 51. Focus on joie de vivre—celebrate being finished with an obligation that was foolish in the first place. A romance that fizzled could once again sizzle. Plan for a sea cruise. Your romantic fantasies could be fulfilled as a result.

Thursday, August 24 (Moon in Gemini to Cancer 6 p.m.)   The answer to your question: Your cycle is high. This is the time to break through, to express your personal style, to make a fresh start in a new direction. Don't take too seriously a broken promise. Whatever was broken today will be repaired within 24 hours. An Aquarian initiates a creative policy.

Friday, August 25 (Moon in Cancer)   Go slow. Prepare for a busy weekend during which the question of marriage will loom large. The financial picture will be much better than you originally anticipated. You'll locate a lost key. An article you have been seeking suddenly appears almost as if by magic. A Cancer is involved.

Saturday, August 26 (Moon in Cancer to Leo 7:17 p.m.)   Lucky lottery: 3, 4, 30, 1, 8, 9. Your cycle continues high and your judgment and intuition are on target. You'll be saying, "This is one Saturday night I won't soon forget!" You'll be very social. People vie for your company. Your fitness report is excellent, so you have every reason to celebrate!

Sunday, August 27 (Moon in Leo)   A relative entertains, playing the role of a stand-up comedian. Someone reminds you, "After all, this is Sunday and we should pay the day respect!" A rare chance exists to correct your past mistakes, to emerge from your emotional shell, and to tell the world, "You don't really scare me!"

Monday, August 28 (Moon in Leo to Virgo 7:56 p.m.)   Get ready for challenge, change, and a variety of experiences and sensations. Another Gemini approaches, declaring, "I am intrigued by you. We are so

much alike that I am falling head-over-heels for you!"
Remain calm, cool, and collected—don't believe everything you hear!

Tuesday, August 29 (Moon in Virgo)   The new moon in Virgo relates to your home, building material, security, household products, and a decision associated with a long-term relationship. The spotlight is on your lifestyle, the need to beautify your surroundings, and the acquisition of an art object, a luxury item, or musical instrument.

Wednesday, August 30 (Moon in Virgo to Libra 9:34 p.m.)   It's an excellent opportunity to perfect your techniques, to catch up on an assignment that was left for another time. Show off your psychic ability; entertain by reading minds. The answers are found behind the scenes—be careful; avoid self-deception. Virgo plays a top role.

Thursday, August 31 (Moon in Libra)   On this last day of August, the spotlight is on romance, style, creativity, and decisions relating to a change of pace, or a change in relationship or marital status. An older person, perhaps your parent, employer, or instructor, will state, "You have advanced beautifully and I have every faith in you!"

SEPTEMBER 2000

Friday, September 1 (Moon in Libra)   On this first day of September, with the moon in Libra, your creative juices stir. Focus on beauty, art, music, your lifestyle, home, and marital status. Taurus, Libra, and Scorpio play leading roles, and will have these letters in their names—F, O, X.

Saturday, September 2 (Moon in Libra to Scorpio 1:56 a.m.)   For racing luck, these selections apply to all tracks: Post position special—number 1 p.p. in the sixth race. Pick six: 2, 7, 1, 3, 6, 5. Watch for these letters in the names of potential winning horses or jockeys: G, P, Y. Hot daily doubles: 2 and 7, 7 and 7, 5 and 4. Horses that run well on muddy tracks will be in the money.

Sunday, September 3 (Moon in Scorpio)   Power, passion, creativity, and the settling of a dispute—all are featured on this Sunday. Your opinions are sought concerning a project requiring a deadline or funding. Spiritual growth is featured. You'll be surprised by the fact that you have more allies than you anticipated.

Monday, September 4 (Moon in Scorpio to Sagittarius 10:10 a.m.)   On this Monday, you'll feel as if you can conquer the world once you're ready to give it up! Philosophical themes dominate—within 24 hours, a decision is reached in connection with a journey or love relationship. Aries and Libra figure prominently.

Tuesday, September 5 (Moon in Sagittarius)   The answer to your question: Yes, a fresh start is necessary; travel conditions are good. Make room for adventure and romance. Imprint your own style; don't follow others. You'll feel like a star in a movie featuring your life and your exploits. Leo and Aquarius are in this picture, and have these letters in their names—A, S, J.

Wednesday, September 6 (Moon in Sagittarius to Capricorn 10:10 a.m.)   Lucky lottery: 9, 39, 3, 30, 12, 6. The spotlight falls on cooperative efforts, dealing with restaurant management, or making a major decision in connection with your direction, motivation or marital status. Capricorn and Cancer figure in this dynamic scenario.

Thursday, September 7 (Moon in Capricorn)   Define terms; check the legal aspects of money you are handling for another person. You will learn more about tax and license requirements—deal also with insurance and other payments. Sagittarius and another Gemini dominate, and have these letters in their names—C, L, U.

Friday, September 8 (Moon in Capricorn)   Lucky numbers: 8, 1, 18. The Capricorn moon relates to interest rates, the financial status of your partner or mate, and news about a possible inheritance. Take a hard-nosed approach—those who attempt to soften your attitude are acting out of selfish reasons.

Saturday, September 9 (Moon in Capricorn to Aquarius 10:46 a.m.)   Within 24 hours you'll get news about the distribution of your product in a distant city or foreign land. Focus on idealism, romance, and spiritual awareness. The spotlight is on written material, change, travel, and variety. Lucky lottery: 5, 50, 1, 10, 12, 18.

Sunday, September 10 (Moon in Aquarius)   Beautify your surroundings, the emphasis is on decorating and remodeling. Look surprised when this surprise arrives in the form of a gift—an art object or luxury item. Taurus, Libra, and Scorpio play leading roles, and will have these letters in their names—F, O, X.

Monday, September 11 (Moon in Aquarius to Pisces 10:35 p.m.)   Focus on a means of transportation. Check your automobile batteries, water, and oil. Someone you trusted to do this did not remember or deliberately forgot. Pisces and Virgo figure in this outstanding scenario, and have these initials in their names—G, P, Y.

Tuesday, September 12 (Moon in Pisces)   For racing luck, these selections apply to all tracks. Post position special—number 8 p.p. in the ninth race. Pick six: 8, 5, 2, 2, 1, 7. Watch for these letters in the names of potential winning horses or jockeys: H, Q, Z. Hot daily doubles: 8 and 5, 3 and 7, 1 and 8. Favorites win; jockeys mount veteran horses giving them superb rides.

Wednesday, September 13 (Moon in Pisces)   The full moon in Pisces relates to your career, the fulfillment of an ambition, and being near a resort featuring boats, swimming, and water sports. Your psychic faculties are activated—you'll sense when something of importance is to happen. A mystery person is part of this scenario. A Pisces could play an important role in your future.

Thursday, September 14 (Moon in Pisces to Aries 8:01 a.m.)   Let go of the status quo; create your own fortune; read your future and make it come true. Special: Avoid lifting heavy objects. Release yourself from a relationship that finds you being taken for granted. An opportunity exists to be free of an unsavory situation.

Friday, September 15 (Moon in Aries)   The moon in Aries relates to your eleventh house—this means that you win friends and influence people, that you have extraordinary luck in matters of speculation. Set your sights on a goal, proceed with confidence. A Cancer plays an astounding role.

Saturday, September 16 (Moon in Aries to Taurus 3:06 p.m.)   Lucky lottery: 9, 10, 12, 13, 40, 42. Some people will comment, "Odds seem to mean nothing to you. You win even when it seems impossible!" Elements of timing and luck ride with you, especially in connection with Sagittarius and another Gemini.

Sunday, September 17 (Moon in Taurus)   The emphasis is on the need to review material, check sources, and be aware of details that you ordinarily would skip over. Scorpio and Taurus persons play meaningful roles, and will have these letters in their names—D, M, V. You will have luck with the number 4.

Monday, September 18 (Moon in Taurus to Gemini 8:23 p.m.)   The lunar position accents secrets, glamour, mystery, intrigue, and private meetings. A clandestine relationship comes to light, which involves possessions and money. A short trip may be necessary in order to obtain a legal document. A flirtation with Virgo is exciting, but might cost more than you originally anticipated.

Tuesday, September 19 (Moon in Gemini)   Beware of a family member who says, "I want your opinion." It will not be your opinion that he wants, but your approval. Forewarned is forearmed—don't get involved in a family dispute that is tiresome and endless. Taurus plays the top role.

Wednesday, September 20 (Moon in Gemini to Cancer 12:16 p.m.)   For racing luck, these selections apply to all tracks: Post position special—number 7 p.p. in the third race. Pick six: 1, 7, 7, 3, 3, 8. Watch for these letters in the names of potential winning horses or jockeys: G, P, Y. Hot daily doubles: 1 and 7, 5 and 2, 3 and 4. Pisces jockeys ride winners; some will be long shots.

Thursday, September 21 (Moon in Cancer)   Focus on investments, security, insurance, and the possible sale or purchase of an automobile. A power struggle ensues in areas of your career or your business. A love relationship will prove durable, despite controversy and separation. Capricorn and Cancer-born persons play leading roles, and have these letters in their names—H, Q, Z.

Friday, September 22 (Moon in Cancer)   Mission completed! Search for the missing link in connection with security. Special locks will be completed, and you'll have reason to be grateful. The moon position highlights the value of your personal possessions, your ability to locate lost items, and a reunion with a family member who states, "I really cannot stand being distanced from you!"

Saturday, September 23 (Moon in Cancer to Leo 3:01 a.m.)   Lucky lottery: 1, 5, 50, 27, 13, 22. Activities are due to pile up, one upon the other. Trips, relatives, and new acquaintances are featured. You'll be saying, "This is one Saturday I won't soon forget" and later you'll declare, "A real Saturday Night Live!"

Sunday, September 24 (Moon in Leo)   Young persons dominate today's scenario. A Sunday outing at a park or amusement area could be featured. Do plenty of explaining. Take poetic license. Focus on color coordination, entertainment, and showmanship. The spotlight is on your family. Excellent cuisine is prepared by a Cancer.

Monday, September 25 (Moon in Leo to Virgo 5:03 a.m.)   Lucky numbers: 3, 25, 5. Pay attention to your hobbies, particularly involving stamp and coin collections. A household pet, likely a kitten, requires more than usual affection. Sagittarius and another Gemini play astonishing roles.

Tuesday, September 26 (Moon in Virgo)   Apparent coincidences take on a religious significance. Read between the lines; don't rely on others to check your source material. Rebuild, rewrite, review, and let others know there are two ways to do something—"The wrong way and my way!"

Wednesday, September 27 (Moon in Virgo to Libra 7:23 a.m.)   The new moon in Libra relates to physical attraction, children, challenge, and a variety of sensations. Remember the aphorism: "Lose your mind and come to your senses!" Let freedom ring! As restrictions are removed, express your feelings to a special person. Your lucky number is 5.

Thursday, September 28 (Moon in Libra)   The spotlight falls on where you live, and on a relationship with a family member who knows the price of everything and the value of nothing. Be respectful but skeptical—trust your own judgment in connection with purchases involving clothing, art objects, and luxury items. Libra is involved.

Friday, September 29 (Moon in Libra to Scorpio 11:31 a.m.)   Play the waiting game; realize that within 24 hours a relationship will be made crystal clear to you. You will know where you stand and what to do about it. Meantime, perfect your techniques, streamline your procedures, and give full play to your psychic impressions. Pisces plays a role.

Saturday, September 30 (Moon in Scorpio)   On this last day of September, with the moon in Scorpio, choose these numbers for your lucky lottery: 24, 18, 17, 12, 33, 16. You'll be trusted with a mission that appears to be impossible. The element of timing is featured; a deadline is involved; negotiations with higher-ups are featured. You will more than hold your own!

OCTOBER 2000

Sunday, October 1 (Moon in Scorpio to Sagittarius 6:51 p.m.)   On this Sunday, the first day of October, your spiritual values surface. The Neptune keynote blends with your Mercury—you're full of information about psychic phenomena and Bible miracles. Pisces and Virgo play outstanding roles, and have these letters in their names—G, P, Y.

Monday, October 2 (Moon in Sagittarius)   A dichotomy—one half of your life is dominated today by spiritual values, the other half by material necessities. Relationships pull in two directions—you might understand and thrive, but your partner or mate experiences utter confusion. You will have luck with the number 8.

Tuesday, October 3 (Moon in Sagittarius)   Attention revolves around distance, communication, language, and romance on the high seas. The lunar position highlights public relations, responses to your efforts, and how you view the world. Your marital status will loom large. Aries and Libra figure in this complex scenario.

Wednesday, October 4 (Moon in Sagittarius to Capricorn 5:44 a.m.)   Make a fresh start. Take the initiative. Locate missing articles. Find out where the money went. The eighth-house influence exemplifies mystery, intrigue, the occult, and possessions and money owned by other people. You'll be regarded as a trusted associate. Your lucky number is 1.

Thursday, October 5 (Moon in Capricorn) A decision is reached concerning your financial arrangements, partnership, and marriage. Prediction: This is one Thursday you won't soon forget! Cancer and Capricorn play featured roles, and they could have these letters in their names—B, K, T. Your lucky number is 2.

Friday, October 6 (Moon in Capricorn to Aquarius 6:34 p.m.) For racing luck, these selections apply to all tracks: Post position special—number 5 p.p. in the seventh race. Pick six: 3, 3, 5, 1, 4, 2. Watch for these letters in the names of potential winning horses or jockeys: C, L, U. Hot daily doubles: 3 and 3, 7 and 2, 3 and 4. Gemini jockeys ride and win with long shots!

Saturday, October 7 (Moon in Aquarius) Lucky lottery: 4, 12, 7, 2, 20, 18. Check your source material. Vital information is obtained by reading between the lines. The lunar aspect coincides with travel, publishing, philosophy, and the dynamic experience of self-realization. Scorpio plays a top role.

Sunday, October 8 (Moon in Aquarius) Gain is indicated via words, both verbal and written. The Aquarian moon tells of correspondence and communication with an unusual person living in a foreign land. Refuse to be blocked by the experiences of other people—you deserve better, and you will be treated differently!

Monday, October 9 (Moon in Aquarius to Pisces 6:37 a.m.) The Pisces moon relates to your career, ambition, and associations with community leaders. Someone in a position of authority will be in danger in connection with water. The fickle finger of fate points to you for a possible takeover. A Libra figures prominently.

Tuesday, October 10 (Moon in Pisces) Time for a "time-out." Play the waiting game, seeing people and relationships as they are and not as you wish they could be. Protect yourself in close quarters; someone attempts to land a sucker punch. Pisces and Virgo play outstanding roles, and they could have these initials in their names—G, P, Y.

Wednesday, October 11 (Moon in Pisces to Aries 3:52 p.m.)   Lucky lottery: 12, 7, 1, 10, 6, 18. Within 24 hours, you will be able to call your own shots and to maintain creative control. Tonight, reach a new understanding with someone of the opposite sex who makes protestations of love, but does little to demonstrate it.

Thursday, October 12 (Moon in Aries)   Stress universal appeal; you'll hear these words, "You make people feel comfortable to be with you!" Free yourself from a foolish obligation or an unsavory situation. Distance and language barriers will be overcome. Aries and Libra figure in today's dramatic scenario.

Friday, October 13 (Moon in Aries to Taurus 10:06 p.m.)   You will not be unlucky! The full moon in your eleventh house guarantees excellent results in matters of finance or romance. The financial picture is bright; a loss will be recovered. A family member asserts, "You are the only responsible one; I depend upon you!"

Saturday, October 14 (Moon in Taurus)   Celebrate with your family! Don't wander too far from home. Liquid refreshments are served by a Cancer who also cooks up a storm. The spotlight is on publicity, public relations, legal rights, and your marital status. Attention will revolve around your home, security, family, direction, and motivation.

Sunday, October 15 (Moon in Taurus)   Triple plays are executed in sports events, especially baseball. You could be in on it in connection with a financial coup. You'll muse, "This is certainly unexpected, and the most unusual Sunday I've experienced in a month of Sundays!" A Sagittarian is in the picture.

Monday, October 16 (Moon in Taurus to Gemini 2:19 a.m.)   Don't equate a delay with defeat. An unexpected array of details creates second thoughts, but eventually you'll endure and succeed. Scorpio and Taurus play fascinating roles, and they could have these letters in their names: D, M, V. Read between the lines!

Tuesday, October 17 (Moon in Gemini)   The moon is in your sign; your cycle is high; you could hit the emotional and financial jackpots! Rely on your own judgment and intuition—romance and creativity are featured. You exude personal magnetism and an aura of sensuality and sex appeal. Virgo plays a role.

Wednesday, October 18 (Moon in Gemini to Cancer 5:38 a.m.)   For racing luck, these selections apply at all tracks: Post position special—number 2 p.p. in the fourth race. Pick six: 1, 2, 5, 2, 3, 2. Watch for these letters in the names of potential winning horses or jockeys: F, O, X. Hot daily doubles: 1 and 2, 6 and 6, 4 and 5. Local jockeys win; more favorites than usual will be in the money.

Thursday, October 19 (Moon in Cancer)   Stop, look, listen! Obey traffic rules; play the waiting game; highlight moderation in all areas, including alcohol. Financial affairs are slow. Your stocks need and take a breather. Follow through on a psychic impression—someone is trying to tell you something.

Friday, October 20 (Moon in Cancer to Leo 8:43 a.m.) What held you back and slowed your promotional process will be removed within 24 hours. Meantime, verify your views; open the lines of communication; make amends to a Cancer who feels neglected. You might be musing, "I wish people would pay special attention and spoil me!"

Saturday, October 21 (Moon in Leo)   Lucky lottery: 21, 5, 50, 12, 18, 17. You'll receive proof that what goes around comes around! A relationship that went off track is back. The ball is in your court, so make a decision whether to go forward or to forget it. Aries and Libra are involved.

Sunday, October 22 (Moon in Leo to Virgo 11:54 a.m.)
Refuse to be exploited by someone who claims to be a master hypnotist. Wear bright colors, make personal appearances, and explain your views in a dynamic, entertaining way. Leo and Aquarius figure in this scenario, and have these letters in their names—A, S, J.

Monday, October 23 (Moon in Virgo) The Virgo moon relates to your home, security, family relationships, and negotiations to determine property value. Food plays a role. The question of restaurant management will be the subject of a lively discussion. In effect, you'll be pulled in two directions at once.

Tuesday, October 24 (Moon in Virgo to Libra 3:31 p.m.) Relief from a burden! Your working and living quarters improve in air quality, light, and equipment. Tonight is an excellent time for social activities, especially those that include Sagittarius and another Gemini. Explore, investigate, advertise, and publish for the purpose of getting your message across.

Wednesday, October 25 (Moon in Libra) Lucky lottery: 4, 25, 7, 6, 12, 50. Attention revolves around repair work, household pets, and the necessity for double-checking your source material. Someone who once claimed you did not know how to concentrate will take back those words. Taurus is in the picture.

Thursday, October 26 (Moon in Libra to Scorpio 8:25 p.m.) You'll be saying, "Freedom at last! I'm going to write, travel, and be available for romance!" Virgo, Sagittarius, and another Gemini will play outstanding roles, and they could have these letters in their names— E, N, W. Your lucky number is 5.

Friday, October 27 (Moon in Scorpio) The new moon in Scorpio relates to basic issues, getting things fixed, cooking utensils, and reaching an agreement with a coworker to end a foolish dispute. Music plays; you'll be involved with art, literature, and sound equipment. An Aries figures prominently.

Saturday, October 28 (Moon in Scorpio)   For racing
luck, these selections apply at all tracks: Post position
special—number 1 p.p. in the sixth race. Pick six: 3, 7,
1, 2, 4, 1. Watch for these letters in the names of potential winning horses or jockeys: G, P, Y. Hot daily doubles: 3 and 7, 2 and 4, 1 and 7. Mild favorites win; look
for spectacular rides by Pisces jockeys.

***Sunday, October 29—Daylight Saving Time Ends (Moon
in Scorpio to Sagittarius 2:42 a.m.)***   What was de-
layed will arrive—overtime may be necessary. You'll
have more responsibility and a legitimate opportunity
for promotion. The Sagittarian moon, plus Saturn keynote, points to legal affairs, cooperative efforts, partnership, and marriage.

Monday, October 30 (Moon in Sagittarius)   A re-
striction is lifted, freeing you to express love and possibly propose marriage. A foreign land is involved. You'll
remember this as being one of the most romantic days,
when your fantasies are fulfilled. As October nears an
end, you'll feel vital, dynamic, sensual. Libra is involved.

***Tuesday, October 31 (Moon in Sagittarius to Capricorn
1:03 p.m.)***   On this Halloween and National Magic
Day, a visitor from South America could create a blend
of pleasure and complications. Stress independence,
making a fresh start in a new direction. Wear bright
colors. Be receptive to romance. Leo and Aquarius play
leading roles, and have these initials in their names—A,
S, J.

NOVEMBER 2000

Wednesday, November 1 (Moon in Capricorn)
Take a new approach to the financial status of someone
close to you. Today's Capricorn moon relates to accounting procedures, discoveries associated with treasure
maps, and hidden wealth. Leo and Aquarius play out-

standing roles, and have these letters in their names—
A, S, J. Your lucky number is 8.

Thursday, November 2 (Moon in Capricorn)   For
racing luck, these selections apply to all tracks: Post position special—number 8 p.p. in the first race. Pick six: 8,
5, 4, 2, 6, 3. Watch for these letters in the names of
potential winning horses or jockeys: I and R. Hot daily
doubles: 8 and 5, 3 and 6, 4 and 7. Aries jockeys mount
long shots and bring them in the money.

**Friday, November 3 (Moon in Capricorn to Aquarius
1:41 a.m.)**   You'll rediscover what once was familiar—sights, sounds, and people. Make a fresh start; imprint your style; make crystal clear that you will not
move except of your own accord! Leo will play a dramatic role, and will have these letters in a name—A, S, J.

Saturday, November 4 (Moon in Aquarius)   Lucky
lottery: 2, 11, 12, 18, 22, 5. Attention revolves around
family relationships, the value of property, and a decision in connection with marriage—these will loom large.
The Aquarian moon relates to publishing, communication, spiritual values, and a journey.

**Sunday, November 5 (Moon in Aquarius to Pisces 2:15
p.m.)**   Highlight diversity, versatility, and philosophical studies. A realization hits home, "There is so much
more to know than is revealed by my five senses!" Some
people will contend that you are delving too deep into
metaphysical waters. A Sagittarian declares, "You most
certainly are on the right track!"

Monday, November 6 (Moon in Pisces)   Revise, review, rewrite, and rebuild—a chance exists to take complete charge of your own destiny. A flirtation lends spice,
but know when to say, "Enough is enough!" Taurus,
Leo, and Scorpio figure in this exciting scenario, and
they will have these letters in their names—D, M, V.

Tuesday, November 7 (Moon in Pisces)   For racing
luck, these selections apply to all tracks: Post position

special—number 3 p.p. in the second race. Pick six: 2, 3, 5, 5, 1, 8. Be alert for these letters in the names of potential winning horses or jockeys: E, N, W. Hot daily doubles: 2 and 3, 5 and 4, 5 and 5. Gemini, Virgo, and Sagittarius jockeys will be in the money.

Wednesday, November 8 (Moon in Pisces to Aries 12:03 a.m.) Lucky lottery: 6, 12, 18, 28, 13, 42. The Aries moon relates to that section of your horoscope associated with the fulfillment of desires and the ability to win friends and influence people. Financial aid is obtained in connection with the purchase of property or a home. Libra is involved.

Thursday, November 9 (Moon in Aries) Lucky numbers: 7, 1, 10. Define your terms; refuse to be rushed or cajoled into making a snap decision. Find out exactly where you stand and why—take nothing for granted! What is expected of you and what you anticipate in return—answer those questions! Pisces plays a role.

Friday, November 10 (Moon in Aries to Taurus 6:13 a.m.) On this Friday you sum up: What have I accomplished? Where do I go from here? Is love really for me? Is my love unrequited? Those questions whirl around in your mind. Cancer and Capricorn play meaningful roles, and will have these letters in their names—H, Q, Z.

Saturday, November 11 (Moon in Taurus) The full moon in Taurus relates to secrets, clandestine arrangements, and a visit to home or hospital to make contact with someone who is creative, dynamic, and has your best interests at heart. The networking process gets started with Aries. Lucky lottery: 1, 19, 29, 49, 13, 4.

Sunday, November 12 (Moon in Taurus to Gemini 9:29 a.m.) The light shines bright! Darker areas of your life receive the benefit of greater illumination. Focus on discovery, your pioneering spirit, exploration, and a serious discussion involving your soul. Leo and Aquarius play featured roles, and will have these letters in their names—A, S, J.

Monday, November 13 (Moon in Gemini)   The moon in your sign emphasizes initiative, personality, productivity, and sex appeal. Show the courage of your convictions, letting go of a losing proposition and extricating yourself from an unsavory situation. Your judgment and intuition hit the bull's-eye. Cancer and Capricorn will figure in today's dramatic scenario.

Tuesday, November 14 (Moon in Gemini to Cancer 11:22 a.m.)   An unusual Tuesday! There's plenty of reason to celebrate. After the Sword of Damocles is removed, circumstances turn in your favor. Now you can afford to be selective, choosing only the best and halting any tendency to compromise. Sagittarius and another Gemini figure in this exciting scenario.

Wednesday, November 15 (Moon in Cancer)   Lucky lottery: 4, 44, 22, 12, 9, 18. What appears to be a barrier or a signal for defeat will do a turnabout, boomeranging in your favor. Taurus, Leo, and Scorpio play fascinating roles, and they could have these letters in their names: D, M, V. Read between the lines!

Thursday, November 16 (Moon in Cancer to Leo 1:20 p.m.)   Attention revolves around writing and your special way with words. Money is involved. Investment procedures require review—you are on the verge of "hitting the jackpot." Dining out tonight fits the bill—Virgo, Sagittarius, and another Gemini figure in this scenario. Your fortunate number is 5.

Friday, November 17 (Moon in Leo)   Go slow, insisting on clarity and getting promises in writing. Remember the aphorism: "A verbal contract is not worth the paper it's written on!" Pisces is persuasive, but likely not to offer anything except sweet whispers. A domestic adjustment is involved.

Saturday, November 18 (Moon in Leo to Virgo 4:17 p.m.)   There is good fortune in matters of speculation if you stick with long shots. At the track, choose horses that run well in mud—if it rains, you might strike it rich! See people and relationships as they are, not merely as you wish they might be. A Virgo plays an outstanding role.

Sunday, November 19 (Moon in Virgo)   Focus on practicality, lining up priorities, and dealing with a heavy-handed Capricorn who states, "I am running the show!" Remember, it takes two to tango—permit your actions to speak louder than sharp words. A Cancer native makes a declaration of loyalty: "I remain your obedient servant!"

Monday, November 20 (Moon in Virgo to Libra 8:36 p.m.)   Complete a mission, looking beyond the immediate. Get a valid estimate of the worth of your property. Focus on language, communication, distance, and a love relationship that grows strong, despite a temporary separation. An Aries or Libra plays a starring role, and has these letters in a name—I and R.

Tuesday, November 21 (Moon in Libra)   The answer to your question: Yes, it is love. Lust is also part of this relationship, but it blends with true feelings. Leo and Aquarius play fascinating roles, and are likely to have these letters in their names: A, S, J. Your lucky number is 1.

Wednesday, November 22 (Moon in Libra)   Lucky Lottery: 22, 33, 18, 17, 40, 4. You exude an aura of creativity, style, panache, sensuality, and sex appeal. In your cycle high, take the initiative, realizing that circumstances are moving in your favor, despite the naysayers. Don't ask too many questions—just be glad that everything seems to be going your way!

Thursday, November 23 (Moon in Libra to Scorpio 2:34 a.m.)   The Scorpio moon on this Thanksgiving relates to your ability to express your feelings. Someone usually in the background will insist on the spotlight. This is likely to be a Scorpio who has something meaningful to say. It will be a joyous Thanksgiving when you will have much to be thankful for.

Friday, November 24 (Moon in Scorpio) Take a stand, refusing to be bullied. Spell out rights and permissions and make your meanings crystal clear to those who seem to doubt you. A Taurus becomes your secret ally. Work previously shunted aside gets done. You won't be alone. True friendship will be revealed.

Saturday, November 25 (Moon in Scorpio to Sagittarius 10:34 a.m.) The Sagittarius new moon relates to actions, attitudes, and resolutions about a partnership or marriage—or both. A legal agreement can be revised to suit your needs and desires. Be analytical and do not ask for more than you can handle. Virgo plays a top role.

Sunday, November 26 (Moon in Sagittarius) Attention revolves around your home, family, security, excellent cuisine, and questions about legal rights and your marital status. By going slow, you win; if you attempt to go fast, you lose. Legal ramifications of a venture should be carefully noted and studied. Libra plays a role.

Monday, November 27 (Moon in Sagittarius to Capricorn 8:58 p.m.) You are in rhythm with your time. This means you are not going in the opposite direction of your own fate. Realize it and respond accordingly. A psychic impression is valid. Follow through and don't be discouraged by those who know the price of everything and value of nothing.

Tuesday, November 28 (Moon in Capricorn) The spotlight revolves around banking procedures, interest rates, and accounting methods. Let it be known that you intend to see and review everything! Capricorn and Cancer are in this picture, and they will have these letters in their names: H, Q, Z. Your lucky number is 8.

Wednesday, November 29 (Moon in Capricorn)
What had been a burden will be removed—thank your
lucky stars! Make travel plans. In the not-too-distant future, you'll meet your soulmate. This encounter could
take place while attending a conference or meeting relating to international affairs or education. Aries is
represented.

Thursday, November 30 (Moon in Capricorn to Aquar-
ius 9:27 a.m.)   This last day of November will be like
a new beginning. Within 24 hours, the lunar position will
highlight romance, style, and creativity. You'll be saying,
"Love is not dead after all!" Tonight sparks fly. The
force that brought you together with a special person
will reignite—you'll be planning ahead for exciting, creative times.

DECEMBER 2000

Friday, December 1 (Moon in Aquarius)   On this
last month of the year 2000, the keynote for the first day
is Mars. The moon is in Aquarius—very fitting indeed!
Before December is finished, you will have delved deep
into what the 21st century portends. Pay special attention to the use of language.

Saturday, December 2 (Moon in Aquarius to Pisces
10:24 p.m.)   On this Saturday, you make fresh contacts. Explore further studies of the mantic arts and sciences that include astrology, Kabbala, and number
mysticism. On a more mundane level, you are physically
attracted and, if single, could meet your soulmate. Your
lucky number is 1.

Sunday, December 3 (Moon in Pisces)   Attention revolves around your family, home, security, and pleasant
surprises. The Pisces moon relates to leadership, dignity,
and your ability to overcome obstacles in the way of
progress. A Cancer extends a dinner invitation—lose no
time in accepting! Capricorn is also in the picture.

Monday, December 4 (Moon in Pisces)   The Jupiter keynote promises joy, frivolity, and the recognition of spiritual values. The focus is also on travel, publishing, advertising, and getting your message across. Sagittarius and another Gemini play leading roles, and they could have these letters in their names—C, L, U.

Tuesday, December 5 (Moon in Pisces to Aries 9:19 a.m.)   For racing luck, these selections apply to all tracks: Post position special—number 4 p.p. in the fourth race. Pick six: 2, 1, 2, 4, 8, 3. Watch for these letters in the names of potential winning horses or jockeys: D, M, V. Hot daily doubles: 2 and 1, 4 and 4, 6 and 8. Scorpio jockeys mount favorites and will be in the money.

Wednesday, December 6 (Moon in Aries)   Lucky lottery: 5, 19, 1, 10, 22, 12. Get ready for change, travel, studies, and a variety of contacts with charming Mercurial individuals who read, write, and talk. Virgo, Sagittarius, and another Gemini figure in this dynamic scenario, and they will have these letters in their names—E, N, W.

Thursday, December 7 (Moon in Aries to Taurus 4:28 p.m.)   The spotlight falls on where you live, your lifestyle, and your building material. There's music in your life and your marital status is in the spotlight. During this cycle, your voice is different—just ask your friends! They will say, "You most certainly do sound different than you did yesterday!"

Friday, December 8 (Moon in Taurus)   This could be the precursor to a weekend featuring meaningful meditation. The Taurus moon relates to your twelfth house, Neptune keynote, which adds up to self-realization. You'll be asking, "Why am I here and what should I be doing about it?" Pisces is involved.

Saturday, December 9 (Moon in Taurus to Gemini 7:52 p.m.)   Finish what you start. Look beyond the immediate. Indications point to the fact that you might hit the financial jackpot. Within 24 hours you'll be saying, "I seem to do the right thing at the right time almost effortlessly!" Capricorn and Cancer are in the picture, and could have these letters in their names—H, Q, Z.

Sunday, December 10 (Moon in Gemini)   On this Sunday, the moon enters your sign, which coincides with your high cycle, a time when your judgment and intuition are honed to razor-sharpness. Take the initiative. Make a fresh start. You can open doors on professional and personal levels. Reignite the spark that first brought you together with your current lover or mate.

Monday, December 11 (Moon in Gemini to Cancer 8:50 p.m.)   The full moon in Gemini tells of romance and of emotional responses in a special relationship. Show your independence of thought and action—do not follow others. Let them follow you if they so desire. You'll be told, "You're sexy!"

Tuesday, December 12 (Moon in Cancer)   The moon is in its own sign, Cancer, which relates to your money and your income. It could mean the end of a financial drought. Just 24 hours ago, you walked on air in connection with emotional excitement, sensuality, loving, and being loved. That feeling blends, today, with a sense of material security.

Wednesday, December 13 (Moon in Cancer to Leo 9:10 p.m.)   Lucky lottery: 12, 2, 4, 40, 13, 22. The emphasis is on your ability to transform an apparent loss into a victory. You'll locate articles that had been long missing. No longer will there be a cutoff in connection with your income potential. Another Gemini is involved.

Thursday, December 14 (Moon in Leo)   A relationship that ended abruptly might not be the end at all! A short trip out of town figures prominently, and it could involve a sudden, dramatic reunion. Taurus, Leo, and Scorpio play outstanding roles, and they could have these letters in their names—D, M, V.

Friday, December 15 (Moon in Leo to Virgo 10:31 p.m.)   Focus on reading and writing, and on telling stories to illustrate your beliefs. The Leo moon high-lights versatility, diversity, color coordination, entertainment, and showmanship. The pressure is on; you are up to it—furthermore, you'll enjoy every minute of it! Virgo is in this picture.

Saturday, December 16 (Moon in Virgo) On this Saturday, you discover that a family member is actually your best friend. A financial logjam breaks; gifts are received; a party is in order. Dance to your own tune. Questions concerning career and marriage loom large. Your lucky number is 6.

Sunday, December 17 (Moon in Virgo) You'll be musing, "Everything falls into place as planned." Today's Neptune keynote highlights spirituality, illusion, and the fact that the mirage is not only visible, but will turn out to be real. Special attention will revolve around real estate, property values, and your marital status.

Monday, December 18 (Moon in Virgo to Libra 2:02 a.m.) The Libra moon relates to that section of your horoscope associated with romance, the stirring of creative juices, and a physical attraction, and unique contacts with children. The Saturn keynote brings you down to earth in connection with the person who will share intimacies with you.

Tuesday, December 19 (Moon in Libra) You'll charm sophisticated, educated persons who invite you to travel, to study, and to elevate your own position. Today's planets give you the kind of universal appeal that overcomes class distinctions, as well as distance and language barriers. Aries and Libra play featured roles, and have these initials in their names—I and R.

Wednesday, December 20 (Moon in Libra to Scorpio 8:13 a.m.) Lucky lottery: 1, 2, 20, 4, 40, 6. Make a fresh start. Take the initiative in presenting a unique format. Within 24 hours, the results of your efforts will prove you are on the right track. Repair work may be necessary, so check electrical outlets and keep your resolutions concerning exercise, diet, and nutrition.

Thursday, December 21 (Moon in Scorpio) The Scorpio moon tells of relations with coworkers and contacts with intelligent people who share your beliefs and interests. A serious discussion in a group that resembles Mensa will revolve around a sex manual. Capricorn and Cancer persons are in the picture, and they will have these letters in their names—B, K, T.

Friday, December 22 (Moon in Scorpio to Sagittarius 4:58 p.m.) You'll be asking, "Is this déjà vu?" Today's scenario highlights familiar faces and places—during a social affair you meet someone whose facial features resemble your own. Oddly enough, that person could also be a Gemini! Your lucky number is 3.

Saturday, December 23 (Moon in Sagittarius) For racing luck, these selections apply at all tracks: Post position special—number 4 p.p. in the ninth race. Pick six: 8, 5, 4, 3, 1, 7. Watch for these letters in the names of potential winning horses or jockeys: D, M, V. Hot daily doubles: 8 and 5, 7 and 4, 2 and 1. Taurus and Scorpio jockeys will be in the money.

Sunday, December 24 (Moon in Sagittarius) A lively Christmas Eve! A world traveler could be in your company. Gifts received include periodical subscriptions, books, and luggage. A flirtation is okay, as long as no one is hurt and you don't act foolishly. The spiritual significance of the holiday will be discussed. You are encouraged to put your views in writing.

Monday, December 25 (Moon in Sagittarius to Capricorn 3:55 a.m.) The new moon, solar eclipse is in Capricorn on this Christmas Day, directly relating to your eighth house. The house of mystery. Your counsel is sought concerning the assets of others. The focus will be on tax and license requirements, as well as on banking and investment procedures. A Libra figures prominently.

Tuesday, December 26 (Moon in Capricorn)   Get ready for New Year's Eve! It certainly will be a momentous time—the dawning of the year 2001 and getting accustomed to the 21st century. As a Gemini, you will have much to do with the future—your own and that of others. Pisces and Virgo play prominent roles, and they will have these letters in their names—G, P, Y.

Wednesday, December 27 (Moon in Capricorn to Aquarius 4:27 p.m.)   Lucky lottery: 10, 12, 28, 13, 15, 1. Within 24 hours, travel plans will be completed. You'll know where you are to be on New Year's Eve, and you'll decide whether or not a relationship is serious enough to develop into a change of your matrimonial situation. A Cancer is involved.

Thursday, December 28 (Moon in Aquarius)   The Aquarian moon tells of communication with someone concerned with numerology, astrology, spiritualism, and extrasensory perception. You might be musing, "What took me so long to wake up to these subjects!" Accent the unorthodox, using elements of timing and surprise.

Friday, December 29 (Moon in Aquarius)   A Leo insists, "I must be with you New Year's Eve!" This person could liven up any party—be wary, however, since the elements of envy and jealousy are likely to be present. The answer to your question: Yes, let go of your usual routine—create your own tradition. Do things your way!

Saturday, December 30 (Moon in Aquarius to Pisces 5:29 p.m.)   Check the location and invitation list of tomorrow night's celebration. If circumstances prevent you from attending a party, remember that being alone has nothing to do with being lonely. You can, after all, be lonely in a crowd. Capricorn is involved.

Sunday, December 31 (Moon in Pisces)   A fun-filled New Year's Eve! The Jupiter keynote indicates that those who speak many languages will be in your company. Dispositions of people are favorable. The Pisces moon indicates, among other things, that alcohol will flow freely. Warning: Don't make promises you can't keep, including marriage proposals!

Happy New Year!

ABOUT THE AUTHOR

Born on August 5, 1926, in Philadelphia, Omarr was the only person ever given full-time duty in the U.S. Army as an astrologer. He also is regarded as the most erudite astrologer of our time and the best known, through his syndicated column (300 newspapers) and his radio and television programs (he is Merv Griffin's "resident astrologer"). Omarr has been called the most "knowledgeable astrologer since Evangeline Adams." His forecasts of Nixon's downfall, the end of World War II in mid-August of 1945, the assassination of John F. Kennedy, Roosevelt's election to the fourth term and his death in office . . . these and many others are on the record and quoted enough to be considered "legendary."

ABOUT THIS SERIES
This is one of a series of twelve
Day-by-Day Astrological Guides
for the signs of 2000
by Sydney Omarr

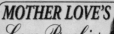